I Begin My Life All Over

Also by Lillian Faderman

Speaking for Ourselves: American Ethnic Writing
(with Barbara Bradshaw)

From the Barrio: A Chicano Anthology
(with Luis Omar Salinas)

Surpassing the Love of Men: Romantic Friendship and Love between Women from the Renaissance to the Present

Scotch Verdict

Odd Girls and Twilight Lovers

Chloe Plus Olivia

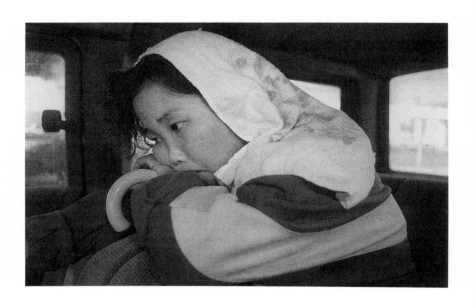

I Begin My Life All Over

The Hmong
and
the American
Immigrant
Experience

Lillian Faderman
with Ghia Xiong

Beacon Press
Boston

Beacon Press
25 Beacon Street
Boston, Massachusetts 02108-2892

Beacon Press books
are published under the auspices of
the Unitarian Universalist Association of Congregations.

03 02 01 00 99 98   8 7 6 5 4 3 2 1

Photographs by Mike Chen: pages 34, 39, 79, 93, 108, 114, 120, 145, 157, 165, 183, 231
Photographs by Mary Lommori courtesy of the *Fresno Bee*: pages iv, 24, 31, 44, 63, 67, 72, 82, 89, 91, 95, 100, 103, 117, 126, 211, 221, 225
Map by Emily Lieb: page 6

Book design by [sic]
Composition by Wilsted & Taylor Publishing Services

Library of Congress Cataloging-in-Publication Data

Faderman, Lillian.
    I begin my life all over : the Hmong and the American immigrant
    experience / Lillian Faderman with Ghia Xiong.
        p. cm.
    ISBN 0-8070-7234-6 (cloth)
    1. Hmong Americans—Cultural assimilation.   2. Hmong
    Americans—Ethnic identity.   3. Refugees—United States—
    History—20th century.   I. Xiong, Ghia.   II. Title.
    E184.H55F33   1998
    305.895′942073—dc21   97-27119

There are only two or three human stories, and they
go on repeating themselves as fiercely as if they had never
happened before.

Willa Cather

In memory of my mother, through whom I lived the immigrant experience

To my son, Avrom, who is an American

And to Xia, my eight-year-old friend, who is the future

Contents

Prologue: A Personal (and Not So Personal) Story   *xiii*
A Note on Methodology   *xix*
Acknowledgments   *xxiii*
Introduction: The Hmong   1
The Narrators   15

Part I: The End of a Way of Life
    The Village   25
    The Escape   43
    The Camp   66

Part II: Becoming American
    To a Promised Land   83
    Shamanism, Christianity, and Modern Medicine   102
    Women and Men   125
    Battles between the Generations   164
    Gangs   185
    Being American   210

Epilogues
    Another Personal Story   243
    Ghia   252
Glossary   255
Bibliography   259

A Personal (and Not So Personal) Story

When I first came to central California in 1967 to teach at California State University in Fresno, I, a Jew with black hair and brown eyes, whose mother came from a shtetl in Eastern Europe, stood out distinctly in a vast sea of blond-haired and blue-eyed "Americans." But the ethnic makeup of the university began to change in the 1970s, and by the 1980s, as large numbers of young African Americans and Hispanic Americans became the first in their families to go to college, the campus looked very different from what it had been when I arrived. By then, the city of Fresno was beginning to change, too, as chain migrations brought diverse racial and ethnic groups to the area. In the late 1980s both our student and city populations expanded even further with the influx of Southeast Asians who had fled their homelands in what was for them the disastrous aftermath of the Vietnam War.

By 1991, when I returned to California State University, Fresno, after a two-year stint as visiting professor at UCLA, I noticed many students in my writing classes with names that I believed were Chinese: Lee, Yang, Vang, Moua. I soon discovered that they or their parents came from the mountains of Laos, and they were called *Hmong*. Their numbers on campus increased dramatically in the next few years. Their essays for my classes often recalled lives in distant mountain villages or the horrors of trying to escape from Laos by trekking across an enemy-filled jungle or swimming across the treacherous Mekong River. They were describing what to me was a very "interesting," "exotic" world.

But one day one of my Hmong students wrote an essay about his sorrows and frustrations over trying to communicate an idea to his parents and failing. They could not understand the English words he was using, he could not remember or had never learned the Hmong words they might have understood, and he feared that even if he had a better Hmong vocabulary, his parents could not have understood him anyway, because the concepts he wanted to convey had no equivalent in their experiences. I found myself crying—not as I'd cried once or twice before over a poignant escape story or relocation camp story a Hmong student had written, but rather in a very personal way, as though I were crying over my own assiduously repressed, long-forgotten story.

Of course I knew enough about the history of race in America to realize that in many ways the lives of my Hmong students were and would be different from my own life. Though I had had to suffer the stings of anti-Semitism in America, I had also enjoyed many of the privileges that were given to Caucasians here. I understood early that although my mother was not literate in English and only basically literate in Yiddish, I could somehow anyway connect to the old Jewish tradition that valued intellectual achievement; I could make that tradition my own and profit by it in America. Clearly, Jews and the Hmong were dissimilar culturally as well as racially, and that dissimilarity accounted for factors that made my life in this country easier than the lives of the Hmong people around me.

Yet I could not help but be struck by the similarity of so many of our experiences. I was impressed first by some more-or-less superficial similarities of history. For example, both Hmong and Jews have had a diaspora that has sent them to far-flung parts of the world; both usually fled ethnic persecution in one country only to endure it again in a new country; before coming to America large proportions of both groups had long lived in isolated communities, separate from the majority culture around them, often retaining a distinct identity, and yet their languages, Hmong and Yiddish, also had great linguistic admixtures from the places where each group had dwelt.

But much more significant to me than these coincidental similarities of history were the many experiences as immigrants or children of immigrants in America that both groups undeniably shared. The stories of the younger Hmong people I met, first in my classes and then in the larger Hmong community, reflected back to me in so many ways my own story: my struggle, as a child of a Jewish immigrant, to become an American—the conflicting beliefs and language and outlook I had to make sense of; the sorrows of separation from my mother's culture that I endured, as well as the guilt occasioned by that necessary separation; the realization that there was no way I could "go home again" because "home," the roots that I had inherited from her, no longer existed. And the stories of the older Hmong people I met, those who were born in Laotian mountain villages which had been totally unaffected by twentieth-century technology, suggested to me what my mother's experiences must have been when she left her shtetl at the other end of the twentieth century and arrived in the strange new universe of America, where plumbing and electricity and telephones and automobiles were usual. My mother's disorientation and that of the new Hmong immigrants must have been much the same; and their attempts to deal with that disorientation, by desperately trying to reconstruct little ethnic enclaves in America—which, in order to become "American," their children are constrained to leave in all but token ways—are much the same.

Listening to the Hmong people, young and old, who were my narrators for this oral history, I came to better understand my own experience in America. But much of what they told illuminated not just their lives and my life. They were revealing the fabric that has gone into the making of Americans: they were telling the tale of the immigrants and their American children.

The material they provided for this oral history recreates the story of the Hmong people who have settled in America—and certainly there is a good deal that is distinctive in their story. But it also mirrors so much of the history of large numbers of us—how we or those from whom we descended came to this country because only here could we survive or dream; what we learned here about the complexities of surviving or trying to realize our dreams; and how we dealt with the crucible of life here that tested us and altered us and made us Americans.

In part 1 of this book ("The End of a Way of Life"), the older narrators talk about the destruction of their homes during the war in Southeast Asia. They describe how they endured what was almost a genocide, their escape through the jungles of Laos and across the Mekong River, and their lives in relocation camps in Thailand.

In the second part of the book ("Becoming American"), the narrators talk about the pains and joys of life in this country. Many of the narratives point up how lost the older generation is. Before coming here most had never used a flush toilet or heard a radio. They feel hopeless about the demands modern technology makes on them. They have difficulty learning English. They are afraid to learn to drive and are dependent on their American-born or -educated children to take them wherever they need to go. Coming from a culture in which children were totally controlled by their parents, here the older people suffer the humiliation of desperately needing their children to intercede for them in an alien world.

The narratives of this second part of the book also capture the voices of young Hmong people who were born in America or came as little children. They talk about the complex process of becoming Americans in a family of immigrants. They recall the conflicts they've suffered in choosing between shamanism and Western religions, shamanism and modern medicine. They reflect on the problems they've experienced in leaving behind their parents' notions of gender relations and parent-child relations and in learning how to develop new ones. It becomes clear through these interviews that some of the young people have bought the notion of the American Dream in its entirety and are avidly pursuing it, fantasizing about big houses and fancy cars—supported in some cases by M.B.A.'s or medical degrees, supported in other cases by big gang heists. Others of them, the middle generation of Hmong in particular, those who came here as adolescents, often speak of feeling lost and betrayed— unprepared by a late and too meager education for life in a world so different from the one in which they spent their formative years.

The child-of-an-immigrant who still lives inside me was a bit taken aback to discover, as I sat with my intermediary, Ghia Xiong, and interviewed the narrators of this book, that to many of them I was one of the "real Americans," just as the blue-eyed blonds had seemed to me in my younger years. I spoke English without an accent, I drove a car and dressed like a middle-class person, I was comfortable in this country that was still so foreign to them. And I wondered which immigrants of the future, some time in the twenty-first century, startled awake in this strange land, would be looking upon these Hmong people or their descendants as the "real Americans."

The Hmong immigrants and their children who speak in this book have voices that are filled with despair as well as hope, with discovery and loss, and with frustration and satisfaction. They tell the story of America as it is being relived once again, by what is, for now, one of our newest immigrant groups.

A Note on Methodology

Ghia Xiong, who is a native speaker of Hmong, acted as my primary link to Hmong communities. Together we identified types of individuals and salient experiences that were representative of the Hmong in the United States: for example, people who had grown up in Hmong villages in Laos, children who were born in America, women who married before the age of seventeen, boys and girls who belonged to gangs, college students. Contacts were made, with Ghia acting as intermediary, through a variety of Hmong friendship circles, cultural centers, clan affiliations, and student groups.

Ghia's help was invaluable in a number of ways. He instructed me with regard to cultural protocol and linguistic nuance. Not only did he translate if the narrator spoke no English, but he also helped supply the English words when a limited speaker was grasping for an expression that was beyond his or her vocabulary. In addition, he provided me with many historical and factual details; he often asked cogent questions of the narrators about specific events or incidents that I would not have known to ask; and best of all, he introduced me to a courageous, tragic, hopeful, and wonderful community.

In several instances our narrators indicated, or we suspected, that they would be more comfortable in an interview conducted by another Hmong rather than by a non-Hmong. This was true most often if the narrator spoke no English. In those cases Ghia and I discussed what directions he might want to take in the interview, and he served as the interviewer. Proceedings were tape-recorded with the permission of the narrators.

The interviews were conducted primarily in the narrators' own homes, where we felt they would talk more freely than they might in the often-intimidating atmosphere of a faculty office at a university. Several narrators preferred to come to Ghia's home for an interview. And with the assistance of Barbara Blinik, a teacher who introduced us to six high school students, we also conducted interviews on their high school campus.

The interviews were as short or as long as the narrators wanted to make them. Most lasted for about two hours, but several lasted for many, many hours, often punctuated by long, emotional pauses, occasioned by the dredging up of suppressed memories or anger and frustration over current situations. As emotional as these sessions were, however, many narrators told us at the conclusion that they were happy for the opportunity to review their lives, not only for us but for themselves.

Ghia and I devised a list of more than a dozen topics we wished to raise in the interviews, but we quickly realized that the most interesting sessions were those we permitted to become open-ended. Hence, after asking a few factual questions such as "Where were you born?" we tried to determine what story the narrator thought it was important to tell, and we listened, asking questions primarily for clarification. If we knew in advance that the narrator had had experiences in areas in which we were especially interested, we tried to steer the narrative in that direction. For example, we would ask a healer, "Will you tell us about a healing you've done recently?" Thirty-six of the fifty-three people we interviewed are presented in this book.

The narrators' ages span from a girl of eleven to a man who identified himself as being sixty-six. It should be noted that there are few *very old* Hmong people in the United States because the more elderly Hmong were seldom willing or able to make the strenuous journey from Laotian mountain villages, through the war-torn jungles, across the dangerous Mekong River, to the relocation camps in Thailand, and then to America.

Our narrators were all living in central California or North Carolina at the time of the interviews. Since the Hmong are fairly new to the United States, we believed that vast regional differences within American Hmong communities are unlikely, though employment opportunities, which vary geographically, may have affected lifestyles to some extent even among these recent immigrants. In any case, many Hmong in America continue to be nomadic; a number of our narrators had lived within the last decade in Washington, Wisconsin, Oregon, Colorado, Iowa, Minnesota, Hawaii, or in cities in northern and southern California. An indication of this demographic instability is evident in the fact that when we began our interviews in 1994, the city of Fresno, California, had 35,000 Hmong (one of the highest Hmong concentrations in America), most of this Hmong population having arrived in America the mid or late 1980s. In 1996, as we finished our interviews, the Hmong population in Fresno had shrunk by approximately 5,000 (despite high birth rates). A large number of Hmong immigrants had left for North Carolina, where land is perceived to be cheaper and job opportunities more plentiful.

The narrators of this study represent ten of the twenty Hmong clans. Our interviews with young people suggested that despite the historical importance of clan affiliation in traditional Hmong culture, clan distinctions are becoming less significant in the Hmong diaspora in America. Indeed, some young people, particularly those involved in gangs, have formed "voluntary clans" which claim their allegiance more than the traditional Hmong clan into which they were born.

We have usually identified people by their real names if we received permission to do so. However, if the individual engaged in activities that would be considered illegal or socially embarrassing in a Western context (for example, opium use or polygamy) or if the individual was a minor and we could not get parental consent (as for gang members, for example), we have used a pseudonym to identify the narrator.

I have edited these interviews by cutting out material that was repetitious or extraneous to the themes shaped by the nine chapters of this book. Many of the narrators appear in several chapters because their stories address the various themes of those chapters. I have edited grammar largely to the extent that I judged that a statement might be incomprehensible without editing. By letting the narrators speak for themselves, in each of their own distinctive idioms, I hoped to capture their living voices, and to make those voices resound in the reader's ears as they have in mine.

Acknowledgments

I am grateful to the fifty-three members of the Hmong community who so generously shared their time and the stories of their lives. Though not all of their narratives have been included, this book is consistently informed by the knowledge gained from all of them. My greatest thanks go to Ghia Xiong, who served as translator and intermediary between me and the Hmong community. He has been unfailingly helpful, sensitive, intelligent, and patient. This project could never have come to fruition without him.

I would like to thank Barbara Blinik for arranging interviews with her students; Geri Echeverria for sharing her own expertise in oral history; Judy Parker for calling my attention to useful materials; and Phyllis Irwin, Virginia Hales, Anne du Pontavice, and Priscilla Allen, for reading portions of the manuscript during various stages of its development and providing much-needed encouragement.

I am grateful to the members of my department and school and to the best of deans, Dr. Luis Costa, for university research grants and the gift of time which permitted me to complete the manuscript for this book. Sandy Dijkstra, my agent, has continued to be a terrific ally throughout the years. Helene Atwan, my editor at Beacon Press, has been a pleasure to work with, as has my copy editor, Lydia Howarth.

Ghia Xiong and I would like to thank for their much appreciated help and advice, as well as the invaluable knowledge they shared with us, Dr. Serge Lee, Dr. Tony Vang, Dr. Jonas Vangay, Dr. Frank Ng, Mr. Tzer Lee, Mr. Bee Yang, and Mr. Choua Pao Xiong.

Ghia would like to thank "my wife, Hlee Vang, and my daughter, Jaclyn N. Xiong, for understanding why I had many excuses for not being there as a husband and a father; my brother-in-law, Shoua Yang, and sister-in-law, Sia Vang, for aid with transcriptions; my stepfather, Choua Pao (Ger) Xiong, for accepting me into the Xiong clan and giving me love, support, knowledge, and guidance; my mother, Txai Her, for enduring so much suffering to raise so many of us; and all of my half-siblings: Shoo, Sai, Eisen, Adam, Pheng, Dao, and Xia, for cheering me on."

My gratitude, too, goes to all of them.

I Begin My Life All Over

The Hmong

Where the Hmong came from originally is a mystery. Some scholars guess the Hmong roots to be "somewhere in Mesopotamia." That particular speculation is based on Hmong legends which have much in common with Babylonian narratives about the creation of the world, the first man and his trouble-causing wife, and the first sin. Hmong legend even speaks of a messiah who will come to earth in human form, though he will not be of human parents, and lead the Hmong back to their lost homeland.

Other scholars posit the Hmong origin to be Siberia, again based in part on Hmong legends, these alluding to the Hmong once having lived in a region "behind the back of China," where half of the year was always day and the other half was always night, where trees were rare and people wore fur. Still other scholars, who point to the similarity between the Chinese characters used in writing the words "Hmong" and "Mongols," suggest that the Hmong were really Mongolians who overthrew the Han emperor in the thirteenth century and ruled China for almost a hundred years as the Yuan dynasty. And still others point to yet another Hmong legend to argue that the Hmong had always lived in China. According to this legend, the Hmong were once ruled in a particular area of China by a Hmong king with magical powers, who lost the kingdom because he was betrayed by a beautiful Chinese princess, and hence the Hmong were dispersed throughout China.

What is more certain than the origin of the Hmong is their historical presence in China. The Hmong can be traced to settlements in the plains along the Yellow River more than five thousand years ago, from which they later retreated to the mountains of China where they might better defend themselves. Their gradual diaspora south may have started as long ago as 3000 B.C. When the Hmong pulled up roots, which was not infrequently, it was generally because some power had come along to threaten them—through unreasonable and punitive taxation, slavery, or ethnic persecution. The Hmong say they had an ancient written language, which the Chinese forced them to give up under threat of extermination (hence the Hmong language had no written form again until one was developed by missionaries in the 1950s). The Hmong were often in their history like the ancient Israelites who had to flee Egypt and became strangers in a strange land, wanderers, forced to run from attempts at genocide.

Though approximately seven million Hmong remain in China to this day, many Hmong left throughout the centuries in waves of emigration. In the eighteenth century, when the last Hmong king was murdered at the hands of the ruling Chinese dynasty, a great number of Hmong fled into Indochina. It has been claimed that those who remained were forced to wear identifying clothing as a form of ostracism.

Another major emigration occurred under threat of subjugation or massacre about 1810. Many of the fleeing Hmong settled in Vietnam, Thailand, and Southeast Burma. Others, the ancestors of most of the Hmong who are now in America, traveled south across rugged mountains into Laos and then dispersed into various little isolated villages on slopes that were sometimes as high as five thousand feet. There they eked out a living as farmers and hunters. The Hmong maintained their distinctiveness from the majority population that surrounded them, but they sustained their ties with other Hmong in distant villages through a shared religion, language, and history of persecution, much like the Jews who were scattered in shtetlach all over Eastern Europe.

When the Hmong arrived in Laos from China, Laos was already made up of about sixty different ethnic groups who spoke eighty different languages and dialects, so the Hmong were far from being the only group who came to Laos from elsewhere. In their remote mountain settlements they had little contact with the other populations, who generally inhabited the lowland. But the Hmong were despised anyway as intruders into a country not theirs. They were especially despised for religious reasons. Because they were animists, they were particularly resented by the Lao, the largest ethnic group, who were Buddhists. For the century and a half that the Hmong lived in Laos, they were essentially outsiders, tolerated as long as they were largely unseen.

In the highlands of Laos, the Hmong lived their lives much as they had in China. For instance, they continued their usual means of social organization. Traditionally, Hmong society is not a congregation of "individuals" but rather of extended families and large clans, to which one owes great allegiance. About twenty clans were represented in the Hmong's Laotian diaspora (and hence in their present American diaspora). Since clan names are taken as patronymics, there are no more than twenty different last names among the Hmong in Laos and America, though there are different spellings in the Roman alphabet of the same name, such as Lee and Ly. While in the Western world distant cousins are considered to be barely related, among the traditional Hmong those in a particular clan believe themselves to be directly tied to all other members of that clan, though they will never meet all of their "relatives." For example, all "Chang" consider themselves "brothers" or "sisters" to each other, which means that a Chang can never marry another Chang, unless willing to suffer clan ostracism.

Traditional Hmong have wanted to live near clansmen, with whom certain ties of rites and taboos were shared, but because Hmong marriages were necessarily exogamous, it was also important to live near some people who were not of one's clan so that matches could be made. For that reason, though villages varied in size from ten to hundreds of families, they were usually made up of more than one clan.

While women kept their own name when they married, once they became wives their own clan affiliation was of no consequence. They belonged entirely to their husband's clan, and their children always took the father's clan name. In a sense, a man's clan affiliation was more important to him than his marital tie, since the latter could be dissolved through divorce, while his clan affiliation was forever, both for him and for his sons.

The Hmong in Laos were slash-and-burn farmers. They built a village and then cut down trees and shrubs in a nearby forest. After the downed vegetation died, the farmers would burn it, creating ash that richly fertilized the soil, and then they would plant. After a few years, when the soil was depleted, the farmers would move on to a more distant forested area and begin all over again by clearing the vegetation. They had no modern tractors nor other technological conveniences that would make farming less laborious. The land was tilled with a plow drawn by an ox and planted by the men poking holes in the ground with a stick and the women and children dropping seeds into the holes. The farm provided enough beans, melon, yams, corn, and other vegetables for the family to eat and just a bit more to use in bartering for whatever else the family needed. The main cash crop was opium poppies (which families also used for aches and pains, "like Tylenol," as Shone Yang, one of our narrators, explains). The Hmong way of life in Laos remained virtually unchanged for about a century and a half, until the 1950s and 1960s.

By 1887 the French had annexed much of the Vietnamese empire and Cambodia, and six years later they forced Siam to cede all areas they controlled on the left bank of the Mekong River. Laos was thus established as a French protectorate. French interest in the Hmong for almost fifty years was limited to the Hmong farming of opium poppies, which the French made into a big business through export. But during World War II, the Hmong also became useful to the French when Hmong guerrilla soldiers fought the Japanese in the Laotian jungles. This early use of the Hmong to serve European interests was the beginning of a relationship between the Hmong and the West which, after their recruitment into the United States' secret and unsuccessful war against Communism in Laos, would finally catapult the dispossessed Hmong to America.

After World War II, the French were constrained to struggle in Southeast Asia yet again, now to contain the spread of Communism in the region. In 1950, when North Korea invaded South Korea, the United States decided to come to the aid of the

French in Indochina. In 1953 the Viet Minh began to invade northern Laos and the Hmong homelands in order to build trails in Laos to facilitate their takeover of South Vietnam (see map, p. 6). In 1954, President Eisenhower authorized supplies to support the pro-French forces in Laos, but when the Viet Minh Communist forces gained clear control of the north of Laos, the French recognized the futility of their struggle, signed an accord with Ho Chi Minh's government in North Vietnam, and in July 1954, the French withdrew from the region.

Though the accord declared Laos to be a neutral zone, the United States, embracing the domino theory, feared the fall of Laos as a key domino and took steps to prop up the country in order to keep the entire region from collapsing to Communist control. Thus in 1955 the United States set up in Laos a "Program Evaluation Office," a disguised military group sent to advise the Royal Lao Army in their fight against the Laotian Communist faction, the Pathet Lao. By 1959 the U.S. Central Intelligence Agency (CIA) was recruiting Hmong agents to gather intelligence about North Vietnamese movements in Laos. These events clearly marked the beginning of the end for the Hmong's relatively peaceful way of life in the mountains of Laos.

Under President Kennedy, in 1961, the United States, supporting the installation of a strong non-Communist government in Laos, began sending special forces to the area to help train Royal Lao Army soldiers for combat. From that time to 1973, the United States also provided Laos with air support and supplies—but while American involvement in Vietnam was overt, involvement in Laos was a secret that was kept from the American public until years after the war. Because the United States doubted the ability of the Royal Lao Army to defend Laos, still another covert program was established in the early 1960s specifically to train the Hmong to fight, since they were considered to be especially valuable as soldiers because they knew the mountains of Laos well. The Hmong fighting force was put under the control of the CIA, and this agency elevated the only Hmong commissioned officer in the Royal Lao Army, the charismatic Lieutenant Colonel Vang Pao, to the rank of general and encouraged him to organize eighty-four companies of Hmong infantry.

Without America being "officially in Laos," the CIA supplied Vang Pao's forces under the cover of a governmental organization that was supposed to help refugees—the U.S. Agency for Aid and Development. Hmong soldiers were formed into special guerrilla units to harass the Communists with lightning attacks. They were also to block shipments of materiel along the Ho Chi Minh trail that were headed for the Communist Pathet Lao, rescue American pilots whose planes were shot down on bombing runs over northern Laos, and fly U.S.-supplied planes to gather intelligence and to deliver materiel to the two hundred mountain airstrips the Hmong soldiers had built.

Many Hmong soldiers were trained to use advanced weapons and were flooded with modern military equipment. Their monthly salary was six times higher than that of the soldiers in the Royal Lao Army. But glamorous weapons and high salaries were not the primary incentives that persuaded the Hmong to participate in a war that would eventually uproot many of them and leave them with a casualty rate that was proportionally ten times higher than American losses in Vietnam. Most Hmong knew very little about ideology or differences between Communism and Capitalism; the communal farming in which they often happily engaged can even be considered a kind of "communism." But they were convinced by those who recruited them that the North Vietnamese would invade them, take their homes, and subjugate them if they did not fight.

And perhaps they also had another emotional motive in agreeing to fight, one which was not unlike that of the German Jews who fought on the side of the "Fatherland" in World War I: The Lao had long referred to the Hmong as "parasites without a country." They contemptuously called the Hmong people

"Meo," which they may or may not have known was a neutral synonym for "Hmong" in Chinese—but in Laotian the term denoted "slave." Perhaps the Hmong believed that if they helped save Laos from the Communists, those Laotians who opposed Communism might finally treat them as equals rather than with the customary disdain.

If, however, the Hmong hoped their contribution to the fight against Communism would elevate them in Laotian society, the staggering losses they suffered must have tempered that hope. By 1971 many Hmong families had no more males, not even boys as young as ten. In the last years of fighting, 70 percent of the new recruits were between the ages of ten and sixteen because there were so few men left. Boys as tall as a carbine became "carbine soldiers." If a boy was shorter than a carbine, he would be taken into the army in some nonarmed capacity such as a cook's helper or one who clears the runway when a plane is coming in for a landing, a job that Ghia's uncle, Ger Xiong, held when he was twelve years old. Before the war was over about one-third of the entire Laotian Hmong population was killed, including half of all the males over fifteen.

Many of the heaviest battles of the war in Laos were waged near Hmong villages, which meant that great numbers of people had to flee. For as long as the United States was in Southeast Asia, American planes dropped rice, salt, medicine, blankets, canned fish, and even live pigs for the fleeing refugees. But in 1971, the United States, discouraged as the French had been two decades earlier, began cutting down on military air support. In 1974, the U.S. Agency for Aid and Development declared that it would no longer help the refugees, and the CIA withdrew completely in 1975.

The Communists overcame the Royal Lao Army, and in May 1975 the Americans airlifted General Vang Pao to Thailand. For several days America sent cargo planes to assist Vang Pao's supporters in their escape. Over forty thousand refugees headed en masse toward the airlift operation in the city of Long Cheng, where CIA headquarters had been, with all their portable worldly possessions strapped to their backs, but no more than fifteen thousand people were able to get on the planes. The rest were left to find their own way out and were soon joined by more than a hundred thousand other desperate Hmong refugees, who were panicked because they believed that the Communists intended to exterminate all the Hmong who had supported General Vang Pao and the United States.

The Hmong had been given promises by the CIA that even if the war were lost, they would be protected and aided. However, years passed before the United States began to keep those promises: Since American involvement in Laos was not supposed to have existed, the CIA believed it was important to maintain the secret, and they feared that excessive U.S. concern about the plight of the Hmong might be taken as a tacit admission of obligation for services rendered. Though the United States soon began resettling anti-Communist Vietnamese who were uprooted by the war, the Hmong were for a time essentially on their own.

In December 1975 the Pathet Lao Communists formed the Lao People's Democratic Republic. They set up prison labor camps to "reeducate" those who had been instrumental in the fight against them. Reports from survivors depict "reeducation" camps as no different from concentration camps, replete with hard labor, starvation, sadistic torture, and other atrocities. Though the Communists sometimes promised Hmong ex-soldiers that those who had not been leaders would be permitted to resume their old lives, many former soldiers feared to go back to their villages because they were certain they would either be sent to a "reeducation" camp or be killed. Some destroyed their military uniforms, hid their weapons, and slipped back into their villages pretending they had not been soldiers. Many others gathered their families and ran to the nearby jungles where they hid, often for years.

When the Hmong activated the Chao Fa as a resistance movement (see page 45), the Pathet Lao launched air strikes against village and jungle areas that were thought to harbor Chao Fa. With the agreement of the Pathet Lao, sixty thousand Vietnamese troops and thousands more Vietnamese advisors occupied Laos, and especially Hmong villages, in order to help defeat the resisters. The U.S. Congress had passed a quota exemption for Southeast Asian war refugees in 1975, and other Western countries, principally Australia, France, and Canada, also opened their doors to refugees who could make their way out of Communist countries. Thus waves of immigrants now risked their lives to traverse the mined jungles and cross the Mekong River that flows down the borders of northern Laos and Thailand. In decimated numbers the Hmong entered Thailand and were taken to relocation camps. After a period of time, many qualified for resettlement.

If accepted for resettlement consideration, the refugees were sent to processing centers such as Phanat Nikhom where they were given medical screenings and were queried about their family history, military service, and use of opium. Those who were approved for resettlement were given some language instruction and were taught basics such as how to use a telephone or a stove. Missionaries in the camps also tried to "Westernize" the Hmong.

As several of the narrators in chapter 4, "To a Promised Land," suggest, however, the instruction that Hmong refugees received in the relocation camps was far from adequate for many who had lived their whole lives no differently from their ancestors in earlier centuries. But though orientation to Western life was not extensive with regard to formal instruction in the camps, in some ways camp life itself was a foreshadowing of the profound changes that would affect the Hmong immigrants who settled in the West. There were few aspects of their traditional life that were not impacted. For example, young men in the camps feared to engage in the time-honored tradition of kidnap marriage that the Hmong had brought with them from China and then Laos because Thai camp authorities would prosecute if a girl's father complained that she had been abducted, and missionaries too would be vociferous in their disapproval. Traditional healing methods of shamans and herbalists were also challenged through Western medical services that were supplied by relief agencies in the camps. When they first came to the camps, Hmong leaders discouraged their clans from accepting inoculations and other Western medical treatment that the relief agencies offered. But as time wore on, more and more people combined visits to Western doctors and the pharmacy in the camp with their faith in shamanistic healing and herb treatments.

In streams, sometimes greater and sometimes lesser, the Hmong in Laos continued to run from the new Communist government, crossing the Mekong into Thailand and arriving at a relocation camp. Many of them hoped that they would qualify for resettlement; others desired eventually to return to Laos—a dream that was kindled by Vang Pao who was now in the United States and hoping that a resistance movement which he sponsored, the Neo Hom, would soon succeed in making Laos safe for the Hmong once again.

In 1983, the largest of the camps, Ban Vanai, was closed to new arrivals, who were now sent to Chiang Kham, an austere, bare-subsistence camp that made the other camps "look like country clubs," according to observers. In Chiang Kham life was purposely made difficult by the Thai authorities in order to discourage immigration into their country and encourage emigration out of it, to resettlement or, if possible, to repatriation.

Many of the Hmong continued to leave the camps for America throughout the 1980s and 1990s, up to 1996, when the last relocation camp in Thailand was closed. The Hmong who were still there were told by the Thai, who had become increasingly hostile to their unwelcome visitors who had long overstayed their "visit," that they must either resettle in a third country or be repatriated into Laos, as was by now possible for many of them. That year brought one last major immigration of several thousand Hmong into the United States.

In all, about 130,000 Hmong refugees have come to the United States, but the high Hmong birthrate accounts for a much higher American-Hmong population. The Hmong are now spread out over many parts of the country, though particular areas have dense concentrations. For example, St. Paul, Minnesota, is home to about thirty-five thousand Hmong; almost fifty thousand Hmong live in central California, more than thirty thousand of them in the city of Fresno.

Adjustment to life in the United States has been difficult for the Hmong, especially for older people. As one of our narrators, sixty-six-year-old Boua Xa Moua, observed, in their mountain villages the Hmong were free to roam everywhere; now they must learn to wait patiently for the light to turn green and then cross only in the crosswalks. So many of the Hmong's habits and cultural values have been turned upside down in this country. What was legal and socially acceptable in the Hmong village is often criminal or taboo here. In Laos, for example, one could hunt or fish anywhere; in America, as many Hmong have discovered, you can be fined if you haven't first procured hunting or fishing licenses. In Laos, polygamy was legal and not uncommon; here it is against the law and socially condemned. In Laos, opium is not only a cash crop, but people use it regularly to treat headaches; here, of course, one can be sent to jail for growing or using opium. As another of our narrators, Phia Chang, an opium smoker, sadly demonstrates, your moral sense of yourself undergoes a wretched metamorphosis if you are suddenly forced to see your habitual behavior as criminal.

Many honored American values are painfully confusing to the Hmong because they are in opposition to what the Hmong have always cherished. For example, in Laos, what was good for the family superseded individual interest; what was good for the spirit superseded material interest. Yet young Hmong people here realize that if one is to succeed in American terms it is important to adopt the American values of individualism and materialism, and that realization often throws them in conflict with the older generation.

Western sex roles, which are profoundly different from the roles played traditionally by males and females among the Hmong, have been especially problematic. The Hmong family in Laos was emphatically patrilocal, patrilineal, and patriarchal. For Hmong women of the middle generation—those who were born in Southeast Asia but came here before adulthood—life in America can be very confusing. Their mothers had ten or twelve children and spent their entire lives serving their husbands. But these younger Hmong women who were raised in the United States grew up in the midst of a feminist revolution, which they could not escape learning about through American schools and the media. By law or contemporary custom, women are supposed to be equal to men and not their servants. Young Hmong women with middle-class aspirations understand further that you're supposed to want no more than a couple of children; you're supposed to prepare yourself for a career and take that career at least as seriously as you take family life.

Their parents, however, cannot understand such goals. They often pressure their daughters incessantly to marry young and start having children immediately. From our women narrators of the middle generation I often heard painful ambivalence when they talked about how they were pulled between the notions implanted in them by two such disparate cultures. These disturbing contrasts between Hmong cultural tradition and Western life have caused not only confusion in the women but also, as Soua Teng Vang, a fifty-one-year-old immigrant man observed when he talked to us, terrible anguish among Hmong men. Many have been plagued here by various new ills, most notably the baffling Sudden Unexpected Nocturnal Death Syndrome, in which "healthy" victims die in their sleep of causes which cannot be determined. The problems of Hmong men in America are manifold, but certainly among the most traumatic is their struggle in adjusting to new rules and demands in gender relationships.

Generational conflicts have also been disturbing to Hmong family life in America. For example, Hmong parents from Southeast Asia have a hard time understanding the concept of "teenager" when their American-educated children explain their behavior or sense of identity with that word. The parents themselves never experienced adolescence because back in Laos one moved directly from childhood to adulthood. Typically, girls married at fourteen years of age, and boys married when they were only a few years older. In America, when children reach those years usually they do not marry. They stay in school; and when they want to date as their American schoolmates do and engage in other behaviors that would tarnish their reputations under the scrutiny of traditional Hmong standards, their parents feel threatened and frightened.

Parental control of children was unquestioned in Laos.

Here parents feel that they have totally lost control. Most often, they blame the schools in America: for undermining their authority by conflating discipline with child abuse, for failing to inculcate in children the moral feeling of guilt when they behave badly, for teaching their children things the parents regard as outrageous, such as sex education, which, the parents fear, will ruin their children for traditional Hmong life. The parents are also confounded and upset daily by American music and television, which they see as aggressively promulgating images of uninhibited sexuality and therefore contributing to their children's knowledge of "bad things."

The younger generation of Hmong people, those who were born in America, have still another set of struggles and confusions. They often say that they feel they are not 100 percent anything though, as some of our young narrators like Ying Chang and Blia Vang admit, they were brought up on television as much as any American kid is nowadays. Their values and habits have been formed largely by the American media—in startling contrast to their parents' values and habits. Yet it is their parents whom they love and have to live with and not the characters in *Full House*. They want to honor their parents' culture by learning aspects of it, but there is no time to do that in America: How can you learn to do *paj ntaub* (the beautiful Hmong embroidery that dates back centuries to the Hmong diaspora in China) or to play the *qeej* (the traditional Hmong bamboo pipes that always accompanied celebrations and mourning) if you have to do homework and participate in the extra-curricular activities of American schools? Learning about your parents' culture necessarily takes a low priority compared to preparing yourself to succeed in America—which entails learning about the larger American culture. For young people, *tradition* has come to mean dressing up in Hmong "costume" for the New Year or perhaps mastering some "traditional dances," but it cannot be the daily lived experiences of their parents or older siblings.

These quiet and not so quiet turmoils, these personal histories that have been so affected by the sweep of political history which has taken the Hmong from village life that had been unchanged for generations, to the war which uprooted that life, to a vastly different life in America on the cusp of the twenty-first century—these poignant tragedies and testimonies to human endurance have all been recorded in the narratives that follow.

The Narrators

The Older Generation

Phia Chang (pseud.),
a man in his sixties, became an opium smoker in Laos where
many farmers grew opium as a cash crop. He smoked to alleviate aches and pains. Since coming to the United States, he has
struggled to break his opium habit. Phia Chang's narrative
appears in "To a Promised Land."

Khou Her
was born in the mountains of Laos, from which she fled during
the war. She lived in the jungle for more than two years before
escaping to Thailand, where she stayed in two relocation camps
before coming to the United States. She is thirty-nine years old
and a homemaker. Khou Her's narrative appears in "The Village" and "The Camp."

Boua Xa Moua
was born in Laos in 1931. He became an expert *qeej* player as a
young man, playing often for funerals and celebrations. He continues to be well-known as a *qeej* player in Hmong communities in the United States. Boua Xa Moua's narrative appears in
"The Village" and "To a Promised Land."

Yo Moua
was born in Laos in 1957. When he was eighteen he helped his
whole family escape to Thailand before escaping himself. In the
United States he has been active in a movement to preserve the
Hmong language and culture. He works as a Hmong-speaking
assistant in a Headstart Program. Yo Moua's narrative appears
in "The Village."

Doua Vang,
Ghia Xiong's father-in-law, is a shaman and a farmer. He currently resides in a newly formed Hmong community in Albemarle, North Carolina. He is forty-nine years old. Doua Vang's narrative appears in "The Village."

Soua Teng Vang
was born in the village of Xiang Khua, Laos, in 1946. During the war he served in the Lao army as a physician's assistant. He now lives with his wife and several of his children in Fresno, California. Soua Teng Vang's narrative appears in "Women and Men" and "Battles between the Generations."

Chue Vue (pseud.)
was born in Laos thirty-six years ago. Through kidnap marriage she became a third wife in a polygamous household when she was seventeen years old. She has been married for nineteen years. Chue Vue's narrative appears in "Women and Men."

Kia Vue
is forty-two years old. She came to the United States in 1980 with five children and no husband. She was remarried in California but is now living with only two of her sons and two daughters, including a four-year-old. She has not mastered English. Kia Vue's narrative appears in "Battles between the Generations."

Mee Vue,
mother-in-law of Ia Vang Xiong, was born in the Hmong village of Qhov Dav. When the Vietnamese invaded the area, she and her children ran off to the jungle with a group of Chao Fa resistance fighters. She came to the United States to be reunited with a married son, but her other children remain in Southeast Asia. She is in her sixties and has not been able to learn English, but she occupies herself by taking care of her two grandchildren while her son and daughter-in-law work. Mee Vue's narrative appears in "The Escape," "To a Promised Land," and "Being American."

Ger Xiong,
the uncle of Ghia Xiong, worked helping to land allied airplanes on a mountain airstrip when he was twelve years old, in
1965, before joining the army a couple of years later. After the
fall of Laos to the Communists, he became a member of the
Chao Fa resistance movement. In the United States he has been
a prominent leader of the Xiong clan. Ger Xiong's narrative
appears in "The Escape."

Nao Kao Xiong
became a healer in Laos, where he often tended General Vang
Pao's sick and wounded soldiers. He is fifty-nine years old and
is renowned in Hmong communities in America for his ability
to cure spiritual and physical illnesses. Nao Kao Xiong's narrative appears in "Shamanism, Christianity, and Modern
Medicine."

The Middle Generation

Chia Ton Cha
was born in Laos and came to America with his family as a
child. He enlisted in the U.S. Army after graduating from high
school in 1990. His friends still call him "Commando," but he is
presently a college student, majoring in biology, at California
State University, Dominguez Hills. He is twenty-four years old.
Chia Ton Cha's narrative appears in "The Camp" and "Being
American."

Bee Thao
wandered with his family in the jungle for three years after they
escaped from their mountain village in Laos. In 1979 they went
to Thailand where they lived in the Nong Khai and Ban Vanai
relocation camps. Bee Thao came to the United States in 1987,
at the age of sixteen. He is president of the Hmong Student Association at California State University, Fresno, where he is a pre-
dentistry major. Bee Thao's narrative appears in "The Escape,"
"The Camp," "Women and Men," and "Being American."

Phooj Thao (pseud.)
was born in Laos and came to America at the age of nine after
spending four years in a Thai relocation camp. He is presently
working on a master's degree in anthropology and lives with his
wife and infant son. Phooj Thao's narrative appears in "Women
and Men."

Elizabeth Mee Vang
escaped with her family from Laos at the age of four and grew
up in relocation camps. In 1980 the family was brought to Oregon by church sponsors and converted to Christianity. Elizabeth Mee Vang is attending National University and hopes to
become a teacher. She lives with her husband and one child. Elizabeth Mee Vang's narrative appears in "Women and Men."

Tony Vang
was born in 1954. He came to the United States at the age of eighteen, several years in advance of the mass migration of Southeast Asian refugees. Tony Vang attended the University of
Hawaii, graduating with honors, and then went on to receive a
doctorate. He is now a professor of Asian Studies at California
State University, Stanislaus. Tony Vang's narrative appears in
"Being American."

Ghia Xiong
served as translator and community contact for this book. He
was born in the mountains of Laos in 1971. After he and his family escaped from Laos, they lived in the Ban Vanai relocation
camp until 1981, when they came to the United States. Ghia
Xiong is a college student majoring in biological sciences. He
lives in Fresno with his wife and baby daughter, and he works as
a medical technician at Valley Children's Hospital. Ghia Xiong's
narrative appears in "The Village" and "To a Promised Land."

Ia Vang Xiong,
daughter-in-law of Mee Vue, was born in 1971 in Laos. When
she was twelve years old she and her family settled in Minnesota. Ia Vang Xiong is now a third-grade teacher, having been

one of the first Hmong to receive a teaching credential in the state of California. Ia Vang Xiong's narrative appears in "The Escape," "Women and Men," and "Being American."

Mai Xiong (pseud.),
born in 1977, was raised in the United States. She was married at the age of sixteen but continued going to high school. She presently attends junior college and hopes to become a teacher. Mai Xiong, her husband, and their two little children live with her in-laws. Mai Xiong's narrative appears in "Women and Men."

Shoua Xiong
was converted to Christianity as a child when she and her family came to Iowa as refugees under church sponsorship. When she married at the age of fourteen, in 1986, she converted back again to shamanism at her husband's insistence. She has four children. Shoua Xiong's narrative appears in "The Escape," "To a Promised Land," and "Women and Men."

Vicki Xiong
escaped from Laos with her family as a young child. She married while still in high school but waited until after college graduation to have a baby. Her brothers were active gang members, and she is the first in her family to get a college degree. She practices Catholicism with her in-laws and shamanism with her parents. Vicki Xiong's narrative appears in "Shamanism, Christianity, and Modern Medicine," "Gangs," and "Being American."

Zai Xiong
fled with his family from their mountain village when he was six or seven years old, and they lived in the jungle for three years. He was brought up in shamanism but became a Mormon in the United States. He is married and has one son. Zai Xiong's narrative appears in "Shamanism, Christianity, and Modern Medicine," "Women and Men," and "Battles between the Generations."

Chue Yang
was born in Long Cheng and orphaned when he was a child. He
escaped from Laos at the age of seventeen. He learned English
in a special camp in Thailand that was set up for refugees who
were coming to America. He has been in the United States since
1988. Chue Yang's narrative appears in "The Camp."

Ger Yang
was born in Laos and was brought up in the tradition of shamanism. He is one of the first Hmong dentists in America, and
he practices family dentistry in Fresno, California. Dr. Yang, a
father of four, is thirty-four years old. His narrative appears in
"Shamanism, Christianity, and Modern Medicine" and "Battles
between the Generations."

Shone Yang
was born in the Hmong village of Numfan in Laos and came to
the United States as a teenager. He holds a bachelor of science
degree in chemistry and is working in a laboratory. He continues to practice shamanism and to play the *qeej*. He is twenty-
five years old. Shone Yang's narrative appears in "The Village,"
"Shamanism, Christianity, and Modern Medicine," and
"Women and Men."

The Younger Generation

Susie Chang (pseud.)
was raised in Minneapolis, Minnesota, and Fresno, California.
She is sixteen years old and has been a member of a Hmong girl
gang since the age of twelve. Susie Chang's narrative appears in
"Gangs."

Ying Chang (pseud.)
was born in St. Paul, Minnesota. He has been a gangster since
the age of eleven or twelve. Most of his gang friends are in jail or

dead, he says, and he would like to "jump out" of the gang. He has recently gotten a janitorial job. Ying Chang's narrative appears in "Battles between the Generations" and "Gangs."

Pao Her (pseud.),
who came to the United States with his family at the age of four, learned English by watching American television. His parents still speak only Hmong. He is now eighteen years old and is looking for work. Pao Her's narrative appears in "Being American."

Sonny Lee
is a former gangster. He is now married and lives with his wife and his parents in Fresno, California. He is nineteen years old. Sonny Lee's narrative appears in "Gangs."

Phia Lor (pseud.)
is thirteen years old and was born in the United States. He lives in Fresno, California, and belongs to a gang made up of twelve-to fifteen-year-olds. Phia Lor's narrative appears in "Gangs."

Mai Moua (pseud.)
was born in 1978 in a relocation camp and brought to the United States by her family at the age of three. She is a graduating high school senior and says she would like to "go away to college" and become a psychologist. Mai Moua's narrative appears in "Battles between the Generations" and "Being American."

Blia Vang (pseud.)
was born in the United States. She was engaged to a fourteen-year-old boy when she was thirteen years old and a middle school student. As was traditionally appropriate, she lived in his family's home, doing the duties of a wife. However, after several months, she returned to her parents' home. She is now a high school junior. Blia Vang's narrative appears in "Women and Men" and "Battles between the Generations."

"Loco" Vang (pseud.)
is eighteen years old and has been a gang member since the age of twelve. He comes from a family of seven children and says he

gets money to support himself through gang activities. He has been arrested six or seven times. "Loco" Vang's narrative appears in "Gangs."

Susie Vang (pseud.)
is eleven years old and was born in the United States. She is the third child in a family of ten children. Her parents speak only Hmong, but she is bilingual. She calls herself "an American kid." Susie Vang's narrative appears in "Being American."

Mike Yang (pseud.)
was born in Honolulu, Hawaii, in 1978 and came to the mainland as a high school sophomore. He became involved in gang activities and was expelled from school. However, he was permitted to reenter and has received his high school diploma. Mike Yang's narrative appears in "Gangs."

Penny Yang (pseud.)
is seventeen years old and was born in the United States. She is the daughter of a Hmong father and a Japanese mother. She grew up speaking only English. Penny Yang's narrative appears in "Being American."

Part I

The End of a Way of Life

The Village

Like my mother's family in Preil, who lived very much as her ancestors had when they first wandered into that Latvian shtetl generations earlier, the lives of the Laotian Hmong well into the twentieth century changed little from the lives of their great-great-great-grandparents. There was no increase in the range of opportunities from generation to generation. They married young, had many children, kept a modest roof over their heads, and barely managed to get enough to eat.

The roof over my mother's head had been thatched from materials that her great-grandfather and grandfather had gathered from the forest that lay just outside the shtetl. The sides of the house were shingles made from hardwood trees. The floors were dirt. Water had to be carried from a well. There was, of course, no such thing as plumbing. (Most of my life I have called a toilet seat a "board," the English word for the Yiddish *bretl*, which my mother had always used to refer to a toilet seat. It was only recently that I realized *bretl* must have referred to the board with the hole in it on which one sits in an outhouse!)

Like the shtetl home, the Hmong home had not changed its design for generations. It had a thatched roof, generally made of materials such as elephant grass or palm leaves from the nearby jungles. The sides of the house were of shingles or split bamboo. The floors were hard-stomped dirt, on which wood fires could be made for cooking. A man, his wife or wives, all his unmarried children, and generally at least one married son and his wife and their children would live together—sometimes as many as twenty people in a small house of not more than a thousand square feet. There was usually one large room that served as "living room," "dining room," "kitchen," and

◁ A village home

"family room." Off to the sides there were a couple of small bedrooms. "Closets" were planks fastened to the rafters. The furniture consisted of beds and stools woven of bamboo. The family ate at a table—a round tray made of woven bamboo—that was placed on the floor.

Almost all of the family worked the farm, from the little children to the able-bodied grandparents, though the very young were taken care of by a slightly older child or a grandmother or grandfather who was too old for strenuous farm labor. Like Western families who worked together in cottage industries in other centuries, like most of my mother's family—parents, sons, and daughters—who sewed at home for a living, the Hmong family stayed together all day long, everyone engaged in joint work occupations that would give the family enough money to subsist.

Occasionally one child, almost always a boy, might be spared from his farm labors and sent to school, so that his family would have a member who is literate. The schools were set up by the Laotian government. Therefore, students would learn how to read in Lao, and then learn Lao history and a little bit of French, as well as basic subjects such as arithmetic. But such study was not considered essential for most Hmong. They had no formal education, and they knew little Lao and no French, despite the fact that they were living in Laos, and the French had dominated in that country since the nineteenth century. Hmong was for all practical purposes their only language—just as Yiddish was my mother's only language for all practical purposes, though she lived in Latvia, a country that was seldom free from Russian domination in the nineteenth and twentieth centuries. Both communities—the Hmong in Laos and the shtetl Jews in Eastern Europe—were so self-sufficient and geographically or socially insulated, whether by volition or because of hostility toward them, that there was no need for most of the people in those communities to learn Laotian or French, Latvian or Russian.

In the Laotian schools teaching was generally accomplished through the rote method and apparently was very effective with regard to basic subjects. While most of the Hmong population was illiterate, several of our narrators said that all those who attended school even for a short period of time, such as a year or two, learned how to read. Knowing of the functional illiteracy problems in the United States, despite laws that keep students in school until they are sixteen years old, I was surprised—until I remembered that my mother attended school for only about a year in her shtetl, yet she could read the Hebrew prayer book, and in America she often read the *Forwards*, a popular daily Yiddish newspaper. In both the village and the shtetl, children seemed to take very seriously the privilege that was given them to have some respite from manual labors, and they knew they had better learn quickly because the privilege would not last long.

Shamanism, the traditional religion of the Hmong, played a central part in the Hmong villagers' daily lives, since it was both a belief system and a health system. The shaman could heal body or soul through his ability to go into a trance and communicate with spirits from the other world who would inform him what must be done in order to effect a cure. It was the duty of the family whom the shaman was helping to know how much he ought to be paid for his services. The shaman himself never requested remuneration. In his ostensible disinterest in materialism, he was to be a model for the rest of the community who, ideally, cared much more about the undoubted powers of the unseen world than the remote possibility of riches in this world. It is not astonishing to hear that Doua Vang, one of our narrators, gave up a treasure, as he describes it, because to get the treasure would have involved disturbing the resting place of a spirit.

Village life, which had remained so steady and unchanging for generations, was thrown into upheaval in the 1960s as the Hmong were drawn deeply into the war. As a result of the great slaughter of Hmong soldiers and civilians, and a mass exodus from Laos of survivors, many of the villages were emptied of their population and no longer exist.

Doua Vang, Ghia Xiong's father-in-law, has been a shaman for
many years. This experience which he related to us occurred when
he was a young man.

In Laos there was much magic. For instance, in Seng Tong there
was a god whom we offered gifts to yearly. This ensured us that
everyone in the village would have a good harvest season and
everyone would be in good health. This god, Dab Phuaj Thaub,
used to live in the mountain of Phuaj Thaub, but that is all gone
now because a landing strip for airplanes has been built on the
mountain.

I farmed near this mountain. It is huge. People said that
on the very top of the mountain there was a flat valleylike place
where banana trees, pepper trees, sugarcane, some *luam laws*
and *pum hub* all grew. It seemed like there was someone living
there, because whatever grew there was the same kind of thing
that grew in the village. Around that place was just a wild jungle
with tigers roaring and all sorts of creatures crying.

Almost on the top of that mountain there used to be a cave
full of treasure—like it had gold bracelets, silver bracelets, and
valuable coins. Each Hmong New Year, a long, long time ago,
people would go up there and borrow the jewels to wear, and
then they would return them after the New Year. But as more
people were borrowing, there were less jewels being returned.
So people now said that the god hid the treasure away in another cave—or maybe what happened was that since everyone
knew where it was, somebody just robbed the whole treasure.

Anyway, where I farmed there were a lot of tigers, so one
night my friend and I went hunting for them. We were just
going around, scaring them off—we had a flashlight with us.
A few hundred feet away from where I farmed, we came to this
cave. It was a cave that was almost at the top of the mountain,
and near this cave there was a group of monkeys—not a lot of
them, about seven or eight—hanging around all the time. I
used to hear them a lot. Each morning you came out to farm
you could hear them, but it is impossible to kill them. When
you shoot there is no sound at all: what I mean is, the gun won't
fire. This is why the elders say you can't kill them—because

these are the Ghost Monkeys. When I was small I did try to shoot them, but my gun didn't go off. That was a good thing because whoever does kill them, the elders say, they will soon be killing another human or they will die themselves. For example, a friend now living in Merced, Toubee. His son Tia, when we were on our way to Thailand, he shot down a male monkey near the cave. Then, when we got to another village, he was killed. Now his widow wife is in Wisconsin.

So when my friend and I were hunting tigers and we came to this cave near the monkeys, we sneaked around the monkeys and we flashed the light into the cave. It reflected back like there was some shining thing inside. We didn't go in—we ran back home and told my uncle. He said, "It's probably jewels or money in there."

So he went to see a *saub*, and the *saub* told him, "There are two treasures in there." We all went back and we used a ladder to climb up to the cave. It was so dark we had to have our flashlights.

We started digging, and slowly we came on metal bells, swords, bracelets, coins, and other things that are used by humans. Finally we found some human bones and we were very scared. We were scared because my uncle said that maybe this was the cave that used to be Toj Phim Nyaj's living place, and she would capture people and take them up here and eat them. She is a guardian of the mountain caves.

We knew we had really found a treasure place—whether of a god or Toj Phim Nyaj or whatever—and we knew that there would be more jewels if we dug down deeper—but should we do it? We were scared because what if this was really Toj Phim Nyaj's cave? We shouldn't be disturbing her rest place. We thought and thought about it, and finally we knew we must just go away.

How did that treasure come there? Maybe it was the treasure the god had hidden. Or maybe it belonged to the Chao Fa people who did not want to leave Laos when the Vietnamese came. It may be that the god told them to hide here. Many people who did not want to leave hid like that. Then many of them died of sickness, thirst, and hunger. And that place where they died just became forbidden.

When a place like that mountaintop is forbidden for such a reason, no one is allowed to ride horses over it or to wear a hat when they cross it. If they did what they weren't supposed to do, just before they finished crossing that mountain, they would have a bleeding nose and be sick. But when the Americans came during the war, they wanted our soldiers to make an airport where planes can go—right on that mountaintop.

At the time the god was still living there. When the soldiers tried to dig, there were a lot of them getting sick and having nosebleeds. The soldiers would just start working, and slowly, one by one, they all passed out. The Americans thought that the soldiers were lying, so they took a movie camera to see what was going on—and they saw it was true. Then, finally, they had to use dynamite to clear a place for the airplanes on the mountain.

Since the dynamiting, no one got sick when they tried to do anything on that mountaintop. Everything was normal. Now you can climb on top of that mountain and nothing would happen. But the country was lost.

Boua Xa Moua, who became a player of the traditional bamboo pipes in his mountain village in Laos, is now famous for his playing skill in the urban Hmong communities in America.

My father died when I was ten years old, and my mother died when I was very small, so I had to go work for other people. I wore other people's throwaway pants and their shirts that had no sleeves left. I would just work for food. I knew that whatever I needed I would have to get with my own two hands. Though I was very poor, I never let myself depend on other people, because I would feel more ashamed. I was already ashamed of being an orphan child, so for me to go asking for pity would only make me feel worse.

I was so poor all I had was my life to hold on to. When my

Water buffalo in a Hmong village ▷

parents died I felt like I was just a dead person that hadn't yet rotted away. I just ate whatever the people I lived with gave me. I knew I had to work twice-ten times as hard as their sons, because if I didn't they would complain, "Oh, that stupid, big-stomach orphan boy is so lazy. All he wants is food to go in his stomach." Though I was always hungry, I never showed it.

And then, finally, I was old enough to get married. I think that was about 1958. After that I realized, I am somebody. So I began to work very hard for my wife and family. I had twelve children—five daughters and seven sons. It was very important for me to have this many. I needed their help to farm, but even more—it was important because I felt, "I am the one that will give my children relatives." They would not be like me, an orphan child, all alone. I wanted them to be happy—"They will have me as a parent and their other brothers and sisters as relatives later on," I said to myself. I felt I needed to be like a farmer who planted all these children, so that they would have many more children, and at the end we would have a big, powerful, Moua clan. Unfortunately, I guess fate did not help me. I lost four daughters and two sons.

When I was young, I didn't play much with the other boys. I was all by myself. I would just work for my food. I didn't talk that much. I was always quiet. But one thing I did very well was play the bamboo pipes. One of my cousins, Chai Pha, had made a lot of *qeej*—bamboo pipes. My cousins would go around and play at everyone's house for fun, and I would just follow them and listen to the sound of the pipes. I would watch them play and play, but when they gave me a pipe, I was too shy to try. I didn't want to play but I knew all of the songs. I would mumble them every day. When my cousins played, I would try to mumble the songs after them.

Then one day, one of my cousins came up to me and said, "Oh, Boua Xa, you already know how to whistle all of the bamboo songs. Why not learn how to play the pipes?" He went on and on, saying all my cousins played, so why shouldn't I. Finally I thought it would not hurt me to try it.

I was a fast learner, they said. It only took me three days to learn what I needed to know and three months to perfect it.

I guess maybe I was born with a paper from heaven to play the bamboo pipes or something, because I could not believe how fast and how much I knew how to play in three months. Usually it takes people much, much longer than that to learn how to play. I was lucky, I guess. Maybe I had just listened to my cousins so much that it was easy for me. It's not that hard. Once you learn how the bamboo pipes should sound, then it becomes a part of you. You can make it say whatever your heart wants it to say.

I started learning the hard songs first. My master thought if I learned the hard ones first, then I wouldn't have to worry about learning the easier ones. That was what I did, and ever since then, all of the songs I've learned have been in my heart. Almost right away I could play about five hundred of them. I remember them right in my heart. When you have the ear for it, no matter if other people can't play the song right—just as long as they sing it to you, you'll catch on the first time.

Later on, one of my relatives died and there was no *qeej* player in the village, so they came to me and asked if I was willing to play. I soon knew all of the *qeej* songs. There are three different playing styles I had to know to be the *qeej* player for my village. First is just everyday singing songs. These, for example, you can sit at home and play for your children or anyone else. Then after you play it you could sing it to them and explain what you just said through the *qeej*. The second kind of song is for dancing competitions. During the new year the young boys who play the *qeej* would come out and dance for all of the other people to see. They jump, roll on their backs, put the *qeej* between their legs or arms and still are able to play.

The third kind is strictly for the death ceremony, like *qeej tu siav*, "The Saddest Song." This you can play only for a dead person. It guides the spirit to heaven. It is forbidden to play this inside the home. Mainly my job as a *qeej* player at the ceremony is to receive the guests of the dead person. Each time a guest would come, the *qeej* players would play. And each time we play, a drum is hit harder and faster. These together would tell the dead person's relatives inside the home to come out and receive the guests.

When you play *qeej* for a dead person it means you are giving him money. You know the saliva that comes out of the eyes of the *qeej*. The dead person's spirit looks at it as coins dropping from the sky. When you play *qeej tu siav* it tells the spirit that a horse has been caught for him (in this world what it really means is that a coffin has been made for him), and that he will need to get on this horse. The songs of the *qeej* will guide him where to go so that he can reach heaven. When it is breakfast time, you have to play a song that tells the spirit to eat breakfast. Same thing for lunch and dinner. There is a song for everything.

I can play the drum for the ceremony too. The way to play it right is to follow the *qeej* player. If he's standing, then you just hit the side of the drum, "tob lob, tob lob . . . " When he's moving and playing you hit "toog, toog, toog . . . " When he finishes, you just play "toog tob, toog tob . . . " This is very much like today—when young people play some music here. The *qeej* player is like the lead guitarist, and the drum player is like the drummer in a band group. The drummer has to get the beat right and know how and where to hit, to synchronize the sound with the guitar. You see, the same thing goes with the drum player in a death ceremony. He has to know when to make which kind of sound to go along with the *qeej*. I learned it by listening to it.

Shone Yang: "When there was no more money in opium, we grew rice and corn instead to feed the family."

The village where I lived is called Numfan. It was a mixed clans village, very big with about five thousand people. We have like Vang, Yang, Lee, Her, Cha. The small villages have only like a couple hundred people and about one or two clans—maybe Xiong or Moua. My family did farming and raised animals.

◁ Boua Xa Moua now plays the *qeej* in America.

With the animals—there were no fences around them. The animals were free to go all over the village. We put a little string on their nose to show that the animal belonged to someone and is not a wild animal. Everybody knows their own animals, so there is no problem.

As far as farming—every morning we got up, maybe at five o'clock, six o'clock, and we had to walk to the farm, maybe two or three hours. We cannot farm in the village where we live because our farming is slash and burn. If you stay in the same place farming, after about two years there is no more fertility. So each year we had to move the farm to a different area.

My whole family went to the farm every day except for one person who stayed home to take care of the house. The house has no locks and keys like in the United States, so there has to be someone to watch the house. Otherwise somebody would come to steal things. We were very afraid of robbers. The robbers were usually people who were smoking opium, and they don't have much time to farm, so they might come to steal rice or clothing or money.

Many people farm opium like they farm rice and vegetables. It is income for the family. Before 1975, opium was almost every family's jewels. They sold it to anybody who wanted to buy. Afterward, opium became less popular and lost price because, when the Communists took over, we could not sell opium to the French. Then we sold it to only those who really needed it and used it as medicine. Or we kept it to use ourselves as medicine and only sold the surplus. If you would have a problem with your feet or a headache, then you would use it as Tylenol. There were no laws that regulate such things as opium. But some old folks in the village abused the use of it as medicine and got hooked on opium. It's very hard for them to get out of it. Before the Communists came, we farmed about an acre of it, but when there was no more money in opium, we grew rice and corn instead to feed the family.

Khou Her: "There were a lot of fruit trees, so even if our farm turned out bad we still had this forest of fruit to eat."

I lived on the mountain of Phu Kho. The mountain was tall and on top it was flat. That was where we lived. All year long, the clouds would remain with us and we would never get to see the sun, so we couldn't dry the rice in the sun. We would have to dry it over the fire. First we would get the rice stalk and spread it on some long criss-cross wood we made. Then we would take that wood with the rice stalks on top of it and put it high up— maybe ten feet—over a big fire for two or three nights. Then once the rice stalk is dry enough we would take it down and beat the grains of rice off the stalk. Then when we finished that, we collected the grains and crushed them. And then finally we took the crushed rice grains and used a *vab* to separate out the skin until we had just the rice grain by itself. This is very hard work but we had to do it every year when the rice was ready.

Every morning we would be wakened up by the rooster crowing. The women would have to get up alone with their children. Each child had a different thing they were responsible for and they knew what that was. Some of the boys would go and get water, some would feed the animals, and the girls would help make the breakfast. As soon as we did everything we had to do around the house, we would all walk together to the farm. Sometimes it took an hour to make the walk, and sometimes— when the farm was far away—it could take maybe two hours. We would like to be there as early as possible, because that way we would get more done before we got too tired. We worked all morning, from around six o'clock until noon time. Then we would come back into a little house that we built on the farm and eat our lunch together. After that we would head back to the field and work until it was almost dark. Then we would all walk home together.

At my farm we farmed rice, corn, bananas, pineapples, a certain kind of pumpkin, cucumbers. We would plant, take out the weeds, then wait for the crops to grow big and ready for harvest. Our mountain of Phu Kho was so beautiful. Everywhere you looked there were trees, there was water running a lot from all the rain we had. There were a lot of fruit trees, so even if our farm turned out bad we still had this forest of fruit to eat.

Yo Moua: "I wanted to kill ten Vietnamese soldiers for every one village Hmong that died."

When our village was attacked the year was about 1962, so I was still small, about five years old. I had a good little friend, Mee Xiong. The missile hit her house right on target, and she did not have a chance to run. Her body was burned along with her house. When we were running to hide I saw her house burning. I also saw an old lady, just standing in front of her own house and then all of a sudden she fell down, fainted right next to me. I was too small to help her but one of her family members came and carried her off to the jungle with us. I wanted to run out and shoot every Vietnamese soldier. I wanted to kill ten Vietnamese soldiers for every one village Hmong that died. My whole village burned down.

So then we kept moving to other villages. Fitting in was no problem since we were on the same side and the same people. Most of the time we would look for Hmong people of our clan to stay with. But even if we couldn't find people from our own clan, people in other villages would help us. For example, when my father was making his house: It was not only him or my brothers working on the house. The whole village came and helped us. Then when someone else was making their house, my father would go and offer his help.

My parents wanted me to have an education. If it was not for the war, they would have liked for me to become a teacher or a doctor. But it was very hard for me to go to school because each time I tried, the village where we stayed would be attacked, and we were all the time moving on to a new village.

Yo Moua with his wife and children in America ▷

Because everyone was all the time moving, in the schools students were not placed in the grade that corresponded to their age. You could see a fifteen-year-old with a five-year-old in one class. The school was always built by the villagers, and everyone was very organized and willing to help. But we could not stay long.

Each time we ran to another village, we knew the safety of our trip was guarded by a *saub*. He had the name Chua Sue. He was a tall and thin man. His predictions were about 90 percent right. Two examples I remember: Before there were any American planes or French planes that flew over Laos to help us, he said, "There will be rice bags falling from the sky." And he also said long before it happened to us, "When you move out of Laos, you will go to another world. That world will have doors that can open by themselves." Over the years the villagers strongly believed in him.

My parents had always told me about *saub*. They said *saub* are born with their gift. One of the most common type of *saub* is like a fortune teller. They can say what will happen in the future. They can say about disease sickness, like which type of spirit was causing a person to be sick. I, too, believe strongly in the *saub*. The *saub* does not make big money from helping people. If he does accept too much money he might lose his spirit power. He must be careful not to cheat on people.

Ghia Xiong: "I didn't want to carry my pig's dead meat on me."

What I remember most is our small village. I don't even know what it was called, but I remember when I was about six or seven going to the farm with my grandparents. Sometimes they wouldn't let me go because I wasn't any use to them and I would just be in the way. But I would cry and cry until they said, "Okay, you can go." I used to hide in the rice field and eat cucumbers or climb on a log and just look around. Their farm was beautiful, especially when it was around harvesting time, because everything around the field was fresh green and orange. There were a lot of grasshoppers, crickets—insects that just make the farm sound nice. And I could hear the stream flowing down to the valley because most of the farming was on the mountaintop or along the sides of the hills.

Every boy in the village had either a horse or a dog for a pet, but my best pet was a pig. When the mother pig gave birth to a lot of little pigs my mom said, "Ghia, you can have this dark blue one." She was such a cute little pig. Each morning when I brought food to the mother pig and her babies I would feed her first. She got used to me so much that when I brought out the food she would know it was me, and she would run to me. I just fed her first and if the other pigs tried to get her food I scared them away. Even when my brothers went out to bring food to the pigs she would think it was me, so she was the first one to come running. We were best friends. When all the little pigs were grown up my blue one was the cutest and fattest and most playful.

Then came the bad news. I didn't know why, but we had to move. This man, Cha Khai, came to our village. He was supposed to be one of the strongest and smartest soldiers. I remember him showing the villagers some of the guns he took from the Vietnamese soldiers, and he was practising target. He told us that he and his friends went to some Vietnamese camp to try to steal some of their guns. They were caught and his friends were shot to death, but he was able to escape because he was so strong since he knew "strength *kher kong.*" So even though they hit him with bats and shot him on the legs, he managed to kill four or five Vietnamese with his bare hands before he escaped. He came to our village to warn us about the Vietnamese Communists and to tell us that if we wanted to go to Thailand, there will be two men coming in a couple of days to lead us.

My parents right away started packing their things. Mainly it was blankets, cooking pots, and about a hundred pounds of rice. Then my parents wanted to kill my pig. I begged and begged them to just kill the rest of the pigs and let her go. I didn't want my pet to be killed—and I didn't want to move away from the village. Then my stepfather just came up and said, "Son, we have to." Just like that. He was never a talker and he never liked to talk to me. But he said it just like that. So plain. I pleaded with my mom, but it was like she was taking orders from my stepfather. He yelled at her, "Ah, he's only a kid, and a pig is a pig. Kill it."

They grabbed my pig, and my brothers and mother helped to hold her down while my stepfather put a knife into her throat. After, she just lay on the dirt floor with her own blood surrounding. I cried and hated my stepfather so much. Then they all joked at me, "Why are you crying? It was only a pig."

During that journey I didn't eat any of the pig meat at all. I didn't want to carry my pig's dead meat on me, so I got the kitchen pots.

The Escape

Even those Hmong who had not fought against the Communists did not feel safe after the Communist victory. Though the Communists claimed to want only to convert all the Hmong to Communism, many Hmong feared that the Communists really had another agenda, and that was the extermination of the Hmong, as Ghia's uncle, Ger Xiong, says. They suspected that the Communists' attempts to bring them into the fold were merely a pretence. What the Communists really wanted was to lull the Hmong into trusting them and revealing the identity of all of Vang Pao's soldiers. Whether or not extermination was the Communists' intention, they repeatedly gave the Hmong good cause to be wary and good evidence that they respected the Hmong no more than the Lao ever had. For example, a 1977 treaty between the Laotian and Vietnamese Communist governments permitted Vietnamese troops to occupy Hmong villages. Reportedly, they often raped the Hmong women; if a husband complained, he was sent off to reeducation camp.

The Hmong who had not collaborated with the Communists really felt they were "waiting for the other shoe to drop." They feared that the Communists would accuse them all of having been U.S. collaborators, thus making them scapegoats to be blamed because there had been a war in Laos rather than a peaceful Communist takeover. Many Hmong people in America still insist that their fears had not been not unfounded. They say that after the Communist victory in Laos, not only Southeast Asian Communists but also those in Russia and East Germany were calling for the liquidation of the Hmong. The Pathet Lao had accused them of being "mercenaries of the CIA"; and thus the official Pathet Lao newspaper declared (in an all-too-familiar call for a *final solution*): "It is necessary to extirpate, down to the root, the Hmong minority."

Organized resistance seemed crucial, and it came primarily through the Chao Fa, a mystical group that had existed since the early part of the century. The Chao Fa, whose name is translated variously as "Lords of the Sky" or "God's Disciples," saw themselves as spiritually inspired, and they believed a godlike spirit would give them the power to destroy the evil giants of Communism; they conducted religious ceremonies that they thought would protect them in war. Many former soldiers joined the Chao Fa and dug up their abandoned weapons. They were actually able to liberate some of their villages from the Communists, though finally they could not withstand the assault on them by the Vietnamese forces who came to help the Pathet Lao. When the Chao Fa ran to the jungle to hide from the Vietnamese and the Pathet Lao, many noncombatants, such as Mee Vue and her five children, ran with them, certain that the Communists would kill them all if they remained in their villages.

Attacks were launched against the Chao Fa, both in the villages and the jungles, but Hmong civilians were also killed in these attacks which utilized chemical weapons such as napalm and yellow rain. Bombs were often dropped on the farms of the villages just before the harvest, creating widespread starvation. War and its aftermath thus cut the Hmong population of Laos in half.

Just as they had been at other times in their history, as when they fled from China, the Hmong became again like the Israelites on their mass exodus from Egypt. When the Hmong fled their villages, sometimes they traveled in single families, but more usually groups of young men or groups of families traveled together. Those families included little children and tiny babies who were not infrequently sedated with opium lest their cries alert the Communist patrols and endanger everyone. To escape from Laos, the Hmong refugees had to walk through the jungles for days or weeks (and some hid in the jungles for months or years), always at risk of being discovered by patrols, usually with no food except what they could find in the jun-

◁ The Mekong River on the Laos side. Thailand is across the river.

gles—vegetation, bugs, lizards. Their trek through the jungles took them finally to the Mekong River, which they navigated with inner tubes, banana tree trunks, rafts made of bamboo, inflated plastic sacks under their arms—anything that would help them float, as Bee Thao and Shoua Xiong describe. Even at the bank of the river or attempting to cross into Thailand, the Hmong were in danger of being sighted by patrols and killed on the spot.

For a short time, the fleeing Hmong were welcomed in Thailand, as Bee Thao told us he and his family were in 1979. However, when the flood of refugees increased, the Thai became hostile and ugly toward them, demanding money, raping the women, and stealing the few possessions the Hmong had managed to keep with them. The Thai were making it clear that the Hmong were not welcome to stay. Many of the Hmong arrived in Thailand in anguish, not knowing where their loved ones were or even whether they had made it out of Laos alive. All of them were put in relocation camps, where most remained for years, until they could be repatriated or arrange to go to Canada, France, Australia, South America, or the United States— the places that would accept refugees from Laos.

The Hmong refugees' stories of human suffering have been repeated millions of times over. The skin color, the language, the details change; the geography is different, the decade or century may be different, but the heinous brutality of "what man has done to man" remains the same.

Bee Thao: "Maybe tomorrow will be the end of our lives."

Sometimes in the middle of the night, you just had nightmares, bad dreams that made you wake up crying. I dreamt that the Communists came over to our village and they set our house on fire and then they killed my parents and sisters and brothers. I'm the only one that escaped. And I was crying in my dreams, so my mom had to wake me up. When I woke up I was really crying, tears in my eyes, and I was shaking, you know, like that. I talked to my mom and she held me tight while I calmed down because it was only a dream. It was very horrible to live in that situation, day after day.

A couple months after that, the village that was across a small river from us was destroyed, and now we really had to escape. The Communists killed all the people in that village except one who escaped and came and told us. My dad and my other two brothers went over to that village with him and helped bury all those people who died. My dad told us that night when he came back from the village about the people who had been killed—the Vietnamese took off their clothes. He saw one girl who had been raped before she was killed and one of her brothers had been smashed on the head so it was open. Most of them had been killed like they weren't human. It's like hunting for sport instead of having some kind of feeling for them because they're human beings. That's what my dad said to my mom that night when I was only eight years old, but I remember.

At the moment my dad told all that I was shaking, even though I didn't know much about life and death. I was very scared, even though it wasn't us, because I kept picturing those things in my mind already. Eight years old—you can pretty much see, not everything, but a lot of the picture.

And so we all had to run off. We went from cave to cave, from mountain to mountain. We were like fugitives. It was very hard. I would say it was very horrible. There wasn't any hope and there wasn't any future. All we could think is, "Maybe tomorrow will be the end of our lives. Maybe tonight one of us might be killed by the soldiers." You didn't have any confidence in yourself. All you could think is, "If I can survive this moment, then that is the greatest gift I could have." We lived moment to moment and day to day. I told myself, "If my dad or my parents can take me across the Mekong River to the other side, I might have a future. Otherwise, I don't know what is coming up, what is next." I knew about the Mekong River and the other side because my parents talked about it—how we had to make a decision, what we should do, what kind of situation we were facing, what is the next move that we had to do.

So we became fugitives . . . you know, with very little food. Sometimes we lived in caves, and sometimes we lived inside a very . . . I would say a very small house that we would make from stuff we found in the jungle. But you can only live like that, at the most, two months. Then you have to move on to another place and build a new house again. If you live in one place longer than that, then for sure the Communists are going to find you. Just because, you know, consider the way you have to go find your food. Somehow they are going to find your trail. So it is better to live in one place only for a couple of months and move on to another place where they cannot find you.

One evening about six o'clock, when my dad and my other two brothers came back, they told us that the Communists were on the other side of the mountain. So we had to rush everything and move at the moment. We had to walk for five or six hours. That was the hardest thing because we couldn't carry all the stuff we had in the first house. We left a lot of my clothes, and most of my mom's dishes, like pots or plates. We left some of my dad's equipment from when he used to be a soldier. He left boxes with bullets or whatever he put in there. He just buried it, and he said when a couple of months passed and things calmed down, he would go back and dig it up, but he never did. We had to escape right away and walk a far distance, so most of the things that we had had for maybe almost our whole lives we left behind.

There were seven of us, including me. We lived in the jungle like that for three years. Mostly when my parents were gone to look for food—they would search like for three or four hours to feed us a couple of days—we just stayed where they left us, didn't make any noise, because if you made a noise or set up fire maybe the Communists might hear, and they might come and that's a situation that we didn't want to face. We were always told by my parents, "If we're gone, you and your sisters stay where we leave you, please. And don't go out. Don't make any fire. Please don't scream or yell, because what if the Communists hear you guys, and what if they kill you guys?" And I always kept that in mind. Whenever they were gone, we always stayed still, and whatever we did, we kept it quiet.

I felt like I had been locked in a room that is very dark, and I cannot see what is outside. All I can see is the space around myself. There wasn't much that I could look forward to. There wasn't much that you could think you might get—even though you don't get it tomorrow, you might get it next week or next month—there wasn't anything like that.

But for three years my dad didn't want to try to escape to Thailand because a lot of people who tried it got killed, and my dad didn't want to take a chance. Since it was so risky, he wanted to make sure that if we decided to cross, we would get into Thailand safely. I think dying was the key thing that he didn't want to risk. But we had no other choice than to leave Laos sooner or later. We could not go back because my dad and my other two brothers had been soldiers. Before, they had been fighting and killing the Communists, so if we went to the Communists to surrender now, there was a chance they would find out what my dad and brothers had done, and they would kill them. That was the thing my mother didn't want to happen.

Finally my dad decided we had to go to Thailand. That was because whenever we got sick there wasn't anything to make us feel better. No medicine, no hospital. We had some herbs, but it doesn't mean that the herbs are going to help all the time. Sometimes they don't work. My mom got really sick a couple of times. Maybe she was sick with the food that she ate. Somehow it wasn't right to her stomach, so she got very sick for like three or four days. She couldn't even breathe. She had a hard time trying to eat. She had diarrhea a long time. I was very scared because the only thing that went through my mind was, "What if she dies? What if she dies?" You know, "Who should I talk to if I lose her? Who should I look up to? Who's going to wake me up? Who's going to help me? What if she dies and what if the Communists catch me?" So, you know, all kinds of things went through my mind.

I had a fever a couple of times too, but I'm a tough kid, so I didn't get sick that much. But my mom, she got sick a lot. Plus, she was getting old and that always happens. She was like forty.

I think that's the first reason that my father finally said we would try to get to Thailand—because my mom was sick a lot. But also he got tired of running from place to place, mountain to mountain. Like I said, you don't have a future. You live day to day, and that's the second reason. The third reason was, he told us that even though he was old, he would like us to have a better future, to have something that we could look forward to instead of, you know, just staying there without any future or hope.

We had to walk like ten or twelve days, just to reach the Mekong River. The day we actually got to the river, it was past midnight. My dad and my other two brothers and some other cousins that came there too, first they did security for us. They went from this place to that place to make sure there weren't any Communists. They came back and said we can move from here to there, stop there. Then they went again and looked further in the distance and came back to say we can move some more.

Then we got up to the Mekong, and some of the people near us, they were using bamboo. They cut like two or three pieces of bamboo, and they tied it together so they could stay on top, and they tried to swim with the help of the bamboo and some energy. Somehow they could make it through across the river. And some of them had *plab yas*, inner tubes, but not all of the people had them. My dad, he had connections with some people who lived with the Communists. He had some friend— but it's kind of a secret . . . he thought that that helped him to get those tubes for us. He used some of his money to buy the tubes, though he didn't have enough for everyone, so my cousins had to try to swim across with the bamboo.

He gave us each a tube. And then he was in the front, and my brothers next—behind him, then me, and then my mom and the others behind me. He tied a rope to himself and attached it to us. Then every one or two minutes he would turn back to make sure we were still with him. It was exciting. It was exciting. Because, you know, looking back to Laos, you didn't see much hope. You didn't see much anything. But facing Thailand, you saw all kinds of light—houses, the cars moving, all kinds of noise, which made me very excited, which made me very anxious to get there. There was also a lot of fear that morning.

But finally we got to Thailand. . . . I would say about three or four o'clock. There were two Thai people to rescue us, and they took us to the . . . I would say the mayor's house . . . not the mayor, but the head or leader of the village, and we stayed there until the sun came. That was December 1979. At that time they were very nice. At that time people every night crossed the Mekong River to get to Thailand. And the Thai knew for sure it was because of the Communists that people were escaping, so they kind of expected us. They took us to their place, had us take showers, gave some food to us. Later they treated Hmong people badly, but in 1979 they were okay. The last people to cross the Mekong, those are the ones who got . . . I would say destroyed by the Thai people, got robbed, raped, beaten up. But earlier, when we crossed, they treated us with respect, dignity, like that.

We took a shower, and then ate, and actually I took a nap because I was so tired. So I don't know what my dad and the leaders talked about. Somehow, my other brothers and my cousins went to a different house so we had to wait until the morning came. Then the Thai told his . . . I would say his employees, to go and get all the people, which was my family and my cousins. By nine o'clock we had everyone back in the leader's house. Then we had breakfast, and then we had lunch. Past noon, the bus came. I wasn't sure what the bus was for, so I asked my mom and dad. They said we needed to get into the bus and move on to Nong Khai. That was the first camp we lived in.

Mee Vue: "First, though you were scared, you remembered to hang on to all of your kids. Later, when you were more than scared—when you were numb—you just forgot about them, and it's them that were hanging on to you."

I don't know exactly the years or date when we were attacked. I'm old—sixty-five years old—and I can't remember. When we were Chao Fa until now, it's a long time. Little girls and boys from then, that I knew didn't know how to cook or do anything, now I see them again and most of them have already married and started having families already. So it might be over ten [*sic*] years now since we were Chao Fa.

When the Vietnamese came in my village, which had the Hmong name Qhov Dav, there were some people who were saying we should not worry. All we needed to do is just run into the jungle and hide a little bit, then come back. So, because I thought we were going to come back for sure and we would only go hiding for a few hours, I didn't bring anything with me. I didn't bring any extra clothes or food at all. What I had was the clothes I had on, nothing else. It was just like we were going to harvest the rice and then come back. But we went and went, and then I heard guns shooting and missiles exploding into our village. I thought to myself, "Wow, what was that noise that was so loud?" I had never heard anything like it before. But for those people who knew what it was, they told us it was gunshots and missile explosions. We got so scared, we just ran and ran.

Babies and little children were just dragging on their mothers. There were no *nyias* to carry my baby on my back. I had to hold him in my arm and grab all my other children and run into the thick jungle. We waited until dark when the Vietnamese stopped shooting. Then during the night we had the little children go back to the village to steal whatever food they could and bring it back to us in the jungle. After that we just ran and ran in the jungle until we got to another village. I don't even know what it was called.

When we were Chao Fa, hiding in the jungle—I cannot think of any other way we could have been poorer than that. Ever since I was born into this world, my life has never been as bad as being a Chao Fa. There was no food to eat, especially for the little children. Mostly we ate *txoob*—like palm trees but much bigger; you chop the tree down and scoop out the part in the center that you can eat. In the beginning we had a *vab* to separate what we could eat out of the *txoob* because there are two layers. You have to separate out the hard layer of *txoob* and eat the soft part. But later on, when we kept running and hiding, our *vab* got old and all torn apart, so we had to use our hands to separate the two layers and it was very hard. Many of the children could not eat it. Many of them, because they could not eat anything, there was no bowel movement at all for them. A lot of them got very sick and didn't make it. Sometimes though we could find for them *suab mus tij*—that is like a fern. If we couldn't find any of this stuff a lot of times we found *qos npua*, "pig potatoes" we call it, it's like yams which we could slice into thin pieces, sun dry it, then crush it with like—a mortar and pestle. We mix it with water, then steam it and just eat it that way. We couldn't really start any fire because the smoke would show the Vietnamese where we were in the jungle, so it was really hard. I just can't believe it now—when we were Chao Fa everything in the jungle seemed like you could eat it.

But there were so much bombs dropped. It seemed whatever the bombs hit, everything would disappear and you could see a big hole. It exploded so loud I could feel the ground shaking underneath me. When it hit people, I saw them just explode like the bombs exploded. Their body just all over the place. I don't know—I was so scared that I just forgot what scared is in my heart. You're just numbed by the scene in front of you. You just run and hope that it was not you that got hit. At first when you see a few planes flying in, dropping bombs, you know how to be scared and you think you must run for your life. But when there are more planes and more bombs, you're just too scared. You don't even know where to run anymore. Whatever trees you see you just run toward it and try to hide behind it. You hope if the bomb explodes near you, the tree can shield you— or whatever cave you can find, everyone would just squeeze in. If the bombs hit on target, everyone would just die.

There was one time I remember, not too long after we ran

from my village, we were running sort of like across a field, and we were being shot at with big guns and missiles. Everyone was just dying by the second. I ran with my kids hanging on to my arms and holding on my back. I was just stepping on dead people and hoping I could make it somewhere to hide or that they would stop shooting. Babies and children were crying all over the place. I was so scared I didn't look ahead or turn my head and look to see who died. I just looked at my feet running. I waited until I made it to where I could hide and then I looked back. I saw so many relatives dead there—my aunt, brother, cousins, everyone. I was so scared and my heart was just aching. But like I said, in the beginning you knew how to be scared and you wanted to run for your life. Later you just got too scared, and you didn't know where to run. First, though you were scared, you remembered to hang on to all of your kids. Later, when you were more than scared—when you were numb—you just forgot about them, and it's them that were hanging on to you. One holding on to your pants, another dragging on your shirt, another one holding on to your *sev*. Your hands were so shaking that you had no strength to hold on to them any more.

Shoua Xiong: "The shaman said we should have done the spirit name calling, but there was no time."

It all seems like a dream to me, but when I ask my mom, to see if it is a dream, she says it all really happened. Like one time, we were running away from the Communists in the mountains, and it was raining and there was rice growing; there was water running. All I remember is water running, the sound of the stream, and we were spending the night on the other side of the stream. It's raining, it's blurry, it was so slippery. Now I ask my mom, I say, "I remember that we walked through a whole rice field on bare feet and it was so slippery. Is it a dream or did it happen?"

My mother says, "That happened, we been there, spent the night, on the other side of the stream." It's just like a dream.

We went to the jungle to keep us safe—but my grand-mom, she was too old, so she didn't go with us. She stayed and some people came and killed her. They killed her and they fought with the other people left in the village, and then they buried six people in the same grave. My grandmother was the bottom one, that's what I heard. I heard my mother say that my grandmother was the bottom one and they buried them together. So now I've asked my mom, "Was that true or did I dream it?"

And she says, "Yes, it was true."

When we ran out of my village I saw some kind of bomb killing a lady and a baby. The plane came and the people ran to hide in the woods so they can't be seen. She ran out of her house, but her baby was crying and she stopped. They saw her and they bombed her and they killed her and her baby. This seems like a dream memory too, but when I ask my mom she says it really happened, I really saw it.

My dad was strong and determined that we should all go together and get across the Mekong River together and get into Thailand. My uncle said, "A family with kids like you guys should not come with us. We know that you're not going to make it through the whole jungle because it's a long way."

My dad just told him, "We'll try." Some people turned back, but we didn't, we stuck with it. We were so happy after we crossed the river.

We were guided through the jungle to the river by people my father knew. When we got to the jungle they told us, "Every step you take, put your foot inside the footstep of the person who goes in front of you. Follow the same footstep."

My uncle, my mother's brother, he didn't do that. He stepped in a place without a footstep, and that was when the bomb exploded and it killed him. He was not dead yet, but he was big and tall so people could not carry him. He said to us to just leave him there. "I don't want to be a burden to you, so just go and leave me here." We left him in the jungle, so I guess he died or something.

Finally, we were just on the Laos side of the Mekong River, and we were resting there for the night. Then in the morning my mom was about to get some water so she could cook for us. And then at that moment, when my mom said she was going to go, there was shooting. Some people got hurt and they ran past us, and we started running and some people were bloody. I don't know what was going on, because I was still little. But I remember that at the time I was about to eat, so I was running with my spoon. That's all I remember. I ran with my spoon and my sister was still sleeping, and then my mom took the baby. My sister was so sleepy and I ran with my spoon. My dad ran away, and then my mom said, "Come back and get the little girl." My father had to come back and get the little girl, and then we ran. I ran by myself. But then nothing more happened, so we went back to hide for a few more days.

Finally, we got to cross the river. We had to come very early in the morning, when it was still dark. There were a lot of babies crying. My brother was very little and he was crying, and they told my parents to drug him so that he won't be crying. They gave my brother some opium. Then he looked drowsy, sleepy, and he wasn't crying anymore. They gave him a little too much. He almost passed away, but he made it. He just lay there with his eyes closed, and his face turned yellow, no movement, still a little breathing. It seemed like he was gone, but after we crossed the Mekong River, it was morning around seven o'clock, then he started to wake up. It was scary, because they had said, "If you don't put him to sleep, then you can't go with us, because we don't want to get caught." So we had to do everything that would make him quiet.

Everybody had on those . . . life jackets, like. But my family didn't have any so they gave us some plastic bags, and they said, "Blow air into it and tie it, then put it under your arms and waists so you can float." We started doing that, but then we were very lucky because some people came in a boat and then we paid them a lot of money, and they took us across the Mekong River.

After we crossed the Mekong River, we got to Thailand, and my sister, the one I said my father forgot to take, she passed away soon after we crossed the river. She wasn't sick or anything. We were only in Thailand like one day, and she just passed away. I don't know what was wrong or what caused it. A shaman told my mom and dad the reason why she died was because her soul was not with her body. When she was sleeping and my father moved her during the attack, he only moved her body. Her soul was out somewhere playing. So when the soul comes back and the body is not there, the body of the child becomes sick. The shaman said we should have done the spirit name calling, but there was no time.

Ger Xiong, Ghia's uncle, who had been a soldier under General Vang Pao, told us why he kept his rifle with him until he got across the Mekong.

I started in the war about 1965, when I was twelve years old. I watched and guided the landing of airplanes and watched out for people. When there was a plane about to land on the run-way, I would not allow anyone to run across or be near it. Then when I was a little older I joined the army, where I stayed for a long time. One of the worst incidents was in 1972 when I was guarding General Vang Pao's house. These Vietnamese soldiers just jumped over barbed wire and threw bombs at the general's house. They didn't know that really General Vang Pao had already left. They thought he was still in here with us. All of them just wrapped like five grenades together in each of their hands. They jumped in pairs, and when they were in the air they tossed those bombs into the house.

We were on the second story of the house and we were shooting and shooting at them. There were only sixteen of us, but we killed all twenty of them. The only thought that came to my mind was to kill them or they would kill me. If we didn't kill them all, and one of them got through into the house, he would blow up the whole house and all of us would just die with the house. So I didn't care—it was my life or their life.

When the general left the country, the ones who had been soldiers, like me . . . we went back into our villages, but we had to hide what we had been doing. We acted and dressed like ordinary village people. Then the Communists came to my village that we called Phu Kha, and they made a camp there. For three months they were very mean and stubborn. They would order us to dig a hole or deep trench in our house against bombing, and then they would change their mind and say the reason we made the hole was because we wanted to hide the Chao Fa in there. They would try anything like this to make a person look guilty, and they would kick or kill whoever they said was guilty. They were really cruel to the Hmong people. They would not allow us to go to our farms because they thought that if we go out we would communicate with the Chao Fa. When they were angry because they thought the Hmong people were still going to the farm, what they would do is they would burn the whole rice field.

Then they changed their tactic. They wanted to brainwash us and tame us. They figured that after the war there will be many soldiers coming back and joining their families in the village. So instead of looking for the ones who had been soldiers now, they would wait until everyone in the village thought the Communists were good people. Then they would find out who had been the soldiers. But we already saw what they were like. And that's why so many people became Chao Fa.

I couldn't stand the Communists anymore, so during the night time we took our family out of the village to the jungle and six of us men crawled back to the village. We positioned ourselves near the entrance of the Communists' camp. We waited for morning, until we saw five of them come out of the camp. Pha Vue and Ga Vue said, "You guys, let us shoot first." Pha shot one, Ga shot one. What we had was our Hmong guns, *phom gaslasbees*—like rifles. When you shot a Vietnamese and the bullet went through him, he would run like four steps and then fall down. This is what happens when this type of gun shoots someone. The four of us just kept shooting until we killed all of them. There was one that was very strong. He fell on the ground; then, like five minutes later, he was moving. He was trying to crawl back into the camp. I aimed my gun's nozzle at his back and pulled the trigger—"bom! bom!" I shot twice into his back. I was only about a hundred yards away. Then the final shot, I shot him right in the head. You could see his hairs flying off—I was that angry.

For three days, we waited to shoot any Communists that came out. They were too scared. Then we had three of us go to the other side. When the Communists came out to shoot at us, the other three shot them from behind. We trapped all of those Communists. They had no where to go for three days, not even to use the bathroom. So what they did was, they used these empty missile shells. They emptied their ca-ca into them and threw them out of their building. At first we thought it might be grenades or bombs, but it was only shit. Finally we managed to wipe out the whole camp. There were fifty-one of the Communists altogether.

After that we had to be Chao Fa. When you're a Chao Fa the jungle is your home. You don't own anything. Each house in the jungle is only temporary. You make it out of banana leaves. When you want to go to sleep in colder weather you just make a little tent with the banana leaves, like a house, and you cover the floor with the banana leaves. Then you dig a small trench around the little tent, so that when it rains, water would go in the trench. We had no blankets to cover us. Only some of the old soldiers had shoes. It was very hard. I was very tired of running like a wild animal with no home. All I ever thought is to survive from day to day until I got to Thailand.

I never thought of leaving behind my family. One of my hands was holding my child while the other hand was holding my gun. I knew that as long as I had one hand to hold a gun I would keep shooting until all of my family died together. I would never leave my family behind and die somewhere else. If I died, everyone would die. If I lived, everyone would live. That was how I felt at the time. This is why all my family members are here today. If I was like other men, maybe now everyone would be in a different world. But I know that without my family I would be nothing, too, so I never thought about leaving them behind.

For a while, we sneaked into the village called Phu Biab. We could live there because this village still had a lot of Hmong people. It was the same thing again. The Communists had already established their army camp there. For a while they didn't bother us. When the rice was not yet ready to harvest, they left us alone. But when the rice was ready they would send in planes to burn the whole farm. Now why didn't they do that before, when the rice wasn't ready? They would wait until people were hungry and ready to harvest the rice, and then they would bomb it. So we got together, a lot of us men, and we went to shoot at four different Communist camps. What we would do is keep the Communists busy by having them fight with us while the villagers would come from the jungle and harvest whatever was left of the rice field. We would just keep shooting at the camp, and the Communists kept shooting back at us while the villagers gathered all the rice and also the corn and took them into the jungle.

During that time at Phu Biab we also killed one of their generals. To do that we had to let a family surrender themselves to the Vietnamese. Then we used one of their girls to go and sleep with the general for three nights. Really we wanted to know where the general was at. After three nights the girl came back and told us where and in which corner the general was at. The general also had a dog. She said, "This is the corner. Over here is the trench hole the general is in." That night we went. We crawled very close to it, and we threw in eight grenades. All we heard was one dog-bark.

Later the Communists had planes drop bombs with yellow ashes and red ashes on this village. When these ashes got to the villagers they got sick—nosebleeding and stuff like that. Whoever came into contact with these ashes would have nosebleeding or stomach ache. If they didn't smoke opium the pain was so bad, it was no use but to die.

There was one other chemical the Communists used. It was like a rain shower. If it hits you anywhere on your body and you don't cut it off, your skin will just rot until you die. We call it *tshuaj npua*. There were a lot of people dying. I was scared because I thought, "This is something that I can't fight." I thought, "One of these days, it might be me." This was why we ran again into the jungle.

Finally we got to the Mekong, but we couldn't cross. We

already had the tubes on the women and children and—I don't know if it was the Vietnamese or the Thai on the other side, they were shooting at us, "Tho plu! Tho plu!" This was making the water splash at us. I thought to myself, "There was no way we are going to make it across. Even if we did, I know we would get shot." So we ran all night back into the jungle and just slept there.

The next day, we woke up—we didn't realize that we were sleeping alongside a road. We thought we were deep in the jungle. We could have been seen and killed. We were lucky. Right away my brothers and I took our family more into the jungle. I told my brothers the only way we could make it across the river was to find a Lao village and kidnap someone from the countryside or a farm and make them help us across. My older brother didn't want to. He was afraid of death. But I told him, "If you hide here, death will come sooner. If we go and find a Laotian man to help us across, maybe we might have a chance."

When we were almost at a village we heard "ther! ther!"— like someone was chopping down trees. We went toward the sound, but as we got closer it stopped. We lost track of it. Then from there we followed a little stream down. We saw two Laotians with dogs. Luckily, right before where we were hiding, the stream divided. The guy with dogs went off one branch and the other one came straight toward us. I raised the nozzle of my gun right at his chest, and right before he reached us, I just stood up with the nozzle at his chest. I told him, "Can you help us cross the Mekong River? If you do I will give you twenty *choj*." He said, "Oh, the Vietnamese have tied all the boats together, and they guard them so it's hard to get one right now. But when it rains I think I can steal some boats for you." He wanted the twenty *choj*. He said he needed to get another man to help him, and we watched with our guns while he went and got another man. They said, "How many are you?" There was only me and my two brothers here, but we said, "Twenty men with guns."

My oldest brother, he was so scared when we walked with those guys. But for me, my gun's nozzle was right at the back of one of the Laotian men. If they took us to where we would get ambushed he would be the first to be killed. But they kept their bargain, plus they were nice. First they tried to steal the boats for us, but the Communists were guarding the boats too well, even when it started raining. Then they said if we had tubes they would take us to an area they know and was guaranteed safe. If we crossed from there, there wouldn't be any firing from the other side.

My brother went back and took the rest of the family, and the Lao man took us into his home. There we waited until early in the morning. It was easy because the house was right along the Mekong River. When the morning came we all just walked out of their backyard and slid down into the bank of the river. We hurried and blew up all of the tubes, and off we went. I had on my back my oldest son, Chue. Behind me I was dragging my wife, my mom, and two sisters. My two older brothers left their guns along the bank, but I didn't because if we were going to be shot at, I wanted to be able to shoot back, too. I didn't want to give up my gun until I reached Thailand. Then I would just hand over my gun to the Thai police.

Ia Vang Xiong, who is an elementary school teacher in America, told us about getting lost in the jungle when she was a child.

I was about six years old and at that time I had pneumonia or something. I was coughing blood. I was coughing a lot. My father had two wives. His first wife had only two sons and couldn't have anymore, so he married my mother. My mother had a lot of us and we were a very close family. Then my father wanted to make arrangements for us to go to Thailand. What he did was he gave me to his first wife because she didn't have a daughter—she only had two sons. The first wife was to come to Thailand a month ahead of my father and mother so everything would be in place. My mother couldn't leave yet because she had just had my youngest brother and she was recovering from child labor.

So, like I said, I had pneumonia at that time. And my father said to me, "Ia, you go with your Big Mother to a town

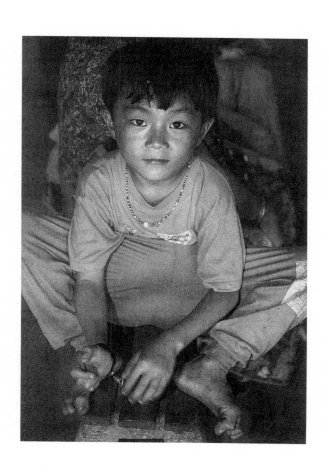

where there's a hospital." That's all I knew. I didn't know I was going to Thailand, that I was escaping. Every person we met, my Big Mother would say she's taking me to a hospital.

Then we came to a group of people and this time my Big Mother didn't tell them she's going to the hospital. All of us together, we walked up the mountain, down the mountain, up the mountain, down the mountain. I was still sick, but I had to do it. We walked only at night when we couldn't see a thing. We were holding on to one another like we were playing train. The first person in line had a flashlight, and everybody else behind was holding on to the person ahead of you because there were a lot of dead trees in the jungle, and there were a lot of trees fallen over. We would trip and fall and get up again. It was so hard. Every couple of minutes I'd fall. The jungle was wet and swampy-like. There were leeches, too. A leech would be on my skin and all over my toes. Sometimes I didn't even have time to stop and peel them off with sticks. Most of them fall off after they have as much blood as possible from you. That was the hardest time. Then you would itch all over, plus it was dark. Ah . . . it felt so miserable. It was so dark. I felt like I was blind. We were walking like that for two nights, all in the dark, and every stranger we saw everybody was so scared of. We were all ready to run in case these strangers were bad.

One time we got to this big river in the middle of the night. It wasn't the Mekong. I don't know what it was. My big brothers were there already, and my father already had arranged for some men to carry us across. They didn't speak Hmong— I think they spoke Kammu. I was so scared, and I was still coughing blood. We crossed and then we came to some village. The people who were the leaders there were expecting us, but they didn't want us travelers mixing with the village people, so they hid us in their rice shed, and we ate in their rice shed. We were sitting there eating and all of a sudden someone came in and said, "There are soldiers following you." My Big Mother and brothers just scattered like rats in every direction, and so did the rest of the people. I didn't know what to do, so I just fol- lowed some people and went with them to hide.

Then, later, when we stopped running, everybody was looking at me, and they said "Whose child? Whose daughter?"

I looked around and I said, "Oh, my gosh, I don't know where my family has gone to." I started to be more afraid, but I had to stay with these people I didn't know.

Good thing the soldiers didn't come because we were peeking from the high mountain to see if the soldiers were in the village—peeking and waiting, peeking and waiting. Everybody was asking me who I am, and I didn't say anything because I didn't know them either. I was just crying. Finally, we went down to the village, and my big brother found me. He hugged me so hard and goes, "I thought I lost you. Don't do that again." I was crying so much. "Don't do that again," he said over and over. "Next time, follow me." So after that we walked and walked, for about three months.

The Camp

Eventually twenty-one relocation camps were established in Thailand, not only for the Hmong but also for the many thousands of fleeing lowland Lao, Cambodians, and Vietnamese. The United Nations High Commissioner on Refugees and various international charitable agencies, most of them related to Christian churches, tried to alleviate horrific camp conditions as much as possible by supplying medical aid, food, and other necessities, but the task was gargantuan. Sanitation was minimal; disease was rampant; malnutrition was common because there was seldom sufficient food to go around; and scarcity was far from the worst of the problems for these refugees whose strenuous escape efforts, fright, and loss of loved ones had physically and emotionally depleted them. Many adults were severely depressed, and suicide was not infrequent.

The refugee camps were, of course, not like concentration camps or the Pathet Lao's "reeducation camps": torture and extermination were not the object. Yet our narrators often described the cruelty and capriciousness of the Thai officials who supervised the camps. The refugees were "inmates," at the mercy of officials, and could be made to suffer if they did not toe the line.

The Thai were apparently genuinely perplexed about how to treat the refugees. Though they did not fight in the war, Thai sympathies were with those who opposed Communism. They were happy for American involvement, so they felt unable to resist American pressure to allow the refugees within their border. However, the Thai resented the burden that had been placed on them because they considered it a potential threat to their economy. Thailand was going through an economic

In the camp ▷

boom as a result of the war and an increasing export market. The Thai feared that a flood of refugees might discourage the new enthusiasm of investors. They also feared that the poor of all underdeveloped countries in the region would take the refugees as an example and would themselves flock to the relative wealth of Thailand.

Several countries, including the United States, ultimately opened their doors to refugees, but more and more continued to flee across the Mekong River into Thailand, and the birthrate in the camps was very high (about three times what it was in the rest of Thailand). The Thai were often agitated at the prospect of being forever stuck with a geometrically multiplying number of immigrants. When resettlement of the refugees into western countries progressed quickly, the Thai were relieved and tended to treat the refugees more generously. But when resettlement slowed, as it did for a period after 1981, the Thai became alarmed. In response they adopted a policy of "humane deterrence," which advocated reducing the meager food rations and support services to even lower levels than had been provided previously. The United States approved the "humane deterrence" policy in the belief that many who were leaving Laos this late were fleeing not war-related political difficulties but economic scarcity, and thus were not owed protection by those who had encouraged the fight against Communism.

Of course the Hmong and other refugees had no desire to stay in the camps of Thailand. They wanted either to go back or to go forward. But even into the 1980s, Vang Pao continued to instruct Hmong refugees to remain in the camps since they were a lot closer to Laos than they would be in the resettlement countries; it would be easier to go home from Thailand when he "retook" Laos. As time passed, terrible conflicts developed within families between those who wanted to remain in the camp until Laos was liberated from the Communists and those who wanted to move on to a third country and try to make a new life there.

Though years passed since they had fled Laos (the median stay in a relocation camp was seven years), many—the older people in particular—clung to the dream of repatriation. They refused to stop believing that they would someday be able to live in Laos again. Frightening stories from resettled relatives about how strange and hard Western life was also discouraged them from wanting to resettle in the West. But many of the younger adults felt they had to risk those difficulties for the sake of their children. Thus, families that had traditionally been extended and very close-knit began to break up. The elderly were now often separated forever from their children and grandchildren when they did not have the energy or inclination to move on and the young were determined (to use a phrase used by so many of our narrators) to begin their lives "all over again."

Camp life, which produced the peculiar anomie of inmate existence, brought about other major changes for the Hmong in its assault on many important aspects of their traditional family dynamics. In Laos, family members were seldom out of one another's sight since they worked the farm together all day long. But camp life became a sad prefiguration of life in the West for many Hmong. No longer under obligation to work side by side with the rest of the family, and without the possibility of absorbing and meaningful occupation, Hmong children, especially boys, ran free. When the family rations did not satisfy hunger pangs they learned to beg or scrounge for food on their own. While they did not form gangs as Hmong boys later did in America, they lived in what was very much, as Chia Ton Cha described it, "a kid society," feeling that their parents, who had been in clear control of the family life in the village, were now essentially powerless.

But not all aspects of camp life were bad for children. In Laos, most Hmong children had no opportunity to go to school; one benefit of the camp was that the Thai Ministry of Education sponsored primary school education for the children, where they could learn basic subjects. Girls as well as boys were encouraged to attend school, though girls seldom continued for very long: In the first grade girls comprised about 45 percent of the students. By the third grade they were only about 25 percent, and by the sixth grade they were 11 percent—yet those figures are surely greater than they would have been in the mountains of Laos.

For the adult males in the camp, there was little to do. The husband of the family, who had been the unquestioned head in an agricultural society, was often unemployed in the camp (though a few men were permitted to work outside, earning a pittance as laborers on Thai people's farms). Time hung heavy on their hands, and most men felt as though they were merely being warehoused. There were few actions they could take to be instrumental in feeding and caring for their family because everyone was essentially at the mercy of camp authorities.

Women fared somewhat better. They continued to have responsibility for children and for running some sort of household, and many women also had another kind of meaningful labor. Relief workers discovered the beautiful stitchery that most Hmong females learned from their mothers. They convinced Hmong women to sew for Western buyers, who were especially excited by story cloths which recorded the harrowing exodus from Hmong villages into Thailand. Sewing provided about 90 percent of the family's earned income in the camps. It even gave occupation to some husbands who made the preliminary sketches for these cloths or handled the business involved in sales.

But it was women who were the most profoundly affected by this commercialization of a skill they had taken for granted. Their money-earning capacity had the potential of giving them at least a modicum of uncustomary independence, and thus it was one more prefiguration of the life they would come to in the West.

Khou Her, who ran from her beautiful mountain of Phu Kho, told us that the camp was like a jail.

We left behind our rice farms, our house, our pigs, chickens, everything, and we came to Thailand, and then they put us in a camp. The camp where we were kept was surrounded by barb wire. No one was allowed to go out without permission. All we could do was wait for our paperwork to be finished so they would let us go to Ban Vanai where it was a little better.

If you tried to leave the camp without permission, the Thai would kick at you or kill you. There was this entranceway that was guarded by the Thai soldiers. And then on the outside there were ministands, like stores. Every morning about a thousand people would just be waiting by the gate for permission to go out and buy food. But most of them had hardly any money to buy anything. Every once in a while people would steal out and work for two or three *npaj*. Then they would have a little money, just enough to buy a bowl of noodles for their whole family.

A lot of the kids looked like those Ethiopian kids on TV. They were so sick that their eyes turned grey. There was nothing to eat almost. The food that was sent into the camp by trucks was only given twice a month. There wasn't enough food to last that long, so my family—we would buy like one bowl of rice noodles with the two or three *npaj* we saved. And we would take it home and give a little bit to each of the children to eat.

We would wait and wait for the next truck of food to arrive. It was almost impossible to survive on what we got. Each time the truck came, they had like a bowl, and they would measure one bowl per a family member. So if you have six people in your family, you will be given six bowls for two weeks. I mean —there is no way. . . . I ate the food so preciously, not to waste a single rice grain. Most of the time I was still very hungry, but I had to give up whatever I could to my children. It was so sad and so hard.

The only happiness there was the sound of the truck coming with food because your stomach knew then that it will be fed soon. You waited and sometimes the truck didn't come and

your stomach would be crying the whole night. In the camp we were in jail, like the chickens and pigs in Laos. We were that helpless and trapped. We ate only what we were given and when we were given, and if they didn't want to give us we would just starve.

Chue Yang: "Every morning around 7:00 A.M. they have songs sung in Thai, like the flag salute."

First they took us to Ban Vanai, and I was lucky because my mother's older sister was there, so I just went and lived with them. Then in 1987, my older brother and I were sent to Chiang Kham, which was not as good a camp. In Ban Vanai there is more flexibility. You have Thai people coming in there to do business, and you have Hmong people selling things in the camp. Furthermore, the camp is not fenced, whereas Chiang Kham is. The fence is made of bamboo and is about eight to ten feet tall. You could see through the cracks—but the guards wouldn't even allow you to peek outside. If you do they could arrest you. Also, if Thai people from the outside brought in goods and you bought—if the soldier saw it—you could be caught for that, too. In this camp no one could do business. Only whoever they agreed on was allowed to sell things. They sold vegetables, chickens—and it was very expensive. For example, if you illegally bought something from the outside, it would cost you about five *npaj*, but if you bought it from the one they allowed to sell in the camp it would be anywhere from ten to twenty *npaj*, so somebody was putting the extra money in their pockets probably.

In Chiang Kham we were very poor, especially in terms of having water. I mean, it's horrible. You think not having money and food is enough, but to not have water—it was hard. They gave each building a schedule as to when you could go and turn on the water. So, for example, if my building's time was at 7:00

◁ Laundry day in the Ban Napho camp

till 8:00, I had to be there just then. Not only that, but they allowed you to take only a certain amount of water. This would depend on the number of family members you have. I mean, talking about scarce! So if you have five people you would get only about five buckets and so on. This was very poor.

Then every morning around 7:00 A.M. they have songs sung in Thai, like the flag salute. They have speakers all over in the camp, so whenever these songs go on, it doesn't matter if you're an adult or children, everyone is supposed to wake up and salute or sing along with the song. You can't walk. You just have to stand up straight, like you respect them. If you don't, you could be jailed for it. Even if you have little children who didn't know anything about it, the parents could be jailed if they didn't make the little kids salute and sing the songs.

Also, every building was given responsibility for taking care of some of the plants planted by them around the building. If the plants die, the whole building is responsible for it. There are other things, like doing free labor for them. Every day a group in the building is taken out to pick up trash around the camp, dig roads, or whatever. Everyone has to do it. There were a lot of things, and it was very hard to follow according to their rules.

Then finally my name was called to go to Phanat Nikhom where I learned English for three months. Here there are better things—more stores, a lot of people like Cambodians, Vietnamese, Lao, and Hmong. They give you certain tests to pass before you can go to the U.S. from there. This is where they check you clean. What I mean is, they check you without clothes on, your urine, your blood. This way they could filter out anyone that is not clean, like if they use drugs or have certain diseases. Everyone is checked there, no exception to it. If you are caught with some disease, it has to be cured first before you can come. Or if you do drugs, you have to be tested clean first before you can come. A lot of people smoked opium, so many people failed. If you don't stop the opium, then you'll likely not come. They have their own place to help you stop smoking and their own hospital to cure your disease.

They taught us a lot of things in that camp. Mainly they

taught us English; second, the laws in America—like when you come there, what you're going to do. They showed a TV show about earlier Hmong people who came to the U.S. and what happened—like not knowing how to use the bathroom, stove, buy foods, or spend money. They also pointed out that we should not believe in commercials because it is tricking people into buying something they don't want. Also they mentioned about gangs and thieves. They mentioned us Hmong people as being the target because we did not speak the language—so when you're carrying things you have to be careful. They also mentioned about crosswalks, where and when you can cross, and stuff like this. They also showed us how to find a job.

When I was learning, I had an American teacher, her name is Suzanne. I know she didn't live here in California, but somewhere in the U.S. She gave me her address, but I have forgotten it. She gave me her address and said she would write to me and I should write back. But at the time I didn't know enough English to write back, so I just said, "No."

Then she said, "Oh, then you don't want to write to me?" This was how I remember what she said. Really, I didn't know how to tell her that I did not know enough English so that I could write her and say how everything is here once I got to the U.S. So rather than saying this I just gave her a dead answer, "No." I still have her picture.

Bee Thao: "I went through a very great moment or years that taught me to believe in myself."

The first camp we came to, Nong Khai, wasn't bad compared to what we went through in Laos. They had food, they had drink, they had bathrooms for us to use; if you got very sick they had a hospital, too. Once in a while they let my dad and me go to a shopping mall outside to buy stuff—such as clothes, shoes, whatever he thought I should have. It was very exciting because you could go there and actually enjoy the moments that you have, instead of—you know—being ready to run, instead of having a feeling, "I have to watch out and be careful." You could go to the mall and you saw people shopping, and you didn't have that fear like back in Laos. It was just a time to think, "Somehow I survived." That was what came through my mind, even though I was only about ten.

We stayed at Nong Khai for about five months, and then they moved us to Ban Vanai, where I lived for seven years, until 1987. There I went to school for the first time, and I learned how to read and write in Thai, I learned how to read in Lao. Every day I went to school and had fun, saw different people, talked to the teacher—and once again, comparing back to Laos, it seemed like things were getting better and better. So I kind of felt that somehow the dark room that I used to live in, now I can leave; I can move outside and actually see the environment.

Even though time and years have passed, those things are always inside my mind. It doesn't matter how many years are ahead of me. Those things will always be inside my heart, and I can always look back to it and say, "Gee, what kind of life I went through!" I can always share those things with my kids in the future or—you know, my grandchild.

So part of it is good. But there are sad parts, too. One sad part is that now I have a feeling that if we had escaped to Thailand before that year we did, and we had come to the United States before that year I came here, somehow I might be a different person than who I am now. My education might be higher. I might have an easier way to understand English, chemistry, or physics. I might have an easier time to get used to all those complicated classes at my college. That's a bad part. But a good part is, you know, it doesn't matter what happens. I went through a very great moment or years that taught me to believe in myself—and taught me to think that nothing is easy. Everything is hard, and if you just have hope or dreams, it might come true, you never know. It also taught me to believe that you do not give up until you die. I have been telling myself that if I hadn't gone through all those things, maybe I might still be living in Laos with the Communists. I might be a farmer instead of a student like I am now.

Another good part is none of our family got killed. We

always escaped. We all came to the United States, except my dad—and except my mom. Him and his second wife who he met at the Ban Vanai camp didn't come here. And my mom didn't come. She died at the camp in July 1986. She died from allergy to some food, because she ate—like a piece of watermelon and two chicken wings. And somehow those mixed together got her very sick. It was the same sickness she got when we were running in the jungle. In the camp she had—like very high fever, and then she got sick—like four days, and then she passed away, because in the camp there wasn't any hospital. . . . There was a hospital but it wasn't that good, so she passed away.

I was the last child she had, and she's the only one that I could always look up to. She's the only one that day and night taught me. Whatever I needed, she was willing to listen to me. She was willing to talk to me, understand my feelings. And she's the only one who wanted me to have a good future. . . . My dad did want me to have a good future, but to me my mom was closer than my dad. So when she died things got complicated. Things got hard. Just a couple of days and she's gone—that's it. And I woke up, she wasn't there. I needed someone to talk to in that camp, she wasn't there. I called her name, she wasn't there—somebody I can talk to. And it was very hard. I went to the cemetery a couple of times just to cry, just to cry there for a couple hours, and then I came home. Sometimes I had dreams that I was talking to her, that I could see her, and then I just woke up—and I cried by myself, without my dad knowing.

A few months after she died they let me leave the camp. They let me move to Bangkok for six months, and then to America. But I came to a point while I was still in the camp that I really missed her. I couldn't eat, I couldn't concentrate. All I could think was, "If I have to go through this kind of stress, it would have been better for me to have died in the jungle instead of going through these things to come to this camp and be alone." The hardest thing was that all my brothers and my sisters, they were married and they had their own families, and they didn't have that much time to spend with me while we were all in the camp. And my dad, you know, a man is different from a woman. He had his own life. He always went out and talked to his wife that he married in the camp and he's still married to now. So I was the only one left behind. And when I went to school there—instead of going and concentrating on whatever the teacher lectured, I just went there and sat and stared and thought, "Why do I have to be me? I had enough torture back in Laos; and now look at me in this camp in Thailand—now I am going through three times the torture I had in Laos." I thought, "Why couldn't God just help her and let me and her go to America, instead of letting her die there, and now I have to leave the camp by myself." I felt very sad and a very emotional pain inside my heart. "She's such a good person. Why did she have to die?" I kept asking. "And then look at her—her body is over here and I have to come to America by myself." So there were a lot of things—a lot of sadness—that went through my head before I came to America.

Chia Ton Cha: "When I missed my mom I would come back."

After we crossed we were taken to Nong Khai camp. If you're a grown-up person, after you're put in there you cannot get out. You have to stay there all the time. But if you were young like me, it looked like it was a joke—if you're under age ten, you could sneak out during the day. You could sneak out of the gate and go play. And at nighttime you could come back, because they're not going to check you. The other people, like my mom, they had to have an ID card to go out, but the kids didn't. Sometimes the guards might chase you a little bit if they saw you going out. Then they'd say, "Oh, he's just a little kid. He'll come back." So they didn't do anything to you.

 As I remember, I used to sneak out a lot. I remember one time sneaking out—I don't know why, I guess maybe I was too hungry—I went to watch two officers eating. They were just eating. I stared at them and one of the officers just gave me

Bee Thao is now a college student. ▷

some good food. He gave me some chicken and sticky rice, so I got one good meal.

The food there was not much. I remember eating rice with salt almost every day, sometimes with chile peppers if I was lucky. They boiled the vegetables with a few chickens. Other food that I remember having was garbage from the ground. Some rotten, unfinished banana, mango, candy, some soft drink. These foods I found usually in the street market or flea market. Sometimes I would wait for an older person and check if he had enough from his drink or finished almost everything from the fruit he ate. If he had enough then I might get the leftovers. If he threw it to the ground, I still would pick it up and clean it out real good.

I was with a bunch of other kids at this time and we all just wandered around, played with beetles or rubber bands, and looked for food to eat. The society I lived in was very much a kid society because I was a kid then and not knowing what real society was. I would say most kids were being neglected every day. The Hmong women were on their own, sewing every day—and the men were off to business, trying to find food for the family. It was a real struggle for them. As far as controlling us kids not to wander around—I believe there was little or no control they had over us kids. We were on our own, playing, but then we always returned home. So that encouraged our parents to forget what we were doing.

What kind of real society was there that we could see? The only sort of clean area out there was the building where you slept. But if you walked like three feet away, you could see a lot of feces around. That camp is always in my memory. Especially the bad smell place. People were too shy during the day. But at night, you could see the people going back and forth, doing their business, three feet from where we slept. That was why I always sneaked out. When you got to the outside you could do almost anything. It's free, and you got fresh air. Even though you didn't have money you could look around in the stores. When I missed my mom I would come back.

Part II

Becoming American

To a Promised Land

The first mass migration of the Hmong into America began about a hundred years after the first mass migration of the Eastern European Jews, which had started in the 1880s and continued to the 1920s. Just before World War I, my mother arrived in New York after a long trip, steerage passage, across the Atlantic. What she saw when she set foot on American soil was dramatically different from the world of her shtetl. My mother was astounded that even the poorest apartments in New York had hot and cold running water and flush toilets and lights that could be turned on and off with the flick of a switch.

The shtetl my mother left in 1914 was in many ways not so different from the Hmong villages of Laos a half-century later. Though the Hmong crossed the Pacific in modern airplanes, they too came from villages where technology had remained unchanged for generations. The strange sights that greeted them when they arrived here were multiplied well beyond those of my mother's day: not only did the marvels and intimidations of plumbing and electricity await them, but also large supermarkets stuffed with food, automobiles everywhere, television sets, VCRs, answering machines, compact discs, computers.

The Jewish immigrants of my mother's generation created their own psychological "shtetl" in the midst of New York City. They arrived by boat on Ellis Island, settled mostly in their self-made ghetto of the Lower East Side (not far from where they disembarked), and remained there for decades. The Hmong immigrants have also sought to recreate their villages in America, though a different era has produced different configurations: They arrived at various international airports across the United States and often traveled to the towns of their white American

◁ Leaving the camp

sponsors, who were usually members of Christian church groups and spoke no Hmong. Because it is now possible to travel across the country much more easily than it was early in the twentieth century, the new immigrants were not constrained to remain in the towns where they first settled. By bus, train, plane, and car, the Hmong followed patterns of chain migration, moving on to various cities across America where other family or clan members had settled. In the midst of urban areas such as St. Paul, Chicago, Seattle, Philadelphia, Fresno, Santa Ana, San Diego, Milwaukee, or Denver, members of clans and extended families created little "village" enclaves, consisting sometimes only of several apartment houses in close proximity or spread out through a few neighborhoods.

My mother was the oldest child of a poor tailor. From the time she was ten years old, she was sent out to work, first as a housemaid and then as a tailor's apprentice. She and her family hoarded kopeks for years so that she could be sent to the land where nobody starved and there were no pogroms. When she reached the Promised Land she was supposed to find a good job or marry a rich man and then bring the whole family over. The task fell to her rather than to a son because the oldest boy was eight years younger than my mother and he limped from a childhood accident. This country, America, the "Golden Land," I heard her call it years later—with how much bitter irony, I don't know—had pulled her and the other early Eastern European Jewish immigrants with its promise of plenty and peace.

The Hmong (very much like the later Jewish immigrants from Europe, who survived World War II and came at midcentury) were mostly pushed rather than pulled. They migrated because their villages were destroyed, their numbers were decimated, and they believed they had reason to fear that the Pathet Lao would kill them all. But the large numbers who chose the United States, instead of the other places that were open to them such as Canada, South America, Australia, or France, came here because they felt something of a pull in the promise America has always seemed to hold out to the tortured and traumatized masses about which Emma Lazarus wrote.

Once they arrived, however, they discovered a multitude

of problems that they did not even have the concepts to dream about back in their Laotian villages or the Thai camps. The specifics are obviously different from what my mother might have experienced, but in a general way I can imagine many similarities. The disorientation must have been much the same. My mother, who came to this country when she was eighteen, and—even more—my aunt, who was already in her midtwenties when she came here, never really stopped being disoriented, though they both died in their eighties. They had been formed in another world, and while they learned to speak enough English to get on, while my mother loved the movies and could tell you the names of all the actors and actresses of her day, they never really mastered the technologically related complexities of the new world. What was entirely obvious to me, having been born here, remained entirely confusing to them. It was my aunt's voice that I heard speaking when Mee Vue described her airplane trip to America ("I didn't know if I was sitting in a house or an airplane or where. I couldn't tell the difference"). Though Mee Vue could find her way in the densest of jungles, the inside of the plane and the airport waiting rooms all looked the same to her. And it was my mother's story I remembered when Shoua Xiong recalled that on her family's first night in America they all nervously stayed up until morning waiting to see if the sun really does rise on this side of the world.

My mother went to school for about a year in her shtetl. Jewish girls were given enough schooling so that they could read the prayers and blessings that would keep the house running. Her meager Yiddish writing skills were of use when she dutifully wrote phonetic letters to her family back in the shtetl. But she never really learned to read or write English. From my first grade on, I was the one who signed my report cards and take-home notices. Many of the Hmong who have come to America were as virtually illiterate as my mother had been. Before the war in Southeast Asia, less than 30 percent of the Hmong were able to read or write. In fact, the Hmong had only the story of an ancient written language until the early 1950s when French and American missionaries developed a Hmong written language using the Roman alphabet. Some adults became literate in the relocation camps in Thailand, and others learned to read in America, but many do not know enough English to use their reading skills for employment or even to sign their children's report cards.

They know their children must learn English in American schools, but they worry the children will forget Hmong. Parents who are interested in preserving the Hmong culture have formed Hmong schools, where the young go to learn to read Hmong and engage in traditional activities after their regular school day is over. Ghia has taken me to visit such a school. The director speaks with great energy about how important it is that the young not forget their past, not forget their parents' travails, not forget what makes them Hmong. I nod in heartfelt agreement. And I remember the Yiddish school I attended briefly as a child, when East Los Angeles still had a sizable Jewish population. I remember the spitball fights in the classroom and the adolescent dirty pictures etched on the already well-scratched and rickety desks, how bored and angry the kids were that they had to sit quietly to learn Yiddish after having sat quietly to learn English all day, and how irrelevant Yiddish school seemed to most of us. I wonder if the children who go to Hmong school in this shabby but very American neighborhood shopping center, surrounded by a vacuum cleaner store on one side and a video rental store on the other, find their experience any more relevant or compelling.

But if the attempt to live straddling two cultures is burdensome for the children, it is mystifying and frustrating for their parents. The children of Hmong immigrants must learn to form an identity; their parents had already formed one, but they found in America that what you were "over there" could not help you "over here." Many have lost the necessary sense of who they are and how that counts in the world. Once, they were in control of their lives. Then they suffered through the traumas of war and the ordeals of their jungle-and-river escape from their homes. After their escape they were forced to cope with the uncertainties, scarcities, and anomie of refugee camp life. And then—if they survived all that, if they managed to come to America—they were forced to start all over again from scratch: no easy task if you possess none of the skills that are requisite in the West on the eve of the twenty-first century. It would be hard under any circumstances to make a new life for yourself if you were not young, but after the trials so many older Hmong people have endured it may be all but impossible. For many, their only hope is that life will be better and easier for their children.

It is especially in the area of work that the older generation of Hmong have suffered a crisis in identity. In Laos, most Hmong were peasant farmers, farming enough for their family to subsist and still have a bit left over with which to barter for the few necessities they could not produce themselves. In America, many attempted to continue with the only work they ever knew, but it is very difficult for an unsophisticated small farmer to make a living here. Farmland is expensive, and the Hmong had no background that would help them understand competitive farming techniques, how to use pesticides, how to irrigate, how to market the produce they've raised. Now sometimes a number of Hmong families cultivate a small plot of land communally. My house, which I bought twenty years ago, was separated from the Good Shepherd Lutheran Church by a three-quarter-acre vacant lot that was overgrown with weeds. About ten years ago the church gave the lot to several Hmong families to cultivate. Almost every day there are many men, women, and children out there working the plot. Now, instead of weeds, luxuriant beans, squash, and corn are growing, but probably not enough to feed all the families well, despite their daily industriousness.

Most of the older Hmong have been on some form of welfare in America, though they continue to make attempts to become self-sufficient. The Hmong, who are used to solving their own problems within the family and the clan, have established here various self-help organizations such as the Lao Family Community which offers vocational training, assists Hmong people in finding jobs, and also tries to serve as a kind of link between the Hmong culture and the American culture to which they must adjust. But despite such efforts, many of the older narrators continue to feel totally overwhelmed by this new world that has proven so difficult to claim as their own. It is hard for older Hmong people to keep from despair; severe depression is rife in the immigrant community.

The older immigrants are something of a "sacrifice generation." To this day, many of them still harbor hopes of going back to Laos, which it is now possible to do. Some have gone back—often to discover how difficult it is to readjust to life in Southeast Asia after life in America. For others, getting to America has been so exhausting that it is virtually impossible to muster the energy for a return trip and an attempt to reassume their old lives. For the young, there is no going back. For better or worse, they are Americans.

I am haunted by a story about a turtle that John Steinbeck tells in *The Grapes of Wrath*. The story is a brief allegory of Steinbeck's larger story in that novel about a poor white family who left Oklahoma during the dust bowl of the 1930s and journeyed to California (their Promised Land) for the sake of their children. In this allegory the turtle laboriously makes its way through a long field of grass, then down a very steep gravel embankment on which it must make frantic efforts not to slip, then up and down a four-inch concrete wall, and then over a highway where a speeding truck touches the edge of its shell and flips it like a tiddlywink. Finally the turtle manages to right itself and succeeds in crawling to the other side of the highway. Somewhere on the course of its journey a few oat seeds had lodged in its shell. Now, on the other side, as it continues to labor along, the seeds fall out into the dirt and stick in the ground. I have always thought that was the story of my mother and me. Now it is the story of the Hmong in America.

First day in America ▷

Mee Vue, who ran through the jungle with her five children cling-
ing to her skirt, told us about her confusion when she journeyed to
America to join her son and her daughter-in-law, Ia Vang Xiong.

In the camp they finally registered me with my youngest son
and his family to come to America. They thought if I was to
come alone I'm too old, so that was why I had to come with Zia.
Like little children, you have to have other people hold your
hand to make it to America.

When I was stepping on the plane I thought to myself,
"Finally I am really going to meet my son Cha Lee in America
and see what America is like." My two oldest sons were separated from me when my husband was very sick, and I stayed
with him until he died. My boys were only in their teens, but
they escaped from Laos with their uncle. Cha Lee came to
America and Zia waited until I got to Thailand with the other
children so he could come to America with me. And finally we
could go, and we could be together with Cha Lee in America.

But despite all this happiness about going to America, I
was worried. First of all, I'm only a farm woman and not a person who knows how to read and write and speak the language. I
told myself then, "I only know how to farm, and if I was to go to
America, I would not know what to do."

But I got on the airplane anyway like they told me to, and
right away, I worried that it was the wrong thing because I did
not know where I was. I could not tell the inside of a building
from the inside of an airplane. So when we were coming to
America, I didn't know if I was sitting in a house or an airplane
or where. I couldn't tell the difference—the inside of a house
was like the inside of an airplane, and the inside of the airplane
was like the inside of a house. We got on, we got off, and I just
sat and sat. I didn't know what was going on the whole time. All
I remember was we were in a big room in a building, and then
we just went to a different room and we were sitting on rows of
chairs. I didn't know each time when we sat if it was the seat in

Preparing chicken in an American kitchen ▷

an airplane or the seat in another airport. Riding the airplane was not at all like sewing the *paj ntaub*, where you know exactly where you're going to stitch next.

So I sat and sat, wherever I was, wherever they told me to sit. Then all of a sudden someone said, "Oh, we are going to land in America." Then I realized I was really in America. I came out, and there were my son Cha Lee and his wife Ia and a whole lot of relatives. It was then that I knew everything was for real, that everyone was real and finally I am in America.

Ghia Xiong: "I had never seen anything like those streetlights and those lights at the airport."

When we arrived in Bangkok from the camp—I was about ten years old—I had never seen anything like those streetlights and those lights at the airport. I sat in a bus in the night and I could see how beautiful it was—so many cars, so many buildings with lights on, and rows and rows of streetlamps. They just formed a straight line down the street, like a diamond necklace of lights.

At the airport, it was late at night, and the lights were like a mini light city—with blue and green and red lights. Then the jumbo jets. They were so beautiful. I just loved to stand at the window in the airport and watch them land and take off on the runway. The first plane they put us on was a green jet but it was too small for all the people. Then they changed us to a great big white 747 plane. Inside it had three aisle of seats that went on and on. It was like a city all by itself.

Ghia Xiong today with his baby and his mother ▷

Shoua Xiong: "We stayed the whole night, watching out the window, to see if the sun will come out."

In the camp my parents couldn't do anything. They just lived day by day and waited to see what would happen. But then we got to come to the United States. We got here after a very long trip, and we thought some Hmong people were going to pick us up at the airport. But instead there was an American guy that came and picked us up. He came and he shook hands with my father and . . . we didn't know what to do. We didn't know how to speak English or anything. He didn't speak Hmong, but he had a Laotian lady with him. My dad knew a little bit of Lao and they communicated. She said, "This is your sponsor." But we couldn't say anything to him and he couldn't say anything to us. We all just smiled and nodded, smiled and nodded. We landed in Des Moines, and they took us to Buffalo Center in Ohio [*sic*].

We were so scared when we first got here because there was so much food everywhere, and lights, and TV—I had never seen television in my whole life. We came and there was TV,—and I saw cartoons on TV. I thought it was weird. I go, "Weird!" They fed us, and then they taught us how to use the stove, refrigerator, everything they thought we should know. Then they went home. I was there watching them teaching my parents. Then, after they left, we tried to turn off the light—and we didn't know how to do it! So, we just kept the light on all day and all night because we didn't know how to turn the switch off. When I think about that I go, "How stupid could we be?"

Then we tried to sleep with the lights on, but we couldn't so my parents decided to try to cook us some food. They turned the stove on. It was not the gas kind; it was the electricity kind. They turned it on, and then it got hot, and then they wanted to turn it off. And they turned the other burner on instead of turning that one off, and then they got four of them on. We didn't know how to turn them off, and it was scary. And then there

At the airport in America ▷

was the refrigerator—it was making some noise, and we got more scared.

They tried to call someone for help, but there was nobody to help us because it was nighttime in Buffalo Center. Nighttime in Thailand, it's morning over here; nighttime over here, it's morning over there. So we stayed the whole night, watching out the window, to see if the sun will come out. It was lonely.

Phia Chang (pseud.): "When I first came here to America I knew that I wanted to stop smoking opium so that I wouldn't have to hide myself from my children."

Back in Laos, the best medicine is opium. We use it for almost all sorts of pain. I started using it a long time ago. After a long day of hard work at the farm, my body could take just so much lifting, cutting, carrying. So when I came home I would just take my little lamp out and melt the cold pig oil that was inside. Then you just roll up a small piece of opium—a little larger than a rice grain—and you stick that piece into a small hole on the pipe, and you just smoke it that way. You have to lay down on one side because it's easier. It would take about an hour before I just fell asleep. Then, when I wake up I feel much better, and I'm ready to go to work again.

I don't really feel bad that I used opium, because there was a good reason for it and I knew what I was doing. I knew I had children to feed and raise. So if I got to smoke opium, it meant my family would get to eat. Another reason why I started using opium was that I had a deep pain in my stomach. I didn't know what it was until I got here to America, and the American doctor told me that I have kidney stones.

You see, I'm a little different from a lot of the opium smokers. If it were not for these things, I would probably choose not to smoke opium. I know that a lot of people who are healthy smoke opium—and they're the ones who don't care about anything. I mean, I do business with these people, and I see how hard it is for them to control themselves. At least I would always still control my desire to a certain point—and I always thought about my family's needs too, not just my need. But with these other smokers, it seems like their desires always come first. I never got all crazy about getting opium. But a lot of those people who smoke it even though they're not sick, many of them just got hooked on it the first time they tried it. For me, I guess I was using it for the right reasons.

At some times I did manage to quit for a while. One of those times was when me and my family were in the camp and we wanted to get to come to America. I knew that I had to stop smoking opium, or else I would fail the physical exam, and my whole family would not be able to come to America. I was very scared when they asked me to give my urine sample and have my chest X-ray done. I was hoping that I had quit long enough before so that they couldn't find out from these tests that I was a smoker. I remember when they brought all of my family back together again into this room. I was looking at the children's dirty hands, dirty feet, torn clothes, and at my wife. And then I thought about how hard we always worked back in Laos, and how hard it was for us to get to this point. I was a very nervous person at this time. If I failed the tests I knew my family would have to remain in this place until I was clean. I heard that a lot of people who smoked opium would never get to come to America because the test showed they weren't clean, so I was really scared.

Then the doctor came in and he said that everyone was clean except for me. I knew right then that it was because I smoked opium. My whole body started to shake. But then he said that they found nothing in my urine. It was only my chest X-ray where they saw something. He asked me, "Did you ever smoke?"

I told him, "No."

Then he went out and came back later and said, "Okay, your family is clear." I was so thankful. The doctor thought the X-ray probably just showed some scarring because I had been exposed to TB.

When I first came here to America I knew that I wanted to stop smoking opium so that I wouldn't have to hide myself from my children. So I went to see an American doctor to find out what was causing me so much pain. I hoped it would be something they could take care of easy. But it wasn't. They told me that I had kidney stones. I couldn't believe what he told me. I was telling myself, "There is no way stones could have gotten inside my kidneys." Then the doctor explained to me what could be some of the causes for this to happen inside my kidneys—like it could be the stream water or the mountain water I drank back in Laos. It could be all those years I was working hard and drinking that bad water.

That doctor said I should have an operation. I was scared because I heard about a lot of people who didn't make it through operations. But I had it done anyway, and once it was done I thought I was cured so I never went back to see that doctor again. I stopped smoking opium and I lived okay for about four years. It was a wonderful feeling not to be embarrassed at yourself all of the time.

But then the pain came back. I took the pain for as long as I could, and then it got worse. I just had to go back to smoking opium again. But like I said before, I never regretted it, because it was only like I was my own doctor. I knew that I was doing the right thing for me, and it has helped me. And how is it worse than when at the hospital the doctors give their patients painkillers with morphine in it? Morphine is made from opium!

The bad thing about opium is like with all drugs—when people can't control it and that's all they want all the time. But when you think about what good opium has done for us, it's a lot. You see, when we were running from the Vietnamese, we had so many crying babies with us. Now, how do you think we all survived? If it wasn't for this opium, everyone would have gotten killed. We gave the opium to the babies to keep them quiet. Yes, some parents didn't know how strong the opium was, and sometimes they gave too much and the baby died. But it was better for that to happen than to have forty or fifty people die. You know, if we had a choice, we would have chosen for no one to die, especially the babies—but we didn't have a choice. And if it were not for us opium smokers who had opium with us to give, many more of our Hmong people might have died.

You know, they say that we opium smokers are beggars and things like that, but I think we did save a lot of people's lives. When their babies were crying and the Vietnamese were chasing everyone, the people would ask, "Oh, does anyone have opium?" or "Where is that uncle that smokes opium? Ask him does he have any left." Like I said, it's a time like this that they call you "uncle," but when that time is finished they don't even want to know you.

It's very hard when you stop and think about it. Many opium smokers don't ever think about it. They don't seem to care. But I'm one of those people . . . I consider myself stuck in the middle, just like many of my children who are stuck in between two cultures. I wanted to quit, but I just can't. It's kind of like my children who can't just quit saying they're Hmong; they can't just say now that they're only American.

You have to remember our Hmong history: In the beginning, it was said, Our Mother of all the Hmong people promised that when she died there would be a plant that would grow out of her breast. And that plant would help to ease all pain. After she died, it was just like she promised. There was a plant that grew out of her grave. And the Hmong went and collected it and learned how to smoke it to ease all their pain. This is why when the poppy of the plant is cut with a small knife, it leaks like the milk of a human. And that's why when Hmong men or women smoke opium, they lay on their side like a baby would lay to suck its mother's breast. This smoke of the opium then will go into the body of the person and help to ease the pain, just like the mother's milk will ease the crying of her baby.

The only difference is that a baby will grow up and learn to quit needing the mother's milk. But because we are old men and women, we don't learn to quit—we learn to need more. That's why many people are addicted to smoking opium.

Boua Xa Moua who, as a young man, learned to play five hundred songs on the qeej *in a couple of months, told us he had difficulty now finding his way in the streets of Fresno.*

Life in America is very tough for me because I'm old. I'm sixty-five now and can't do anything. I would rather go back if I had the choice. I have been here so long, but I have not learned how to speak English or how to write. I tried but it was not easy. It wasn't like when I was learning to play the bamboo pipes. I don't know —I guess as you get older, things just appear harder to learn or something. I am very frustrated. I thought by coming to America I would find a new life. I did—but it is harder than in Laos.

You see, everything in America is confusing. They have red lights, yellow lights, green lights. I have just barely learned what these mean. Then, you see, they have a crosswalk. But we are old—we don't know what it is. We don't care. We would just cross anywhere on the street that we want. But here you cannot cross anywhere you want. You have to find the crosswalk. You have to watch the red light, yellow light, green light.

This is hard enough. But imagine, whenever you want to go anywhere, all the time, you have to wait for someone. I mean, if they don't come, you can't go where you want, because you don't know how to go. I want to go somewhere, and I would like to just walk there. But I'm afraid. There are many streets that are so alike, and I might not find my way back.

For me, I'm lucky. I've been to the Hmong elder place a lot of times, so now I know how to go there. But usually, for most people, you have to wait for someone like your son even to take you to the Hmong elder house, and then you have to wait for him to pick you up again. To do it a couple of times, your son wouldn't mind that too much—but to do it everyday . . . sometimes they get angry. And they don't have the time to always take you where you need to go.

It has been very hard for me. Like I said, if I would have had a choice, I would have remained back in Laos. Or if I could, I would like to go back now. It's much nicer and peaceful back home. Here everything feels too lonely. Everything is too much. I always find myself lost in this world.

Shamanism, Christianity, and Modern Medicine

Ghia has invited me to my first shaman ceremony. His step-father, Choua Pao, is diabetic, has tried one American doctor after another and still feels awful. The doctors tell him there is nothing more they can do for him. It is time to return to the shaman.

I am happy for the opportunity to be present at a shaman ceremony, but I am anxious, too. Will I be in the way? What signs of respect am I supposed to offer? How does one behave?

I arrive at Choua Pao's house at the appointed time. Young men in the front yard are hacking at pieces of wood. They hardly notice I have come because they are so intent on their task. I can see into the garage by the side of the house. A dilapidated Toyota has been parked close to the wall. There is a canvas on the garage floor, and on it an enormous pig lies dead; some elderly men stand over the pig with cleavers. Nobody answers my timid knock at the screen door, so I let myself in. I can see that the small kitchen that is right off the living room is crowded with girls and women cutting vegetables, preparing sauces. A woman who is stirring a large pot over an electric stove has a baby strapped to her back.

The shaman is in the living room. Ghia has told me this shaman has a *neng*, that is, his body hosts a healing spirit. He uses his shaman powers to help people who are physically or emotionally sick: He is like a physician, a psychiatrist, a counselor, all in one. Like healers of other cultures in which health and spirituality are tied together (for example, the root worker among the Africans, the *curandero* among the Latins), the Hmong shaman must communicate directly with the spirit

---

A good luck ceremony for a new arrival ▷

world in order to diagnose ills and determine how to cure them.

The shaman has already begun. He faces an altar on which a light is burning that enables him to see what is ordinarily not seeable, but he does not look at the light. Over his face is a black veil that separates him from the material world. He is already in his trance. He is straddling a bench, riding it as though it were a horse, his whole body shaking as he sits astride his spiritual "charger." His body is present but he is really off in the other world, galloping to find a spirit, a *dab*, who will tell him why Ghia's stepfather is sick and what must be done to cure him: Has one of Choua Pao's three souls gotten lost? Has he been attacked by an offended ancestor spirit or an angered nature spirit or an untamed evil *dab*? Will that spirit be propitiated by the sacrifice of a chicken, or will it demand in exchange for letting Choua Pao's soul return to him a soul of an animal that is weightier than a chicken—a cow perhaps?

The shaman is bouncing up and down on his spirit charger. He will tirelessly ride the charger all over the other world seeking the answers that will help him cure Ghia's stepfather. From time to time the shaman shakes a rattle or beats a sacred gong to frighten off the lurking evil *dab* that he sees.

Three feet away from the shaman the television set is playing an old rerun of a Flintstones cartoon. Five little children sit pressed against each other in front of the set, giggling at every "Yabba, dabba, doo." Ghia's stepfather, clad in western-style pajamas, comes into the room once and massages the shaman's back gently. He too is a shaman, and he knows how the muscles ache when one rides the "charger" hour after hour. He and this shaman are old friends. Choua Pao looks pale and exhausted. He returns to bed, shuffling in his slippers. I sit on the sofa alone, my hands folded, wanting to communicate respect, feeling as foreign as I do in a church. No one pays attention to me or to the shaman.

Three of the older sons come into the room, quickly offer deep bows to the shaman (who, oblivious to them, continues his horse ride in the other world), and then they return to the front yard to cut the wood for the pig that will be barbecued for a feast.

I'm reminded of the synagogue I used to attend with my mother during the High Holidays when I was a child. The women sat upstairs, separate from the men. I was puzzled, angry—not only because the synagogue felt so irrelevant to American-me, and I was forced to sit there with my mother when I would rather be home reading *A Tree Grows in Brooklyn* or *Tom Sawyer*, but also because of the constant coming and going, shuffling of feet, fanning against the heat, whispered conversations. Why was no one listening to the rabbi or the cantor? Was this the way they used to behave in their synagogues in Eastern Europe? Where was reverence?

Now I wonder if what seemed to me to be inattention may have been something different altogether. Perhaps for those Jews, most of them having come to America just a few years earlier, faith was so much a given in their lives, so much a part of their daily experience, that they had no more need to sit gazing in awe at the ceremony before them than a husband of thirty years would need to sit gazing in awe at his beloved wife. Or was the truth that they came to the synagogue for the High Holidays only because that had been their unquestioned habit all through their lives—or because after the Holocaust the remnant felt obligated to honor the memory of the lost in this way?

I cannot be sure what is true here either as I alone sit watching the shaman. Most of the extended family is present today, from the young infant on its mother's back to the old men preparing the pig. All go about their appropriate tasks, preparing a feast to honor the shaman's efforts. Perhaps faith is so much a part of this family's life that they do not need to sit and scrutinize it. The shaman knows his job; he needs no supervision. Does that explain the inattention? For how many in this new world does shamanism remain relevant?

Many of our narrators have said that shamanism is inextricably bound up with Hmong culture. If it ceases to exist the Hmong in America would cease to be Hmong. Yet our young narrators often declared their ambivalence. "Doctorism," as

Shone Yang called it in our interview, threatens to replace shamanistic healing in America. Many Hmong qualify for health benefits that are made available to the poor, and they are sometimes even forced to use the system. I remember a front-page newspaper article about a public child welfare agency suing Hmong parents because they refused to allow their little son's clubfoot (which they believed saved the family from other curses) to be operated on by an orthopedic surgeon.

Christianity threatens shamanism as a religion. The Hmong are besieged by the church groups which often act as their sponsors. These churches very generously provide the Hmong immigrants with places to live, furniture, food, and various services such as taking them shopping in supermarkets (which can be so intimidating to those who have always grown their own food). The church people make themselves indispensable, and sometimes they win the hearts and minds of the Hmong. Some churches are training Hmong ministers to become Christian spiritual leaders to other Hmong, as our narrator Zai Xiong has been trained by the Mormons.

If you are acculturated, an American, no longer a believer in the faith that has been an inseparable part of your ethnic group, what—other than your appearance—makes you a Hmong? What makes me a Jew? After I was no longer required to attend High Holiday services in a synagogue, I put all connection to the Jewish religion behind me. Mostly, I slipped back and forth between atheism and agnosticism. As a young person I had a minor flirtation with Unitarianism because I liked its humanism; and I liked it that the Unitarian church in Los Angeles sponsored a writers' group. If I had to have any religion, I decided for a while, it would be Unitarianism, that very American religion. It felt relevant to me. Judaism wasn't even in the running.

Until I had my son. I had him, first and foremost, because I wanted a child, and I wanted to be a mother. But I had him too because most of my relatives had been killed by the Nazis who were executing Hitler's plan to make the world free of Jews. Of my mother's large family, I was the only one left of my generation. If I had no children, I would be aiding and abetting the horrendous designs of the enemy.

But what did it mean to be a Jew if the religion had no meaning for me? With great anxiety I joined a synagogue when my son was five years old so that he could go to Jewish Bible classes. I started preparing him for Bar Mitzvah long before he left elementary school. I felt great relief when he completed that ceremony so beautifully at the age of thirteen. And great disappointment after the Passover seder last spring, eight years after his Bar Mitzvah, when he disclosed to me without rancor that the seder had little meaning for him and he had gone through the motions of it only because he knew I wanted him to.

I panicked. What makes you a Jew if you find no meaning in the beliefs and customs and rituals that have defined Judaism? How will he be a Jew if he finds the practice of Judaism irrelevant? What have I failed to pass on to him? How have I failed the memory of my slaughtered family?

The anxieties of many of our narrators with regard to their traditional religion are not unlike my own. The convictions of the practicing shamans that we interviewed, such as Nao Kao Xiong, appear to be as powerful today as they have ever been, as is the faith of many of the older generation. Several of our younger narrators—even those who fear that life in America has vitiated Hmong culture because shamanism is endangered—may be emotionally tied to shamanism as the belief system of their formative years, but that bond appears less passionate than sentimental. Some of them see themselves as survivors, remnants, and they feel they are obligated to honor the past by honoring its beliefs. Many are not sure what to believe or what to do. Some hedge their bets, combining shamanism with Christianity, shamanism with Western medicine. They often wonder: What makes you a Hmong if you have put behind you the beliefs and customs and rituals of shamanism? They struggle with the answer.

Nao Kao Xiong: "All of the doctors were very impressed with me."

Back in Laos, I was a healer. I helped cure a lot of General Vang
Pao's soldiers. There were so many soldiers with broken arms,
legs, nonstop bleeding, torn skin. So what I did was, I used my
kher kong. Usually, for most of them, if they had broken legs
they could walk within a week.

The reason I believe in *kher kong* is that it worked for me.
How can you explain why a person's hands, when they use *kher
kong*, cannot be cut by a knife or burnt by steaming water or very
red hot iron rods? I have done these things. Because of that, I
know there has to be some spirit that is making *kher kong* work.

Another example that I do is covering a bowl of water with
a fabric cloth, and the water inside would not come out when I
flip the bowl over. If there is no spirit in *kher kong*, then when
you flipped the bowl the water would just come out. Wa Yang
did not believe me. He said, "Oh, that's nothing. All you have to
do is just cover it with a plastic wrapper and the water will not
come out."

He tried it, and the water poured out. Then he came to me
and said, "Grandpa, it didn't work."

I told him, "Well, you said it would work." Of course it
does not work if you don't know the *kher kong.*

There are many different kinds of *kher kong*—for
strength, to kill, to ward off bad spirits, to heal, for love. Let me
share with you the *kher kong* for love: Back in Laos, there are
kher kong that you can do to young girls, but you must be very,
very careful that your *kher kong* is not done to a married
woman. Love *kher kong* is like a trap, and the girl you are using
your *kher kong* on is like an animal. Somewhere out on the trail,
you do the *kher kong*—and if the girl is the first one to come
onto whatever your *kher kong* trap is, she will fall in love with
you. So for about two weeks this girl that has fallen into your
kher kong trap will not be able to work, do stitchery, or do anything but think about you.

But if it is someone else's wife that comes along, then

◁ Nao Kao Xiong, the shaman, at his altar

you're in big trouble. She will fall in love with you, and her husband and his relatives will come after you. I know that if I teach someone love *kher kong* there will always be trouble. If you do *kher kong* you do not have to say anything out loud—your heart says it, and whoever you are thinking of can't help herself; she would come to you. And then there could be problems: for example, if you were sitting together with a lot of people, and all of a sudden someone's wife comes over to you and whispers how much she loves you, her husband would be mad. And if you do it on a girl, once the *kher kong* wears off, in about one to two years, the girl will begin to really hate you. It'll never be a happy marriage. Or if the marriage does last, then soon one of you will die, because this is the curse for cheating in love.

Kher kong to heal is better. For example, Chong Yia Yang—his wife had an operation done a few years ago. After her surgery, the doctors came to him and told him they could not stop the bleeding. They said, "There's not much we can do for your wife. She is bleeding and she could die. You can go and find your own Hmong doctor or shaman to come and help." So he called me.

When I arrived at Community Hospital, Chong Yia and some of his relatives were there. The hospital was closed for visitation at the time I arrived. But I, being the Hmong doctor, requested that I must see her. They let only me in and no one else. But since I could not speak English, I asked to have someone come in and translate. When I went in I brought with me a *sher qeng* and performed one of my healing *kher kong*. Then I tied that *sher qeng* around her neck. Then I took her hands and looked all over her body. Finally, after this, I came home.

The next morning the doctor came in and talked to Chong Yia and his family. He said, "Where is your Hmong doctor? Is he going to come back this morning?"

The family told the American doctor that they could come and pick me up, and he said that would be a good idea. Once I got there, a translator and I went into Chong Yia's wife's room. Then, when the doctor came in, he said to the nurse, "Yesterday their Hmong doctor came to see her. Has the bleeding stopped?"

Then the nurse replied, "Oh, yesterday he came and did his *kher kong*. Since then the bleeding has stopped all night long." The doctor went up to Chong Yia's wife and checked her.

Then he came up to the translator and just raised his hands and said, "What does the Hmong doctor say?"

Then the translator turned to me and translated to me. I told the translator to say to the doctor, "You did the surgery on this woman. Not only did you cut her rectum, but you also cut some arteries that went to her uterus. This is the reason why she was bleeding so much."

Then the doctor said, "You know this for sure? And how do you know?" Then he asked us to go out and wait until Chong Yia's wife came back from X-ray.

So we went out and waited with the relatives. In about an hour and a half the doctor came back. This time three doctors came, and one of them came kneeling. He said, "We as doctors did not see that she had bleeding of the arteries to the uterus. We even used an endoscopy to go from her mouth to her rectum, and checked again from her rectum back up to her mouth. But the Hmong doctor did nothing but hold her hands, and he told us that her rectum was about to break, that the arteries to her uterus were cut. According to the X-rays, he was correct. We apologize."

All of the doctors were very impressed with me.

What I did was, I held onto her hands; then I squeezed her nails. If everything were okay, after squeezing them, you would see all of the blood in her nails moving back. But what I noticed is a small black line within her nails. When you squeeze you can see the blood flowing or not flowing. If there is bleeding somewhere else, the blood would not be able to fill up her nails, and you can see a small black line.

Right now, though the hospital will allow us to do *kher kong*, and when we bring a string to tie around the person in the hospital they will not say anything, they do not allow us to bring a chicken or burn paper money in the hospital. If you ask them, you can burn incense, but they will not allow you to bring a knife.

There was also another case: This time it involved a

Hmong woman in San Diego. She was in labor, but because she was big and the baby was big, she could not deliver. The doctor had to do a C-section on her. After the surgery, the doctor just stapled the cut back together. Then she came home. Three days later, there was an infection. The cut did not heal; instead it was red and swollen and the staples came off. When the staples came off, all of her intestines came hanging out on both sides.

When they took her to the hospital, the doctors there said that there was not much they could do. The wound was too big and tricky. But the doctors had heard of me, and they told the family there was a Hmong doctor that could probably help. The family told the doctors they didn't care how far away I lived, just as long as they could get me there. So they called me and scheduled a flight for me right away.

When I got there I was directed into her room alone. I didn't know if she was dressed or not dressed. She was just covered by a white cloth. I nearly fainted when I took the white cloth off. All of her intestines were hanging out on the side. My whole body shook. I couldn't stand up. Then the doctor came in and asked me if I could help to heal the wound and put some of the intestines back.

I turned to him. I was angry. I said, "You have the nerve to operate on this patient, and now you're telling me you cannot do anything. If you know how to operate, why can't you put it back together?"

Then he told me, "Yes, I could do it. But only if the skin is not too old or too stretched like hers is from having too many babies."

Then I asked him, "Are you going to do any more surgery?"

He said, "I still will, but only if it is necessary."

After this, an officer came in and he said, "You're the Hmong doctor. Since you came, you have to cure it. If you don't, how would you feel if she dies? And then the family will demand that this doctor be taken to jail. How would you feel?"

There was something else that the officer also said that angered me very much—I don't remember. I hit the doctor twice and hit the officer twice, but they did not leave. I was so angry and scared. Then another officer came in and asked if I could help the woman. I told him I could. Then I asked them to go out, and I said this would take about eight hours.

Then I came to her and used my healing *kher kong* to heal the wound. I would do the *kher kong* on it, then take a break somewhere else, then come back and do it again. I used the *kher kong* about three or four times. Each time I did, the wound got better and better. The intestines that were still hanging would just pull in by themselves. I suspect the reason why the doctor could not staple her back was because she had too much fat around the cut area. Each time they tried stapling back, because of the infection and her fat, the staples would just come off.

Finally, when they came back, the wound had almost healed. They asked me, "How much money do you want?" I asked them how much an operation would be. They said, "About ten thousand dollars." But I told them that for me, I don't want that much.

Then they asked, do I want the hospital to pay me, or should the patient pay me. I said, "I don't know. Whoever you think should pay, I'll take the money from them."

In the end, the family was asked to pay. The patient said that her family was poor, so she would just give me three thousand dollars. I said that was okay, so they paid me one thousand dollars right away. Then, when she was totally cured, she did send the other two thousand dollars to me.

Shone Yang: "Some [Hmong in the U.S.] believe both in the churches and shamanism, and there are some who believe in shamanism and doctorism."

To me, culture is like an ID card. You have to have an ID. If someone asks you "What is your culture," you have to have something to show them. So even though I have been here since I was in my teenage years, everything about our Hmong culture is still very important to me. Shamanism is very, very important. For us, it's like your prayer: You go to your church and you pray;

we talk and we ask our ancestors to guide us and to protect us from evil spirits and bad lucks.

A lot of the times a shaman could help a sick person to get well. I remember my brother got real sick with a high fever, and my parents called a shaman to come and check on him. The shaman said that my brother's spirit had been taken away and we needed to sacrifice a chicken to call his spirit back, and then we needed a pig to sacrifice in exchange for his spirit. We did just like the shaman said, and a few days later my brother was back to normal again.

The shaman knows how it has to be done. He knows whether or not the reason somebody is sick is because they have an ancestor whose spirit is in hardship. When that is the case, sometimes the ancestor keeps bothering the family, making the children cry or making them sick or giving everyone night-mares. The ancestor's spirit doesn't really directly tell the father of the family that it is in hardship and needs help. The spirit tells it indirectly through dreams or sickness or bad lucks. Very often the ancestor might take away the spirit of a person from that family as a sign that the ancestor's spirit needs something.

This is why a shaman plays an important part to the Hmong people. He can give correct interpretation of bad dreams or sickness or bad lucks. For example, if he finds out that the spirit of a member of the family has been stolen by an ancestor he will know how to get it returned. We have to satisfy our ancestor's need with the sacrifice of a pig or a cow or spiritual paper that represents money. If we don't do that the person will have more illness and it will lead to his death.

When we make these sacrifices—like with paper money—it is burned so that it will go up to the ancestor's spirit in a spiritual manner and he will take the money and use it for whatever purpose he needs it; then the spirit of the sick person will be returned in exchange. If we sacrifice a pig or a chicken, we cook it and invite the ancestor to come and join the feast. After this big feast for our ancestors, then a few days later the sick person is better and becomes healthy again.

◁ Blessed by the shaman

People have been trying to make us lose our shaman beliefs for a long time. Before the Vietnam War, there were some French missionaries that came across to our people and converted some to Catholicism. Some shamans even became priests and then forced other Hmong people to convert. Sometimes Hmong people practiced both at once—shamanism and Catholicism. But there were some who still stayed with shamanism only. Like today here in the U.S.: There are Hmong who believe in churches of the Catholics and Christianity, and some who believe both in the churches and shamanism, and there are some who believe in shamanism and doctorism.

But I think less and less people here are believing in shamanism because of the churches and all the doctors and nurses who say they have knowledge and skills to cure people. I think for those who are living in the U.S. now, in ten years they won't be practicing the shaman religion anymore. That is very bad because that is a part of our tradition that is being destroyed. Not only that, it is the *main* core of our culture. What do we have in our culture if we don't have shamanism? It is our tradition, our religion, our medicine—and maybe it will soon be gone.

Vicki Xiong told us about combining Shamanism and Catholicism.

It's hard to give up the spiritual values my parents instilled in me, like spirit calling before the New Year, where they say you have to leave the bad year behind and welcome the good. I liked the ritual. It was a time when your relatives came and visited you from everywhere—I loved that.

My parents still have their old beliefs. Every time somebody gets sick they think it's the spirit so they seek a spirit calling or they get the shaman. It's hard to give that up, too. Though I became a Catholic through my husband, I'm still very influ-

In a doctor's office ▷

I Begin My Life All Over

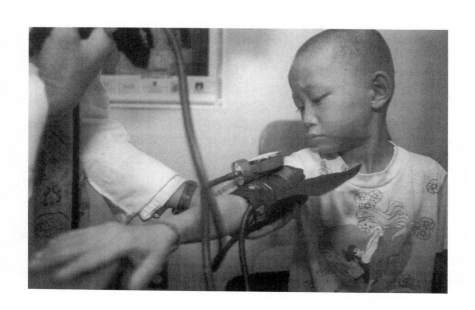

enced by that. Every time my friends get sick, or I get sick, we still want to do that. But since my husband is Catholic, I try not to do it.

I'm very disturbed by this. I always try to put my shamanistic beliefs away, but I still have my parents and they say we should do them. So sometimes, even since I've been married, we do it when we need it. We call a shaman in. Then we would set up a small table as an altar, for his buffalo horns, gong, some incense, two eggs—all set up ready to go. Sometimes we do it plain. Other times we have to sacrifice pigs or chickens, but usually not in the house. For example, the pig is brought in, the shaman does the ceremony on the pig, and then the pig is taken back to the slaughterhouse to be killed.

I think that the reason that it works is because we believe it. It actually does work. I remember when my son Joshua had diarrhea and vomitting for almost a whole month. We took him to see doctors, but they only gave him an antibiotic and it didn't do anything. My mom was very worried and she said we should call a shaman in. Then she asked a shaman to come in and help, so he did. Afterward we had to sacrifice a pig, two or three chickens, and some paper money. And right after that, Joshua was getting better. So I think I . . . that enforces my belief, even though I'm a Catholic. I grew up believing in shamanism, and I still believe it. I think it really works for my friends and me. But because my husband is a strong Catholic, I feel very bad after I do that because I'm in his family and I'm breaking the rules.

Ger Yang, D.D.S., a Western-trained dentist, told us about combining shamanism with modern medicine.

I have a problem educating the Hmong community to understand the health care system. I'm not saying we're bad, but we don't understand. They don't come to you when a problem first develops, but then when they have bad pain, they come and they want you to fix it. It's too late. They don't understand prevention. That's the main problem I have right now. And it's daily with my patients.

They expect the pain to be cured right away. They come to you and demand that you provide them with everything to stop the pain. They don't understand that in health care you can only do one step after another. They expect you to do all the steps at once. For example, when someone comes to me with an infected gum: In that area around the tooth, there's bacteria, and yes, they're in pain. What they don't realize is that before I can remove the tooth, I have to control the infection with antibiotics. So they come in pain, they want me to fix it, and when I write them a prescription for antibiotics they go home complaining that I didn't stop their pain.

Or another example I just had: A patient comes in with a toothache and the X-ray determines that the cavity is deep into the tooth. You tell them, "Well, if you want to fix your tooth you have to do certain steps. First we have to do a root canal. We have to remove the nerve and replace it with an artificial nerve," and so on.

But they don't understand. They just say, "Well, don't drill anything. Just put the filling in. Just block the hole." But you can't. They're going to have more pain if you just block the hole, because there'll be a lot of pressure on the nerve.

Other times, you take X-rays, and you show them there's a cavity there. But because they can't see it with their own eyes, they don't believe it and they don't want you to treat them. I think this is mostly common with the older generation.

Actually, I myself still believe in the shaman along with modern medicine. I grew up living with uncles and relatives who are shamans, and that's my tradition. I saw over and over again how it can help cure a person, though I also know of cases where it doesn't work. As far as my work goes, I know a person's tooth can be in pain and a shaman can cure it with his ceremony. But if the shaman doesn't cure it, it's usually because the tooth is diseased and needs to be removed or treated. That's where I come in.

I mean, as far as shamanism is concerned, let's do it. It's not going to hurt you. Shamanism is not going to take anything

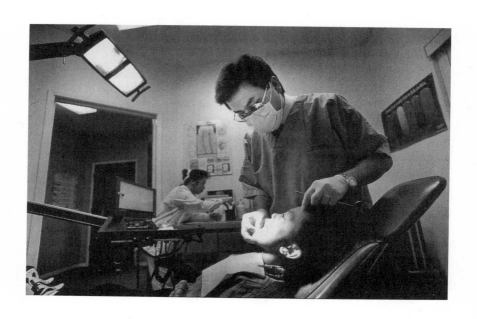

from you. If you don't believe in it, just be quiet. Just don't say this and that and be critical and discourage other people from believing.

Zai Xiong, who was raised in shamanism, told us how he became a Mormon elder.

When I was about sixteen years old, there was one day I came home from high school, I came into my bedroom and sat down at my desk, and I am thinking about life. I guess I kept on hearing about people who are Christians but who are still in the Hmong culture. I heard about this Jesus that people are talking about, how he could restore people with hearing loss and all those things. I had a very bad hearing problem.

According to my parents, when I was a baby they took me down to a swamp and they lay me near some bushes. They said that after that I had a bad spell on me, because there was probably some bad spell where I was laying—or maybe it was a spirit's home and I had crushed it. There was a curse on me, on my hearing, that was brought to me by whatever spirit was there. They tried very hard to fix my ear. They called in the shaman to do a ritual many times. When they looked into my ear they couldn't see anything—only ear fluids that were coming out.

Finally, we came to America. And I kept thinking to myself, "Why, why do I have to be the only child that has to go through all this and not my brothers and sisters?" It really bothered me, especially when I became sixteen and boys and girls were talking together and could hear each other and could carry on a conversation fine.

But one day about that time, when I was asking myself why I had to suffer like that, a missionary couple from the Church of Jesus Christ Latter Day Saints came knocking on the door. They were telling me about this healing power and every-

---

◁ Dr. Ger Yang, D.D.S.

thing. I was really surprised by what they were saying, that I would be able to hear again.

They gave me things to study, and I found out how these things really work. Then I took missionary lessons and they taught me about the purpose of life, where I came from, why I am here, where I am going. They also taught me how I could get my hearing back. I studied everything very careful and I felt very peaceful, comfortable, quiet.

I felt a lot of good things happen to me that year. As a Hmong, I never heard of Christians. But then I found out that the things they were teaching me were true, were essential to life. I took it very seriously to evaluate my life. I sense myself as a minister now, an elder. I understand that the most important principle and doctrine to me is life after death and that after the mortal life in which I am in now, I will be able to go to the next life and be able to gain eternal life.

I prayed a lot about getting my hearing back. I had 50 percent loss, and now after all my prayers I have 85 percent hearing. The answer I got from my prayers was that I needed to see a doctor. It was the prayer that gave me the strong feeling I could hear again. I learned, "After you pray, you do your best to help yourself and God will also help you." My best was to find a doctor to give me some tests, and he said he could do something to gain my hearing back. He found out that I didn't have my eardrum at all in both of my ears. That was why I couldn't hear. He said something got into my ears and I had an infection, and I never had any medication to heal it. He said he was going to use some small part of my skin to make an eardrum.

At first my mom didn't want me to do that. She was scared, and she said that it wouldn't work because they tried everything for the last fourteen years, and they always took me to a shaman. We were active in shamanism. My uncle—my dad's younger brother—is a shaman, and my father is a bamboo pipe player. He plays it very well, and I'm his son, and it was very hard for me to become a Christian. If I would not have had such a faith, such a trust and confidence in who I called upon, then it would be very hard for me to move out of the shaman religion and come into the Christians.

So I had two mixed feelings: One is about my family and relatives, about "What if they disown me? How would I handle that? How will I be living on with my own self in a world where there is so much confusion?"—and at the age of sixteen getting a job is hard. I was afraid of my family loss. But then I told myself, "I have such big faith, I have such great love and concern that I will be able to overcome this."

One afternoon I went to my mother. I had a feeling that I needed to go to her first. And I said, "You know Mother, I found this church that I have a lot of strong feeling about. And this church will be able to provide me with a lot of ideals and help me with healing of my hearing. I will be able to hear again, and then I will be able to hear all of you."

She was very concerned about me going to church. She said, "No, you're the only one who wants to do this. None of your relatives are going, and how can you go by yourself?"

And I said, "You know, Mom, I can handle this. This is America. And this is life in America. America is freedom, freedom of religions."

And my mother said, "But you are still a Hmong. So it doesn't matter where you are, you are still going to be a Hmong. You're not going to church and be a Christian."

I felt hurt. I told her that nobody else could help me with my hearing. "You all have been trying for fourteen years and it hasn't been successful. Now I want to try something new, for me, for my life, and for my future."

After that she just sort of cried and became quiet because she could not answer me. Then she told my father and he said, "You crazy! Why are you doing this when none of your relatives are going?" He yelled at me. It was really bad. I didn't think it was going to be that bad.

He said a bunch of words in Hmong. He said such things like, if he was performing a shaman ritual, being his son I would have to be there. But if I become a Christian person, how will I help him? Why not stay with him and help him out?

So for the first couple of months or so, I was just sneaky. I didn't have a car yet so I just called up the missionary people and told them to pick me up because I don't have a ride. I knew my parents weren't happy with me, but I was too big for them to spank me. And I felt I just had to go to the church meetings, I had to find out more about Jesus.

Once I used to look up to shamans as my spiritual leader. I looked up to them as my healer and I looked up to them as my guide. I guess they did their best to try to heal me, but it didn't work, so maybe it's not good for me. It might work for other people, but for me, no. So after I felt that shamanism wasn't successful for me, for my hearing, I shifted gears and found out about this new doctrine. I felt like, "I will go and find something that heals me, but I will not forget who I am. I will not forget that I am a Hmong."

I told my mother again, "You have tried your best, now I will try mine." So after I told my mom, I just went to the doctor and gave them permission to do whatever they needed to do to make me hear again. With my heart I felt that my prayer had been answered and that everything will be okay. After two hours of surgery, my brother came to pick me up. He shook when he saw all the bandages on my ear. Then after about a week I went back to the doctor and he removed all these bandages: Small sounds became big sounds for me! At sixteen I did all this by myself, because my prayer was answered.

Women and Men

Hmong folklore contains a tale that is very much like the Eve
story in Genesis. The Hmong story claims that the first humans
knew no death and did not have to work because the earth gave
them freely everything they needed. Life was always joyful and
without problems. Then one day a woman drank water from
a forbidden stream and ate a forbidden white strawberry. Because of her transgression, humans had to leave their first home
and were never allowed to return. They had to earn their bread
through hard work, and death came into the world.

For the sins she was thought to have inherited by virtue of
her gender, woman in traditional Hmong culture was treated as
an inferior in a variety of ways. Her inferiority in relation to
males began as early as birth, when the placenta of a boy baby
was honored by being buried next to the center housepost while
that of a girl baby was disposed of by being buried under the
bed. Throughout her life it was not possible to escape an awareness of her bodily inferiority. During her menstrual period and
for one month after giving birth her body was even considered
unclean (which is similar to the view of woman's body during
menses in Orthodox Judaism) or in disequilibrium with
nature.

Women were also reminded of their inferiority in daily
life: A woman had to walk about five paces behind her husband;
she had to serve food to the men of her family first, and only
after they had eaten could she and the other females of the family eat. Her legal status in traditional Hmong society was virtually nonexistent, just as it was for women in the Western world
until the last century. Women were not permitted to speak bind-
ing words or negotiate contracts. Only men could participate in
group governance. Women could attend an assembly, but they
could not vote, even for clan leaders.

Women had little or no control over even the most intimate aspects of their lives. For example, they had virtually no say about whom they would marry. Marriages were often arranged by the parents, but "catch-hand marriage," that is, kidnap marriage, as Shone Yang explains in this part of the book, was also common. Whether the marriage was arranged or forced through kidnap, it would be the woman's male relatives who would ultimately negotiate a marriage contract with the man's male relatives.

The contract generally stipulated the "bride price," which was often paid in silver bars. The greater the girl's virtues, the higher a price her male relatives were justified in asking. If an amiable contract could be worked out, a black umbrella would be hung in the bride's home as a sign to the young men who came to visit that she was taken and no other suitor should have designs on her. After the wedding the umbrella was to be tied closed and brought with the couple to the husband's house where the male elders of the family would untie it.

Polygamy was permissible for Hmong men in Laos, though a 1968 survey reported in Hendricks, Downing, and Deinard's collection of essays *The Hmong in Transition* (1986) showed that only about 20 percent of the men had more than one wife. Wealthy men might marry several wives in order to manifest their wealth, or a clan leader might marry women of other clans in order to gain support from those clans. Sometimes a man might marry the wife of his deceased brother (as has been common among other cultural groups such as the ancient Hebrews). A wife might also request of her husband that he take additional wives who would help her with the housework and fieldwork; or, if a wife could not have a son, she might request that her husband take additional wives to bear children, and as the "Big Wife," she would have a right to claim their sons as her own. The bit of power a woman might have was usually only over other women: for example, First Wife had power over Second Wife, Second Wife had power over Third Wife. The husband was obligated to allay the wives' jealousy by having sexual relations with each of them on a regular basis, but as our interview with Chue Vue reveals, in practice he did not necessarily adhere to his obligations. Because polygamy is illegal in America, when applying to come to the United States men who had multiple wives had to shed all but one wife officially. Unofficially, the practice continues to exist among a few in the immigrant generation in America.

Divorce was permissible among the Hmong in Laos and could even be initiated by the wife, but not without great difficulty. Not only would her family have to return the bride price if she were divorced from her husband, but she would also lose all her rights to any of the children her husband's family wished to keep. Naturally, all able-bodied sons were kept by the husband's family, as were girls who would soon marry and bring a bride price. Since girls typically married between the ages of fourteen and sixteen, the wife would usually lose even her young daughters if she divorced her husband.

Perhaps women felt they could not object strenuously to their inferior positions because they were inculcated with the idea of a "mandate of life," or "a paper from heaven," as Chue Vue says to explain her fatalistic acceptance of being "Third Wife." The "mandate of life" foretells how long one will live and what one's fate will be. Therefore, if a woman is kidnapped and must marry a man she does not love, it is because the mandate, the "paper from heaven," ordained it.

For the Hmong, relations between the sexes started to change in the refugee camps of Thailand. As mentioned before, the change began perhaps when Hmong women learned through relief workers that they could earn money by selling their beautiful stitchery, a new experience which may have planted a seed of independent thought in some. Yet a change in women's view of themselves would undoubtedly have been inevitable even without this phenomenon in the camps: In a 1993 study of the Hmong in contemporary Laos, *Hmong at the Turning Point*, Yang Dao observes that today it is possible for Hmong women in Laos to go to school, and as a result of education many Laotian Hmong women are demanding equal rights. As the twenty-first century approaches, feminist ideas seem to have spread everywhere in the global village, as painful as that may be to those who are not ready for such upheavals of their private worlds.

In the United States, some immigrant women continue to sell their remarkable needlework and occasionally earn more money than their husbands, who often lack any specialized skill that might be marketable in this country. Great numbers of Hmong immigrant men in America are, in fact, unemployed. They are not in the position to discourage their wives from making money, but their wives' greater earning power here is a shock to men who did not doubt their own superior powers back in Laos. Middle-aged male immigrants believe, as fifty-one-year-old Soua Teng Vang told us, that many of the health problems their group suffers here, including Sudden Unexpected Nocturnal Death Syndrome—99 percent of the victims are male—may be attributed to the stress of this new gender inequality. Studies of the syndrome by Adler and by Bliatout bear out its connection to great stress, whatever the cause of the stress.

Hmong women in America have not claimed power easily or uniformly. Most immigrant women are not self-sufficient, and domestic life for them is not appreciably different from what it was back in Laos. Older Hmong women who left Laos after the war, before education was open to females, were inculcated with beliefs of women's inferiority and subservience. Their female children who were raised and educated in America often feel pulled between the image of women that their mothers presented to them and the very different kinds of images that they see in American culture.

I was struck by two particular scenes at the Hmong New Year celebration that Ghia and I attended in Fresno last winter. Both demonstrated to me how little life has changed for some Hmong women here in America and how great the ambivalence toward change is, even on the part of those whose lives have been profoundly metamorphosed through immigration. The first scene was of a family group, all dressed in beautiful blue Hmong traditional garb, whom we wanted to photograph— a prosperous-looking middle-aged man, three adult women of varying ages but all younger than the man, and their many children. Ghia knew what was appropriate: He went directly up to the man to ask permission to photograph him and his family, never making the slightest eye contact with the women. The women and children posed at the man's instructions, and then when we were finished taking pictures the women walked off several steps behind their husband.

The second scene was at the New Year Miss Hmong pageant. The pageant, based on the Miss America idea, is something of a showcase for the marriageable young women in the community. I have been told that the bride price for the winner of the pageant is often ten thousand dollars, four to six thousand dollars above the usual price. This year each young woman appeared first in traditional Hmong dress and then in a western-style evening gown (some organizers wanted to add a bathing suit segment, but they were voted down). Each of the contestants had to give a little speech about herself. One wanted to become a businesswoman, three were going to be doctors, another was going to be a politician and a pilot, one was a future physicist, several were already studying to become teachers. All were going to help their husbands realize the American dream by bringing good salaries into the home. Not one planned to be just a housewife. And their hobbies? "In my spare time I like to help my parents and do work around the house." "My favorite thing to do when I am not studying is cook for the family." "My hobby is taking care of children."

Many young Hmong American women are not at all ambivalent about who and what they want to be, however. They see themselves as equal to men and are demanding that men acknowledge their equality. Their goals are often supported by younger, educated Hmong men, but it is not surprising that men of the older generation have a difficult time with the changing relationship between the sexes in the Hmong American community. In Laos the entire village disapproved of a husband who could not control his wife, so men learned they had to be forceful. Now they are dismayed to see that their sons are not always following their examples of how to treat a wife, and that their daughters have little notion of how a Hmong woman is "supposed to behave."

Most studies of the Hmong community in America suggest rapid changes with regard to attitudes toward women's and men's roles and the family, particularly among younger people. In Laos, a woman's most important job was having children—frequently ten or twelve—who could contribute to the family welfare by their labor on the farm. A 1993 study of Hmong courtship and marriage in the Fresno community by Dana indicates that 95 percent of the young couples interviewed said that "it was not important that they have a lot of children." They expressed a very American awareness of the financial hardships involved in having many children and the difficulty of giving children in a large family "quality time, attention, and love." Both husbands and wives objected to the possibility of their daughters marrying at a young age. Sixty-five percent of those interviewed said they would like their daughter to finish college and have the means to support herself before she considered marriage. Another 15 percent said their daughter should at least finish high school before she considered marriage. While parent-arranged marriages and kidnap marriages had been most common in Laos, none of the marriages in the study began in kidnap, and only 15 percent of the marriages were arranged by relatives. Most commonly, the young couples met in school—far from parental scrutiny.

In another study of 134 Hmong adults in Omaha, Nebraska, published in 1986 in *The Hmong in Transition*, 78 percent of the women interviewed disagreed that in case of divorce it was the husband's right to decide where the children belonged. Seventy-three percent of the interviewees believed "the husband and wife should be equal in power in marriage." Only 7 percent of the women said they would approve of polygamy. Forty-two percent of the interviewees disapproved of the bride-price custom. In Laos, marriage of a Hmong outside the community was almost nonexistent, but about half of these interviewees thought it was acceptable for a Hmong to marry a non-Hmong. From what we observed, it is likely that if the interviews were done today, just a decade later, the responses would indicate an even more emphatic departure from traditional attitudes.

Human beings are capable of such vast changes—such dramatic adaptations to place, circumstances, and opportunity—in so short a period of time. My mother was a universe away from the life of the shtetl where she was born. There, a woman almost invariably married young, had as many children as God would bless her with, served her husband, and was constrained to live what the community would consider a pious life. If her husband was a Talmudic scholar and did not work for pay, she might have a little store that would permit her to make enough money to support the family, but she had no ambitions or possibilities beyond that small sphere. It was pointless to question. There were no choices to be made. One accepted one's fate.

My mother did not get married until she was fifty-eight years old and I was a fourteen-year-old. My biological father, who never married my mother, had been her lover for eight years before I was born. She had had two abortions already, and when she became pregnant with me, he wanted her to have a third. But she was already almost forty-four years old, and she realized that this might be her last opportunity to have a child. She would have to work always; she would be our sole support, but she had a trade and had been self-sufficient since coming to America at the age of eighteen. Several months before I was born, my grandmother, who never left the shtetl, died of cancer; a year after I was born the rest of the family in Latvia was killed by the Nazis. My mother had never told any of them about my existence. How could she explain that her lover would not marry her and she decided to have his child anyway? Such things never happened in the shtetl.

I am a universe away from the life of my mother. It briefly occurred to me as a teenager that I might like to be married, but the impulse passed quickly. I chose to make my life with other women instead of with a husband. Because I knew I would have to support myself always, I chose to get a Ph.D. so that I could have a profession instead of a trade. I desperately wanted to have a child, and I chose to do so by donor insemination. In my mother's world of the immigrant such choices would not have been open to me. Nothing that I am could have existed in my grandmother's world of the shtetl.

As the young Hmong people we spoke to also demonstrated, the choices provided in America have created women and men vastly unlike the people they would have been had they lived in Laos.

Shone Yang, a college student, who is perhaps the most sensitive of all our middle generation narrators to the older culture, told us that traditional Hmong views of courting have not entirely disappeared in America.

One of the old traditional things in Laos was kidnapping a girl as a way to take her for a wife. Today it is still happening in the United States, but not very much, because the girl or her family calls the police. In the old tradition, the man and his friends kidnap her. Then the man sends two people from his clan—they are called *fiv xov*—like negotiators. They go to the girl's house, and first the two men ask politely, "Whose house is this?"

Once they are received into the house, one of the *fiv xov* speaks to the father of the house, while the other *fiv xov* hands out cigarettes to everyone present. This is to let everyone there know that their sister or daughter has gone to the welcoming house of her husband-to-be.

The *fiv xov* who speaks to her father or the other males of the family will usually say something like, "We now have your daughter, but we come in peace. We ask for your forgiveness, and we would like you to accept that our son has taken your daughter for a wife. We come in peace, to let you know that you do not need to worry about your daughter. She is in the house of so-and-so, and their father's name is so-and-so." They leave and in three days the daughter returns with the man who wants to marry her and his negotiators.

If everything goes well then these two men's job is done. They would just return home to the house of the father of the groom-to-be and let everyone know that everything went well. But if the girl's family is not happy, this is the crucial time to prevent the marriage from taking place because any time after this she is no longer considered clean. If they really hate the groom, maybe their first step can be, when the *fiv xov* came and told where their daughter was, her mother could send a few women from the girl's side to go to the house of the boy and get her back—this is like one of the few times the women have a little bit of power. But even at this point it would be a shameful thing for the girl and all the relatives to accept her back. So really—already it is too late to do anything about the kidnap but give in.

If the father has a lot of confusion about what to do about the dowry price or whatever, he would call upon his clan leader, and they will seek out two of their own men to come and have a talk with the groom's men. If everything works out, there's agreement between both clans and money is on the table, then the wedding is on. But first all problems must be settled out, like the dowry price must be set. Sometimes for that part new negotiators are used, and it may take the whole night. Then the wedding would start the following day—or the father of the bride would set it for some other time soon.

But the bride's parents do not like it often, because they do not have much choices. Sometimes if they don't like the groom they will try to set the dowry very high. But even at this time, the parents don't have much choice except to go along with the marriage. Maybe they do not like the groom, but they will be ashamed because if they say they do not want the marriage the groom's men will remind them, "We took your daughter for three nights and she may not be a virgin anymore. It will be useless to have her back. Everyone around will know that she has been taken as a wife for three nights and that will ruin her reputation. She will not have any good chance for a future husband if she doesn't take our son."

Usually then, the girl's parents will have no choice but giving in. Almost never does a girl come back to her parents' house to live if she has been kidnapped. So you can see why Hmong parents do not let their daughters go out too much, and it's hard for me—for any man—to find a date with a Hmong girl, even in the U.S. The parents do not want to lose their choices to kidnap.

Before I can even see a girl, her parents have to trust me and like me for their future son-in-law. They will inspect not just me but my whole family and my clan for bad luck or for genetic disorders. They will ask me every bit of my background, and if I am from a clan that has given her clan no respect, I might as well just say goodbye to the girl, I might as well just go kick the curb now. If I am from a clan that they have nothing against, then I can try to win that girl's heart.

But even then I would not have anything like an American date with her. To you—to Americans—to date is to get to know each other on the first date. But in our culture, we have to have the girl's parents' permission, and then we can get to know her in her house. There is just no such thing as real American-style "dates" like going out alone together. And even if we can go to her house, we are almost never alone with her. If the mother cannot sit there, she will have one of the brothers or sisters sit with us. So you can see that privacy for us dating couples is definitely not the same as for Americans. The only privacy we might get is when we are visiting at her house and talking and talking until everyone in her family has gone to sleep. Then maybe we can get just one hour of nice and private talking. Other than that, our best hope is to meet each other at school for a little private talk.

If her parents give permission for me to go and do visiting, mostly I can get to know her family and her way of life with her family. But her parents will judge me very quickly, and if they don't like me they won't even talk to me. I can't go back. If they liked me, they will try to convince their daughter that I should be the chosen one. But I have not been so lucky yet.

It's hard to find an American kind of date with Hmong girls because in most families even here in America, they would like to still keep the old traditional way of dating. The girl's parents and relatives will say that if the girl went out of the house for dating now, she would not turn out to be a very good housewife and she would have no respect for her family. If she said to her parents that she wanted American-style dates her parents would say to her, "We raised you to be big and full grown, and now you want to ruin our reputation."

The parents are afraid not just of kidnapping but of other kinds of losing face. For instance, if some relative saw their daughter kissing in public or things like that, like American girls do, they would say it is a shame, it is obscene stuff to see that happening. Then rumors would start going around that she is a whore, and she could easily lose face. Not only that, but her parents and relatives would say she is worthless—and she would think she is worthless, too, because the rumors would be so strong that she wouldn't be able to take it. Usually the parents believe in other people's rumors—they would easily fall for it and put their daughter in a bad situation where she would suffer emotionally.

Maybe a few Hmong parents here in the U.S. do allow their daughters to go out, but one thing they always do: They have one of the girl's little brothers or sisters go on the date also. By making sure the girl is never alone with a man the parents think they can keep their choices open about who they want to marry her off to.

Chue Vue (pseud.): "Everyone has their own fate. I think mine was to be what I am today, a third wife."

I've been married for over eighteen years to my husband. I married him when I was about seventeen years old in Ban Vanai. When he was coming to see me, I knew that he already had two wives, but in my culture I was supposed to be polite to all the men that came to visit me, whether they had another wife or they didn't. I was supposed to respect them and try to talk to all of them the same way as if I were talking to just one of them.

I didn't really have strong feelings for any of them. The reason I didn't have strong love for any of those men was that I felt I had no choice in who I would marry. I knew that I could like this guy or that guy—but then I might be kidnapped by another guy, maybe someone I didn't love, but I would have to be his wife anyway. You see, once you're kidnapped and you enter the man's house, once you've been in there for a night, the chances of your coming back to your parents are not good. It wouldn't matter if you really wanted to come back. So you see, I knew I would have no choice. I might love someone and then be kidnapped by someone else and forced to live with that person.

That's what happened to me. One of my big thoughts when I was single was never to be a wife to someone who already had other wives. I thought that if I became a second wife, everyone would talk about me. But I was kidnapped— I was kidnapped to be a third wife. And, even though I wanted to, it was really impossible to go back to my parents because I knew they would lose face.

But then I realized I shouldn't feel terrible because I was not the only person in the whole world to become a third wife. It was really common at the time. So, over all, I didn't feel anything bad about it. It was part of the Hmong culture. At times I felt proud that I was married to an important man. I know a lot of other women would want to be in my shoes. I would rather marry someone like this and be his third wife than marry a "nobody" and be his only wife. I know I would probably have had to work a lot harder for everything if I had married a nobody.

Yet I do have to say that the thought of sharing always bothered me. If I were to really have a choice, I would rather not share. But at the time polygamy was so common back there. There were many men that had more than just three wives. Some had as many as five wives. There could be even more if a man wanted it.

The important thing about polygamy is that all the women have to cooperate. This is hard. When I came to live with my husband and his other two wives, I felt very embarrassed. But there was little competition from them when it came to sharing time with our husband. I was a lot younger than they were. In the beginning I felt I had to be the one to work the hardest so I would impress the other wives. But my husband didn't seem to want me to worry about it. Sometimes he would tell me that I shouldn't work too hard, that the other wives should do the work. Well, I think this issue got so big that the other wives didn't like me. They thought I should be the one who had to work the hardest, and my husband thought they should be the ones to work harder.

There are a lot of arguments among the wives in these situations. Usually the first wives have most of the right. I guess as the youngest I felt the weakest. But I did have my husband mostly on my side, so everything kind of balanced itself. Most of the conflict I felt was just personality problems between the other two wives. Finally, his first wife could not take this anymore, so she left my husband. After the first wife left, the second wife and I got along better, so everything worked out great.

I remember that everything always seemed so hard in the first year when I married my husband. But after I had my first child, nothing more mattered to me. As a matter of fact, I felt more powerful. I could then say that I was really part of the clan or family. I knew then I would stay with my husband for the rest of my life. I knew my child and I needed the support from him and his other wives. Actually, the second wife was really pleased and helped out a lot. During the first month she helped cook for me, took care of my baby, took care of the family. I didn't have to depend much on my husband. It was really great.

Now, in America, this polygamy thing has not really bothered me. I guess I learned to live with it. To me, after so many years, I see a beauty in all of this. Second Wife's children are my children, and my children are her children. They all call me mother, just like they call her mother. So there is always a special love flowing between the family. But I would not like to see my daughters in my position—especially not in America because I know they have choices that I didn't have.

If I had to do it all over again, how would it be? I don't know. I think I would like to have a husband that I didn't share. I would like to see how that would feel. But everyone has their own fate. I think mine was to be what I am today, a third wife. Maybe in the next life, if I get a paper from heaven, then I might get what I want.

I have known many other women who told me that they too didn't want to be Second Wife or Third Wife, but many of them, like myself, came to accept that it happened because it was our fate. This is why many of us are still in polygamy today. But I don't see the younger generation practicing polygamy anymore. This is really good—that there is one wife to one husband and the children have just one mother. You don't have to go through all these mixed feelings about the children and about sharing your husband.

Phooj Thao (pseud.) told us about an Americanized version of "catch-hand" marriage, which did not work for him.

I was about nineteen years old and I was in junior college. I really fell in love with this girl. She was a Hmong but her family was also Christian and mine wasn't. Maybe that's why her family didn't like me that much. I don't know. Anyway, we were both in the same classes, and we liked to be together a lot whenever we could. We really wanted to go out together on the weekends and at night, but we knew that probably her family wouldn't let her date because, even though they were Christian, they were still Hmong. So every chance we had in school and for as much as we could after classes we would stay together. Then a few times I went over to her house to visit her family, and I thought everything went okay, but probably it didn't.

We spent all the time we could together after school, every day. We were really in love and we wanted to be married. After we decided that, I asked her to come home with me one day when we got out of school, and she said, "Okay, I will do it."

She came with me, and my father was at home. I said to him, "Father, I have brought a wife home." He looked surprised and shocked, and he would not say anything right away. I was worrying, wondering what was going through his mind. My girlfriend—I will call her Mai but that was not her real name—she was worrying too. Then he said to her that she should go home now and he would think about what to do. But Mai told him that since she was already here she did not want to go back to her parents' home because that would be hard for her.

Finally my father said, "Okay, I will call my relatives and ask for two negotiators to go and tell her parents."

Mai and me were very scared because—you know—it felt like I was really helpless. I could not do anything to help us both. Everything had to be done by my father and my relatives. It was up to them whether I would get a wife or not.

After the negotiators went over there to her parents, her mother called me on the telephone and she said, "Do you really love my girl? Are you really serious about wanting to marry her?"

"Yes," I said, "I love her, and that's why I want to marry her." That was it. She hung up and I thought everything was going to be okay.

But maybe an hour later her sisters and a few other ladies showed up at my house, and they wanted to drag her home—by the hair, in front of my whole family. All of my brothers and relatives were there, and they were all helpless. I tried to plead with her sisters because I knew them very well from high school and even before, but they would not listen to me. My whole family begged them, too. Nothing helped, and they made her go home with them and she did.

But that was not the end of it, because the next day we saw each other at school again. She told me that no matter what, she really loved me. She said she wanted to be with me and she would come home with me again. So we drove to my house— and there was her family's car and some ladies waiting inside it. They were going to do the same thing all over again. That was when I stepped on the gas and we drove off to some quiet place.

Then I told her there in the car, "You know, I'm helpless and so is my clan. If you want to marry me, it is up to you to do something." She was crying and I felt like crying too, and she said she would beg her mother and try to get her mother to agree to us being married.

The minute we got back to my house, three or four ladies jumped out of her family's car and started pulling her hair and trying to drag her away from me. We tried to hold on to each other as tight as we could. This older lady hit me over and over, and she scratched my face and arms. She just wanted to make me let go of Mai. I felt bad about hitting those ladies back, so I could not defend myself. Mai was pleading with them and crying that she did not want to go.

Finally my father came out of the house, and he told the ladies, "Let's go inside and we can talk." But they didn't want to talk because they thought it would make them lose face, because they had come to do their duty and they weren't supposed to let anything get in the way of it. They didn't care about anything except being able to return my girl to her parents. Finally, they came inside my house. Maybe they were ashamed at all the people in the neighborhood looking to see what was going on. But no matter what my father said to them, they yelled rude things to him.

I guess my father got really angry himself, because then he said, "Okay, if you guys want to call the police, go ahead and call them." He was probably thinking there were a lot of cases in Fresno like this before, and when the cops come if the girl doesn't want to go back to her family, they won't do anything.

One of those ladies left the house to call the police. My girl and me just sat on the sofa holding on to each other and we didn't say anything.

But the other ladies kept yelling bad language at her and saying things to her like, "You don't even know how to cook for yourself. All you know how to do is boil water and pour it over those noodles. How can you be a daughter-in-law?" I guess they wanted my parents to hear that. And some of them yelled, "Why do you want to marry that guy?" They just wanted to humiliate us, to make us feel hurt and bad—which I did.

I didn't know what to do, so then I just kept pleading with them and bowing to them. That didn't help either. They didn't care. To them, I did not exist at all.

It took a long time before the policemen came. The ladies didn't stop trying to drag her and pull her out of the house again. She and I pleaded to them. I bowed again and again to them. But it was no use.

So finally the cops came, and I knew everything was up to her now. Maybe it will be okay, I thought, because after all that bad language and hitting and hair pulling from the ladies, she still had not left me.

But she did not say anything to the police, and that was when she let the ladies pull her away. She was crying, but she did not open her mouth.

I did not see her at school again. They must have made her quit school. When I tried to call her house, whoever answered just said, "She's not coming," and they hung up on me.

Elizabeth Mee Vang: "I was committing the crime of the world because I would not let him marry another wife."

I have had culture conflicts over being a Hmong woman in the U.S. constantly, every day, every minute of my life. When I was young I had to decide, "Should I date? Should I have sex before marriage? Should I just kind of be assertive? Was I going to marry a Christian guy or a regular Hmong guy?" It was so difficult. If I was American I would not have all this in my head, but I was always, always into a culture clash.

I grew up as a Christian girl, but in the Hmong community the man is supposed to be more superior than his wife. They believe the woman should stay home, babysit, just clean the house. I was totally the opposite. This is why when I got married I had problems with my mother-in-law. And then my husband wanted to marry a second wife, and everyone was against me. I was committing the crime of the world because I would not let him marry another wife—because I said I wanted a divorce if he married another wife.

Everything . . . every minute of my life . . . right now . . . I'm trying to get over this culture clash with men and women. But I feel that as long as I know who I am and what I believe in . . . I believe there are certain things in the Hmong culture that should be kept and remembered and practiced, like respecting the elders is good. But there are certain things that you must let go of, like marrying a second wife or having a mistress all the time. We should never, never, never practice that again. If my husband marries another wife, and she's having his child— I think it needs to be clear cut that if he's going to do that, I should be allowed to divorce, and I should be allowed to marry another man.

Men don't consider that when they have another wife it hurts us women. They think it's okay with us just because they are our men. Those women back in Laos could accept such things, but not me. I want just one man by me, and I want to be the only woman by him. I never got the chance to ask men how they would feel if I was sleeping with two men. I'm sure they would be as mad as we women are when we see they sleep with two women. But men don't understand—marrying two wives . . .

I would just like for men to see us women having two husbands, and then see how they feel. Men are the most jealous of all. They get mad at you even if you're just talking to your cousin who happens to be a man, if they don't know him. They think, "Oh, it's her boyfriend," and they get mad at us. Everything we do is wrong. What is wrong with these men? We Hmong women are human, too. I just hate it that everything we do is wrong, wrong, wrong.

I know that in the community there are some women that are accepting their husbands having a second wife. I don't know how these women could do it, but I guess their brain must be working wrong. Many of them are happy, too, so I'm surprised. I don't know why, but I guess they just learn to accept it. But I must try to influence the younger ones not to practice this.

I always have problems with my in-laws over such things. They always believe in this crazy thing about men being the superior ones—superior beings, and women must do everything they say. You must save face. I don't believe in that. I believe in being direct, being able to speak to someone's face if you don't like what they do. But in my culture you must save face, so you must not prove your husband wrong in front of his relatives. A wife can only tell him indirectly if something is wrong or she can only get someone else to tell him that whatever he's doing is wrong. This is a stupid way of doing things.

I'm really different from my mom because I'm facing all these problems. I don't know if my mom faced them, but it's very hard for me and I'm very frustrated. My mom, she wants me to be a good wife, obey my husband, all that. But I find it very hard to do when I know what he is doing is wrong and I can't even confront him directly. Maybe what is different about me compared to my parents is that I have become an American citizen. I have made America my home. For them, they still think Laos is their place, and they hope that someday they can return there.

But I can't see any educated girls here living the way a lot of the older women that I know live. It's like they've been living under their husbands' feet for so long that they don't realize it. They haven't seen any freedom so they don't know how good it is to be free—not to be told what to do, to share the housework, to go out to dinner or a movie. They don't see that. But for girls who grew up here, almost everyone I guess is feeling what I'm feeling. Because if their husband is still very old-culture oriented . . . it's very frustrating unless a man knows how to love her very much.

Soua Teng Vang: "Is a Hmong man a man when he can't control his wife?"

Here I feel like I . . . like all the Hmong men . . . our worse problem is, is a Hmong man a man when he can't control his wife? In our culture he would not be called a man.

Here in the United States I can't control my wife. If we got into a little argument and we fought a little bit, she would call the police, and I would be the one that is arrested—not the woman. I am mad. Most of the time the police would be on her side more than my side. Here I can't believe women are having so much rights. They can drive and do whatever they want. Hmong women are really changing. I am confused.

I don't know what to do. It seems like anything I do I could get in trouble for. I guess this might be one of the reasons why our Hmong men die in our sleep, why we have sudden death syndrome. First we had a tragic war, and now our young men can't really deal with the change in our caste system. Women are supposed to serve their husband, but now they are arguing that sharing the duty is better. This makes many Hmong men feel stressful—to argue everyday about equality around the house.

Shoua Xiong told us that she married at the age of fourteen and reconverted to the traditional Hmong religion just a few years after she and her family were brought to Buffalo Center, Iowa, by a Christian church group.

I liked it before I was married when I was a Christian because it was peaceful and you didn't have to do all the shaman things. You just go to church on Sunday and the rest of the day you don't do anything. I don't like the way the shamans do, but I don't have a choice. I do what my husband does because when I married him my parents said I should do everything that he wanted or his family would not like me. My mother said, "Now that they own you, you belong to them, so you have to do whatever they want you to do."

It was sad. It seemed like you're not belonging to your family anymore. You belong to someone else. It's like they buy you from your family, and it's like they own you. You can't be who you were when you were still living with your parents. I was fourteen when I got married, and I didn't know anything. I didn't even know how to cook because I got married too young—I don't know why. If I was smart then like today, I wouldn't get married.

Probably I got married because I felt too much pressure when I was still with my parents. They wouldn't let me do anything—not like those people in the 1990s where you go to a party or something. My parents wouldn't let me go anywhere. I couldn't do anything that would offend my father or make him look bad. I was scared of him. I felt he had too much power and I was under his control. I guess I got married because one time, before I was married, I went out with the person who's my husband now. I lied to my parents that I was going to a friend's birthday party, and I went out with him to this party—and then I just came home. But my parents had called my friend's house to ask for me, and they said I wasn't there and there wasn't any birthday party. When I came home my dad said, "You lied to us!"

And I told them, "That's the only way I could get out—because you don't let me go out, this is the only way."

My mother lectured me. My dad was mad at my mom because he felt she didn't take good care of me, she wasn't a good mother, and I wasn't a good daughter—that's why I did what I did. He would say it was all her fault. She would get in trouble. I didn't do it again because I love my mother and I didn't want to get her into trouble with my father. And that's why I married my husband—so there wouldn't be those problems anymore.

Fourteen was not too young to get married for the Hmong—it was just the right age. That's because with the Hmong people, when you're eighteen they consider you too old. But I consider myself getting married too young—I regret it. I have three girls and a boy now and I don't have any education. If I was smarter I would have waited and gone to school and gotten some more education and gotten a good job instead of staying home watching the baby—stuck at home every day now. But if I waited too long the community people would think that I might not be a good person and that's why nobody had already married me. That's what a lot of people say. If you're not married, then they think, "Oh, she must be bad or something. That's why no one wants to take her." If you're married, if someone takes you, then they say, "Oh, she must be good, that's why someone wants her." This is how the rumors go with our Hmong people.

It's hard when you get married at fourteen—when you go to school and you're just starting high school or you're in middle school and you're married already. For the Hmong people it was okay; but for the American people, they still think you're a baby. They say, "Is it hard?" or "It's weird that you got married so young!"

I don't know. . . . I felt okay, but a lot of the American people said it's too young. And the teachers—they felt sorry for me. They said I should stay single and do whatever I want in school. Sometimes this makes you feel embarrassed. But I chose to get married, so it's not a big deal.

In my sophomore year I had an English teacher. She was loving. I got sick and I lost a lot of weight, and she said she wished I wasn't married so she could take care of me herself.

She said, "Look at you now. You look so pale. You lost a lot of energy. I wish I had a couch here for you to rest." But then, that was the way it is. . . . At the time I had a miscarriage—I had some kind of seizure—and I was weak but I went to school, and she felt sorry for me. She said, "You're still too young to have a baby."

Well, I felt sorry for myself, too. I wished I could still be single like she said, so I wouldn't have all these problems.

There's still a lot of problems. In our culture it looks like the woman is not important. They're just like—*housewife*. They know nothing, and the husband is the head of the household. So you have to do whatever the man says, and whatever you say—it just isn't important to the man. They don't listen to anything you say, but you got to listen to everything they say. They say "Do it!" and you do it. If you don't do it, you're going to end up no good. When I compare myself to the Americans I feel like I'm in a prison. I can't do anything that I want—like men can go out, enjoy themselves like the American men, but we can't.

When you are married, the romantic passion is gone. The husband changes, the wife changes. You argue, you fight—even though when you're boyfriend and girlfriend you never want to fight and you always say good things to each other. You never see the bad things when you're boyfriend and girlfriend. But when you're married, it's different. They change after they get married.

I wish I could have the freedom of American women. But I don't think it could ever happen because that's the way it is. I wish it could happen, but in our culture the women can't do anything. All they do back in our country is cook and have babies—that's all. Back in our country a man can have as many wives as he wants. In this country a Hmong man can only have one wife, but he can still have an affair. For the American people, a husband can only have one wife—but he can have as many affairs as he wants and the lady can have affairs too. And it's okay with the man. With our people, though, if they found out that you're a married lady and you have an affair, there's going to be rumors, and then your husband's going to divorce you. And after he divorced you nobody will want to marry you because they would say that you're a bad lady, a bad wife, you're a married lady and you have an affair. For men, they can do what they want and there's no rumors. It's different.

I guess even though I went to school here and everything, my life is the same as my mom's. I follow the older generation because I follow what my husband says. So for me, it's still the same. Nothing changes. But nowadays some people do change: When they get married they move out of the family. I've been married to my husband for ten years, and we still live with his family. That's the way he wants it to be—because mostly in our country the wife stays with her parents-in-law until they pass away or something. Her job is to take care of them. And that's what I have to do.

Even if I consider myself half American, I can't do like the Americans do. I'm still Hmong. I can only do the way the Hmong people do, follow the steps the Hmong people do. Even if I wish to be different I know it would never happen. But sometimes I think, "If I could make myself good, my daughters could be good too. But if I'm not good and don't go to college or anything, my daughters won't go to college." I wish I could set an example for them. If I go to college, they would have to go to college. If they see I didn't go to college, they won't feel like going either. I want my daughters to have a nice life, a good job, so they don't have to be like me—staying home, never getting what I want. Whatever I want, I don't get it, because I don't have the money. I wanted to go places—like Hawaii, France. A lot of it is romantic—like a fantasy—but still, I wish someday I could go.

Mai Xiong (pseud.): "When I told my husband about other families not following that rule, he said, 'It's our Hmong culture!'"

I'm taking Spanish this year because I want to know a lot of languages. I really like to help people so I'm going to be a teacher. I see my people—like the girls—that don't get to go to school a lot. They just get married and have kids and all that stuff. So I want to help them and be a model to them.

I'm married too. I'm nineteen now and I got married when I was sixteen, when I started my freshman year in high school. I have two kids already. It's kind of hard, you know, because people depend on you. But me, I'm kind of lucky. I have a mother-in-law and father-in-law who help me take care of the kids so I can come to school.

Usually it would be very hard because in my culture, the daughter-in-law is supposed to do all the work, like make dinner for the family—and in my family we have thirteen. I still have to do the dinner, but my mother-in-law, she's kind of nice and she helps me. Still, I do have to clean and cook a lot for them. And so the earliest I can do my homework is nine o'clock—usually it's ten o'clock. Then I go to bed about eleven o'clock. I don't think I get to spend enough time on my homework, but sometimes during lunch time, I go get my lunch and then do more homework while I eat.

My mother-in-law really understands how hard it is, so she tries to make it easier. You know, like sometimes when I come home from school, she will already have cooked because she knows I might be tired. So all I have to do is set up the dishes on the table and do the dishes afterwards. Officially, it's not her job to help me—but, you know, she's not that old, thirty-something, so she still wants to do it. But sometimes, she's sick or tired, so when I come home I have to cook. When my younger brother-in-law marries, he and his wife will come live with my in-laws and at that time if we want we can leave. I hope we'll leave because it's overcrowded.

Even though my mother-in-law helps me, I think she doesn't understand why I want to keep going to school. One time on a weekend, I was sitting in the bedroom and my mother-in-law and my cousin were talking. It was about education, and my mother-in-law says, "Girls are not supposed to keep going to school after they finish high school. They should just go and work and help support their family because money is very important right now." This is what she said. But I really think it's okay with her that I want to go to school full time because she knows how important education is to me.

Still, though, it's hard because we have such a big family. Some of my friends, they have a small family, and they only have to cook one time each night. But, you know, in my culture, my husband . . . you know, their culture—I cannot eat with my husband and father-in-law. So every night we have to eat like, two dinners. I have to put the food on the table for my husband and father-in-law. And after they eat, the women get to eat. It's kind of hard and it takes a lot of time.

Then I clean up and then two or three times every night I have to take care of my baby's bottle. I go do my homework, and I come back into the room and all of the dishes are still on the table, even though I cleaned them up once already. That's because I have all these little brothers- and sisters-in-law. They go cook by themselves and they don't clean up all that stuff, so I have to do it. I think it's very hard for me, but when I was living with my parents I was the oldest girl, so I had to do all those things there too. I never get much time to study.

Since I've always done like this—even in my parents' house, cooking two or three times a night, I don't complain. But you know, when my brother-in-law gets married and he brings his wife here, they're not going to want to live long here like we have—for four years almost. I have some cousins who got married, and they said it was too hard to live with their in-laws and cook two and three times every night, so they and their husband went off to live by themselves. All of them are going to school, and not too many are willing to do all that plus homework and taking care of the babies. I feel I still belong to the true Hmong culture more than anything, and what a daughter-in-law is supposed to do, she does. But what I fear we will see is for the daughters-in-law who were raised here and have become more Americanized, it would be very hard for them to go back to this traditional role and do all these things.

I never yet said to my in-laws that maybe we could have just one dinner every night, but I said it to my husband. He said, "That's their culture"—his parents, he meant. He said, "When we move out we can eat together. But you know, when my sons grow up and they get married, they'll want to eat separate too." So, I don't know. Now, not all of the Hmong men eat first in this country. But when I told my husband about other families not following that rule, he said, "It's our Hmong culture!"

Zai Xiong: "I have actually talked to my dad and asked him, 'Why do you guys have to do this to your wife?'"

I'm a Mormon now, but I don't believe in polygamy for anybody. When the Mormons did it in the 1800s there was good reason. A lot of their men went to war and were killed. There were a lot of women and children and no one to take care of them, no food for them. So some of the men had to take care of the families left without husbands who lived right next door to them, and before they could do this they got permission from the church leaders.

But when the Hmong used to take more than one wife in Laos, I think they did it for pride. Or sometimes they took another wife because the first wife couldn't have more babies, and they were very concerned about having a lot of offspring. I feel very against such practices because I've seen a lot of broken homes, a lot of misconceptions. They couldn't even support one family, so how could they afford another one? How can they just have children, and then the children can't get an education or don't have anywhere to go?

When I was a kid I didn't think much about these things, but now that I'm older, I think deeper. And I learned things from the United States and also the Church. I learned about the respect that a husband and wife should have for each other. It hurts now when I think back to how my dad treated my mother, or how men used to go out and grab any virgin they wanted— kidnap her and any problems would be resolved later. That's not fair.

I have actually talked to my dad and asked him, "Why do you guys have to do this to your wife?"

And he would just . . . "You're just a kid. You don't know nothing." That's all I get. I have to respect him, but it's very hard for me to communicate with him on these personal things.

My wife, she was just fifteen when I married her. Now she's sixteen. Before I married her, I gave it a lot of thought. I went and looked at her family. They had eleven kids and her dad was not very kind. They are still sort of like back in Laos. I felt very sorry for the children. In fact, the oldest son doesn't want to live there anymore. So I thought—there she is, living there; she's beautiful, kind, her knowledge of goodness is high, and she wants to live in goodness. But how can she practice that at home when there is no love in her home. Two parents supporting eleven kids—that is a lot of responsibility.

I said to her, "What if I take care of you? Then they'll only have ten to take care of, and I can take care of you good. I can help you a lot. You don't have to ask your mom or dad for money. You don't have to hear your dad yelling at you, slap you, do this and that to you. I have a feeling that you have a soft heart and understanding. You want to do what is right. Why don't you help me and I'll help you? My parents are not Christian and your parents are not Christian, but I am a Christian and you are a Christian, so you will be able to help me, and I will be able to help you." I came to see her for a year.

Her mother was glad that her daughter was seeing me. She wanted her to marry me because she didn't want her daughter to go through suffering like she had gone through. Her mother feels like she has been married to the wrong man for many years because her husband gave her no kindness, no respect, no love, no help. When she was in Laos she was forced to marry quickly. She had no choice because there was an old man, sixty years old, who was after her. He was very rich, and he wanted to marry her. Her family was forcing her to marry him. They had already taken money from him in return for the promise that he would have her. Then the man who became my wife's father suddenly came over the night before she was supposed to marry.

My mother-in-law says to me now that she had no choice; if she didn't marry this young man right away, the next day she would be forced to marry the old one. So she went with the man who became my wife's father; she ran away with him because she was young and she didn't want to spend the rest of her life with an old man. At first sight, she agreed to marry the man who is now her husband. When she ran away her parents had to give the old man his money back, and they were very mad at her.

I've been married about ten months. I ain't going to be like those men I have seen in my culture. I will treat my wife just like I would treat myself. I would never force her to do anything against her will. I will say things to her only like the things I would want to hear myself.

Bee Thao came to America as an adolescent, after losing his mother in the relocation camp. He told us he often has conflicts about gender relations with his older siblings, who came to America when they were in their twenties and thirties.

To me and my friends that are the same age, it doesn't matter if you're man or woman. You have equal opportunity to become whatever you want. If you have the skill, if you have the power, then do it. So it doesn't bother us that much if a woman is successful. But to the older people, they do have that negative feeling that a woman cannot be a leader. In a way, I kind of feel sad. Like I said to my older brother, "You know, we are living in a different society. This is now, and that was then. Now you should only keep those things that will help in the future. And the rest, just let them go. You know, try to adapt to whatever the society has." But he's thirty-something, and even though we talk so much, he still has very strong beliefs in the culture back in Laos.

He still believes that men eat first and then women can eat. I don't think such things will be a problem for me. When I get married, it won't matter. She can sit with me and my friends. We can eat together. That's the way I want it. I had a situation like that last year. When I graduated from City College with my A.A. degree, all my brothers, they collected money and they bought a cow, and then they killed it to make a party for me. I invited all my friends—you know, girls, boys, women, and men—to come over. And then, instead of having just the men eat first, I had all my friends go together. And I told my brothers, that's the way I like it, and that's the way I think we should do it. And they did accept the way that I proposed to them.

But in many cases, it's not only the men who are to blame. Like my sister-in-law and my sister—when they have some kind of party, the men eat first, and then the ladies. But one of the reasons that the men eat first is because the ladies don't fight for their right. The men say, "You ladies eat second," and that's it. They never argue with the men. They never give them a good reason that they should eat at the same table. But I think that in the future Hmong women should stand for their right, prove it to the men that they should eat together. They should not push themselves down. I think most of the Hmong women, they push themselves down so much. That's why they don't have much power.

My older niece and I argue about that. I explain to her she should stand for her right. But she always says, "Well, that's okay. Eating with the men . . . they talk different things, they tell different stories than the women. It would be like sitting there and being ignored. So it's better to sit with the women. We have something in common. We can talk about something that we really enjoy, instead of sitting with the men and listening to them talk about different stories that we don't even want to hear."

But she married her husband back in Laos. Their feeling is different from what we have, and it's very hard to combine them. They have a different idea and we have a different idea. Someday it will come together. But it will take time to break the barrier. You've got to take them and move them step by step. But I think ten to fifteen years from now, we're gonna come together and be like Americans.

First the men eat. ▷

Blia Vang (pseud.): "Once you get married, it's like they lock you up in prison."

I was in a relationship a few years ago, when I was a freshman in high school, and my boyfriend asked me to marry him. At the time, when you're thirteen or fourteen, you don't know what you're doing. We were just boyfriend, girlfriend. We didn't even know each other. But we got kind of engaged for a couple of months, and I went to live with him and his family.

My mom, she was crying. Everybody—they wouldn't let me go. But then I was stupid. I said, "You know, no matter what happens, I'm going and you can't stop me. If you don't let me go right now, then I'll just take off later."

So then they said, "If that's what makes you happy, then fine." But I was making a big mistake at that moment. He was born in Laos and he was just a year older than me—so, like fourteen. When you live together you get to know each other and to understand how you are. And then you know that there's no way you can spend the rest of your life with this person.

I lived with him and his family. They didn't like me because in our culture the parents have an ideal daughter-in-law that they've always wanted. So if their son marries someone different from that, they'll look at her and say, "Oh, she's not good." I know a lot of my friends are married, and they have the same problem with their in-laws—because my friends are really Americanized now, and their in-laws are not Americanized at all.

They expected me to wake up every morning earlier than them, cook for the children, clean up the house, and everything. If I go to school that's okay, but then I got to come straight home from school, don't talk to anyone, don't have no friends, nothing. Just come straight home, do my homework, and then cook. After that, go finish my homework and just go to sleep. Same thing every day. I didn't like it at all. I didn't like being ordered around.

Maybe in Laos it would be the same situation, but here you have more freedom; you get used to going out. Then once you get married, it's like they lock you up in prison. They close out all of your friends, don't allow you to go out. You start missing those things, especially when you're in your teenage years. Those are the years you're supposed to have the most fun. But if you're married you don't have time for fun. I even had to depend on them for a ride, to take me to the store and everything. It's so hard.

And his parents were really old-fashioned. The way they do their things, the way they cook their meals, the way they run their household. It's really old-fashioned, like in Laos or something. And I was born here, not in Laos. I wasn't taught the things they were doing. They were eating different kinds of food, cooked differently, with different spices. Like they were used to cooking without fish sauce. So everytime I put fish sauce in, his mom would complain, "I don't like it. How come you always put it in there? It stinks." She would hate the smell of it, and she would go outside.

So then I just wanted to come back home, and my parents wouldn't let me. I tried to come back three or four times, and they wouldn't let me at all—because they said in our culture it's not right for the daughter to come back. They kept sending me right back to his house, and I was—like, "Gosh, you guys don't want me to be happy. If you know what's right for me you would let me back here so I could live my life. I can't live a life over there because it's too hard."

And they just said, "You need to try. If you don't love him now, just live with him anyway and you'll learn to love him."

I was—like, "That's wrong, because I don't even have any feeling for him. How can you learn to love a person?"

So they said it was my choice when I went. And I say, "Yeah, but it's my choice to come back now!"

I wanted to come back, and they wouldn't let me. They said it was against their culture, and most important of all, they're afraid of losing face. It's especially hard for my dad because he was a Vang, and it's like everyone respected the Vang clan. My grandpop, he was well respected, so my dad didn't want me to come back at all. The first time I tried to come back home, my mom understood and she wanted me back. But my dad was—like, "No, she can't stay!"

I had to go back to my in-laws, but then I just told my parents, "If you guys don't let me come back, I'll just wait until I'm eighteen and I'll move out and live by myself."

And they said, "You're not supposed to. You're a Hmong."

So I said, "When I'm eighteen I'll be able to do what I want, and you can't stop me anymore because this is America. Just watch me. You won't be able to stop me."

They said, "You're not an American. You're Hmong. Whatever you do, you can't change the fact that you're Hmong. Even if you try to run away, everything will always follow behind you."

Whenever I tried to return home, his parents and his relatives came and took me back to their house again. Then my relatives and their relatives had a meeting—my uncles, my grandpop, their uncles and their grandpop. So it's like the old people, they're making the decision. They were saying that I'm a girl and I should listen to them. They lectured to me and I felt bad because there was nothing I could do. I just sat there and listened to them. This happened like three times. They would just be lecturing me, and I had it all memorized in my head. I knew exactly what they were going to say, and I thought, "Oh, get it over with. I know what you're going to say already. Just hurry up."

My boyfriend and I both agreed that we didn't want this relationship. I kept telling my parents that he didn't want me and I didn't want him either; but my parents said since I was already engaged, just stay that way. Then his parents started saying bad things about me and spreading rumors, like I was lazy, I wouldn't do anything a daughter-in-law should do, or that I've been seeing other people. And his dad told me, "If you want to go back home we don't care, because there are other daughters-in-law we could get."

In order for me get to stay home finally, I had to convince my mom. I did a lot of crying. I did a lot of expression of how I felt. I said, "I can't live like that no more. It's torturing me. They're taking my life away from me. They're turning me into something else." So—finally—I got to come back home.

Ia Vang Xiong, who trekked through the jungles with Big Mother, her father's first wife, told us how she convinced her family that in America males and females are equal.

I know my family depended on me verbally—to help them with translation—since I was in the seventh grade, even though I only spoke a little English. My older brother would take me everywhere he had to go. I remember the first time he asked me—I was like twelve or thirteen: "Ia, let's go get telephone numbers." When we got to the telephone place he said, "You tell them you want a new number." I really didn't know how, but I did it anyway. We got the telephone. I got the telephone for us so my brother knew I could do it each time anything had to be done.

I remember another time, just before that, in Minnesota. All of my brothers and sisters couldn't understand what our landlord wanted. First my brothers said they understood something like, "Our landlord wants us to pay more money." But I understood it differently. I said, "The landlord says that if we're going to move to California now we probably will not get our deposit back." We were all debating. Nobody knew what he said for sure.

Then my father said, "Oh, you guys. I believe Ia more. I don't think they want us to pay them more. I think they're not giving us our deposit money back." But it was then that I realized that because nobody knew for sure, they needed me to do well, so I could understand more, so I could do the translation for them. And I needed to do well for myself, too.

Each time they asked me to do something, I knew they gave me all their power, they put all their trust in me, and that empowered me to want to do better. I would always think, "I got the power and I have to do it for them." And each time I did well, they praised me.

But my father used to tell people—and I heard it over and over again—that he wished I had been a boy, he wished me to be a boy, how come I was a girl. To their perception, in the old days, a girl gets married, and she married into another family.

She becomes a member of another family, and if she can do good services, it's for the other family that she does it—it's not good for you. The boys, they stay in your family, and if they're smart they can be a help to you. So over and over again he wished that I was a boy.

But even then, I always felt that it doesn't matter if you're a boy or a girl. If it is your parents, when they're in need you'll do everything in your power to help them. I wished he would understand that and value me as he valued a boy, you know. It was sad for me. He gave a lot of support to his boys, and he gave me very little, even though I was advancing much more than my brothers. That hurt me emotionally a lot because I knew he loved me less.

After I got married, I went back, and he was still saying that. I had enough guts to tell him, "All the time I was a kid you were saying you were sorry I wasn't a boy, you loved your boys more, you gave them all the support. You always gave them a break, a hand, gave them money and so on. But because of that I wanted to prove to you that I could do better, and I did better, I even became a teacher. They didn't care about doing better, because whether or not they did, you loved them anyway, you gave them money anyway. For me, I had to prove myself to you." And I just hoped he understood it.

I'm now a fighter to get equality for women—and for my people, for my ethnic group, for the Hmongs. I'm a fighter for the Hmong community. I'm a fighter for the Hmong women in the community. I try to defend women's views and always be out there, not bashing but saying what we women feel is right.

Like one time, in a Hmong radio talk show, the president of the Hmong Council, who has a Ph.D. in Psychology, said, "We will take any girl, thirteen and up, to be in the Miss Hmong pageant." I was shocked when he said this. I was so mad. I was a junior in college at that time. I called up and said, "Wait a minute, how could you take a thirteen-year-old girl and say she's Miss Hmong? That's only promoting younger marriage because once they've gotten the name Miss Hmong, by the next year they're going to be married. And that's the kind of role model we're all going to have. Those of us who are in college right now don't need that."

The president argued and argued with me. And I said, "All of you down there are guys. You don't have one woman down there to make the decision with you. How could you do that? Aren't you funded by the government? You are, so you're supposed to follow the affirmative action form."

Then he said, "Okay, why don't you be one of the judges."

And I go, "I would love to be on your board. But I know you wouldn't be on my side anyway. You wouldn't let me do any good."

But I guess he understood the message because the next week he announced that the minimum age for the Miss Hmong pageant was fifteen.

Last year my father was real sick, and he had two heart bypasses. He was close to death, and I was the one who did the translating at the hospital. He didn't trust anybody else. He wanted me to talk to the doctor. He wanted me to get the medication. He wanted me there when they did the angiogram. He wanted me at his bedside. I had my school get a substitute teacher for my class. Everytime he called me I was there.

Well, two weeks ago we were at my parents' house and we were discussing looks. I said, "Dad, people don't usually think I'm Hmong at all. Even Japanese people come up to me and start speaking Japanese. They think I look Japanese. But when Chinese people see me, they think I'm Chinese."

Everyone was always getting me mixed up with other Asian people. Then my family started joking that maybe I wasn't a Hmong at all. They joked that maybe my mother cheated or something. After we all had fun laughing one of my brothers said, "Too bad you're a girl because you're so smart."

And then my father said, "At this time and age it makes no difference whether she's a girl. Here in America there is no difference."

Battles between the Generations

Children in Laos had a clear picture of family hierarchy. They, of course, were at the bottom. Their father was at the top, and his wife or wives were somewhere in between. The father worked his farm, and the women and children helped him. Age and gender counted for a good deal both within the family and outside. For instance: Within the family, the oldest son had far more prerogatives than the younger children, and they were to respect him just as he and they respected their father; if there was a family problem so severe that the father needed help in solving it he might consult his own father or, in especially difficult cases, he might go outside his family to consult the elders, a group that consisted of the wisest men of the clan. There was little room for divergence from this hierarchy.

But in America, every aspect of the hierarchy has virtually fallen apart. Many Hmong women are demanding equality and, as discussed earlier, they are sometimes even better able than their husbands to contribute to the family income. The elders often feel robbed of their power because they don't know how to maneuver in this strange country. It's hard to present yourself as a wise man if your sons or daughters have to teach you how to cross the street or dial the phone. The elders feel they have been reduced to helpless children, as they so often complain. Nor can grandparents generally serve in their traditional roles as revered old members of the household who share their wisdom with their sons and hand down to their grandchildren the fascinating lore of the past. Often the grandparents no longer live with their grandchildren and the rest of the extended family, as they invariably did in Laos. And even if they do live with or near their grandchildren they sometimes have

Dressing for the Hmong New Year ▷

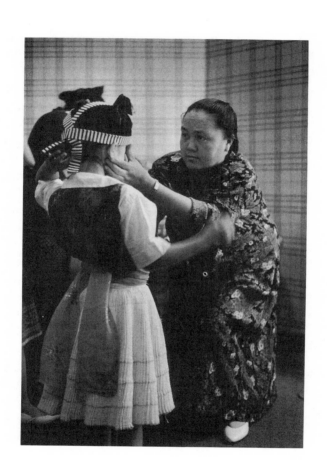

difficulty communicating with them because the grandparents generally speak little or no English, and the grandchildren often know very little Hmong.

The young understand much more easily than their parents and grandparents what must be done to live in this country. They are the ones who can deal with the differences in language and customs and Western technology, and though they themselves do not always feel comfortable with American ways, they see their elders as being completely out of touch. Parents may have pride in their children's knowledge and ability to act as Americans, but they often also feel shame that their children know more than they do. As Kia Vue says, it's humiliating when your four-year-old daughter, who goes to an American Head Start school, can write her name better than you can.

This new family configuration creates pain for the parents, but it also creates great independence for the children, a trait that is counter to traditional cultures but is very useful for making your way in America. How did I feel when I was ten years old and my aunt asked me to address Rosh Hashana cards for her, or my mother asked me to interpret the directions on some pharmaceutical for her? I felt important and empowered, as though I understood how to operate in the world, as though I were practically an adult. I felt smarter and stronger than the adults closest to me. Sometimes I felt like they were the children and I was the parent. But I also felt sad that they were so helpless, and scared because I knew that they didn't understand enough about the system to help me make my way in it. If I were ever to make my way, I realized, I would have to do it by myself.

At about that same time, I was also saddened by my realization that I could not really talk to my mother anymore. My Yiddish vocabulary stopped growing when I started school and English became important for me. At home, my mother would talk to me in Yiddish and I would answer her in English. But her English was almost as limited as my Yiddish. Our communication was merely about the basics—"What do you want for supper?" "When will you be back?"—because we didn't share the words for more profound thoughts or feelings. And very soon—because I was being formed more and more through what I learned in school and from my American peers—there were also many values and outlooks we didn't share. Even had we had the words to talk to each other, how could we communicate? How could I tell her my very American ambitions and desires or the intellectual ideas I was engaged in through school? We lived in the same home, but a part of me belonged to a world where she had no place.

I was as ambivalent about the situation as many of our young Hmong narrators are who are trying desperately to become Americanized—who *are* becoming Americanized through their exposure to school, peers, television, music—but who feel guilty about rejecting their parents' values and failing to measure up to their parents' notions of a good child. After all, it is for their parents that they feel their deepest emotional allegiance, yet they and their parents don't share a world anymore—or rather, they cannot bring their parents into that other world in which they live, where they themselves are not yet entirely comfortable. They feel stuck between two worlds, or marginal in each world. Yet despite such guilt and ambivalences, the one thing about which they are certain is that their parents' "good child" cannot thrive in America—and that their parents are totally ignorant of what it takes to thrive here.

The parents, for their part, in a very natural panic at losing influence over their children, often resort to the means of controlling a recalcitrant child that is most familiar to them: corporal punishment. In Laos, for a loving parent to beat a child until he was bruised was considered an appropriate, tried-and-true method of teaching him. Hmong parents are puzzled when their American children accuse them of "child abuse," as they learned at school such treatment is called. They are devastated when the children threaten to report them to the authorities, as their American teachers informed them they should do if they are being abused. The children learn on American television and from their school that "good parents" talk to their kids in order to correct faulty behavior. But Hmong parents don't have the words their American children will understand.

The parents feel helpless, too, because their children's peer group has more influence on them than do the parents. In their peer group Hmong children develop the notion that they have a right to personal freedom, a totally foreign concept to their parents who believe that life is not about exercising individual freedom but rather about fulfilling your obligations to family and clan. The notion of personal freedom is especially problematic for parents with regard to their girls. Hmong girls look around them and see the latitude that teenage girls have in America, and they demand such latitude themselves. The parents are horrified because they believe that one of their primary duties is to watch over a daughter carefully in order to protect her reputation, to make sure that she won't be considered sullied goods by potential in-laws. Since parents and children no longer labor together on the family farm—in America everyone goes his or her separate way each day—the parents can't control their children as they could back in Laos. They lament because they see all aspects of family life deteriorating, along with the rest of the Hmong culture in America. They often despair that America is ruining their children, that their relationships with their children would have been much better had they not had to leave Southeast Asia.

But for their part, the children see their behavior as acculturation and as survival. I was about eleven when I started calling myself a "typical teen" and a "be-bopper," cracking gum, buying movie magazines and trying to fix my unruly Semitic locks in the style of Doris Day, pulling my halter top low (as I'd seen Rita Hayworth do) over my nonexistent breasts. In our furnished room my mother was weeping and tearing her hair because she had failed in her duty to bring her brothers and sisters to America, and they had disappeared during the Holocaust, and now it was clear that they had been killed by the Nazis. I was running off to be with my best friend, Magdalena Hernandez—"Maggie." We listened to Sinatra records and did pretend swoons over Frankie, as we'd seen teenage girls do in the movie newsreels. We were learning to be American—whatever that meant.

Soua Teng Vang, who despaired over male-female relations in America, told us that he is also confounded by parent-child relations here.

I grew up in Xieng Khouang. My parents first thought that getting an education was useless, it wasn't worth it. But then they thought that just in case things turned out all right with the country it would be good to have someone in the family who could read and write, so I was sent to school until the sixth grade. We learned so much that graduating from the sixth grade is more than graduating from junior high school in the U.S.

There is a nice rule in the school there. The teacher is the parent or father of all of his students. He disciplines whenever he wants to make sure that all of his students learn. If necessary he could hit them. The parents would not have anything to say. In school the teacher has the authority and the parents don't. When a child comes home from school, the responsibility is back to the parents.

My teachers in Laos were not like the kind of teachers here in America. You see, my children—when they go to school here, I am still responsible and the teacher isn't. The teacher doesn't have the right to discipline your child to learn. But in Laos, the teacher can do whatever is necessary. For example, if a student doesn't learn, one of his punishments would be to stand in front of the class for maybe fifteen or thirty minutes, one of his feet extending out, both arms held away from his sides. He would have to be holding two rocks that weigh maybe two to five pounds each in his hands. During this time the teacher would come with a stick and hit his arms to keep it straight. Another thing would be to have some spiny rocks, and what a student would do is kneel on these rocks with arms extended out for fifteen to thirty minutes. Then after the time is up the teacher would come and ask you what you need to do in order not to get into this position again. So you would have to say that you would try harder and really memorize whatever phrases or poem he gives you. This really puts pressure on the student to learn and behave in class.

I remember I had a friend who was whispering to his girlfriend in the class to give him some answer. He was caught red-handed. The teacher told him to hit his girlfriend on the head for telling him the answer. It wasn't him that got the painful punishment, but he had to do it to her. This way it makes both persons feel bad, so they won't do it again.

When something like that happened to me, it was the first and last time because it was so embarrassing for me. There was this one time I had to go up and stand in front of the class holding the two rocks. I was so ashamed in front of my classmates that I did not dare look up. I just tried to hold on for as long and as still as I could until my time was up. There was no one laughing because everyone was scared to be in my position. But when that was happening to me, and all during that day, a lot of thoughts were going through my mind. I told myself I would try hard and study harder the next time. I got mad at myself for not studying or doing the work. I hated to be in this position. I told myself I would do whatever I have to do so that I would never be in this position again. And I did study and I did do well after that incident. It really changed the way I do things.

Another thing we had in that school was a dress code. Everyone was to dress alike. All of the girls wore the same color blouse and skirt. The boys wore the same shirts and pants. We weren't allowed to have long hair. Boys—their hair had to be neatly combed. And the girls' hair had to be braided or tied. No one was to wear dirty clothes and have messy hair. Shoes—that was the exception. Those who had them, they wore them. Those who didn't have them, the teacher didn't do anything. Shoes were something they couldn't really enforce because the people weren't rich enough to afford shoes after buying the clothes. But nails—they had to be clean and cut. You couldn't have long dirty nails. Often times, students would forget to cut their nails, so before everyone goes out on their break, the teacher would close the door. He would check everyone's nails. If they were long and dirty, he would hit them, either with a ruler or some thin, flat, long wooden stick. Other times, he had students hit each other. I remember my nails being hit, and it was painful. It felt like it was bleeding inside the nail, but it wasn't. This always reminded me to check my nails. Such things scared many of the students into making sure they were clean and neatly dressed.

I feel this way is good, and I never thought of it as being abused. It might look abusing, but it is just a way to make a student more serious about school. You can't just come and play around. You come to learn, and if you neglect to do something, this disciplining method always reminds you to try harder. If the schooling system here would be strict like when I was learning, I know for sure my children and other children would learn more. The schools here are too liberal. They are showing my children freedom. For those who know what freedom is, those who are adjusted to it—like the American kids—maybe it is all right. But my children have never seen what freedom is like. For many years, all they knew is about the war and a lot of suffering. When they go to school and hear about freedom, they literally take it as *free*. They come home and they think they are free. They go play and have fun without worrying because they know they are free. When you discipline them with a stick, they tell the teacher you beat them up—and they say that is child abuse. It is against the law to hit your own children.

I don't understand it. If the school doesn't want to take responsibility in disciplining our kids, why not let us do our own disciplining? I was beaten a lot more than I swat my kids, and yet I accepted that it wasn't an abuse—it was a warning that I should try harder.

Here, you can't discipline your kids because it's child abuse, and the teachers can't discipline your child because they have no authority. How could a child learn how to act? Here a child doesn't learn unless he's been in a gang and now he's running for his life. That's when he learns, but then it's too late. I see these things happen more and more. There are more and more young Hmong gang members. It scares me a lot about the Hmong people. We were peaceful. But now, when our Hmong children find a little bit of freedom here in America, they don't know how to control themselves. To our Hmong kids, freedom is fun. It's like the saying: the Hmong children here are like farm cows that have just found some wonderful tasty hay to eat. To move them you have to use a stick to make them notice. If you don't, they will just keep eating until there is no more hay left.

I'm afraid our younger generation who find this hay, they all become gang members. Not only are there are more and more each day, but also they are younger and younger. Most of our kids are already into gangs and only a few are finally getting out of it and moving on to college and making something with their life. How else could it be? The school doesn't want me to hit my kids, but how then can I make them feel responsibility when they get in trouble? I know lecturing doesn't work because—look, there are so many Asian gangs out there. Why not let me do what my parents did? I turned out to be good!

When I swat my kids, I swat them because they did something bad. If I lecture them they will think, "Oh, see, we don't get hit, only a lecture. We'll do it again." I only swat my kids when they are a certain age—from like six to fourteen. This is a critical age, when I feel I must control my kids. I must make them feel I am the father, and if they don't do good in school or do something wrong, I am there to let them know. When they pass this age they are already grown up. I consider them grown-up and adult when they know how to talk to a girl. Then I know they will remember my discipline because they would feel ashamed in front of their girlfriend if they didn't do right and got hit again. But if I can't discipline my children when they are younger, it will be hard to control them when they are a teenager. I know I have to guide them through their young age. Then, by the time they know how to talk to a girl, they will thank me for being mean. It was only for their own good.

Ying Chang (pseud.): "I was so angry, I wished she would have hit me harder so I could die."

I see myself as Hmong-American. Most of my life I was raised here, but my true background is that I'm a Hmong, and I can't really say that I'm an American. I am Hmong and proud to be a Hmong and I like being a Hmong. For example, if I was to be in a pack of Americans and they said, "If you want to be our friend you have to be an American, you have to get away from those Asian people, you have to dye your hair," I would never do that. I would always say, "I'm a Hmong and I'm proud of my traditions."

But I can still see some things that are not good. My parents, they came from a different place, and they don't know what society is like here and they don't know how to teach you. Like when I was small, they would always call you "punk, punk, punk." Even though you don't feel like a punk, they always called you punk. So when they call you something you don't want to be, finally you get mad and you say, "What the hell, my parents are always calling me punk, so it doesn't matter if I join the punks. Why shouldn't I go into a gang?"

They didn't raise me the right way. They didn't treat me nice. There isn't a time when my parents would read me a story book or tell me not to do this or it's okay that you did such-and-such but just don't do it again. My parents would just yell at me, everything I did, yell, yell, and call me a name. It's tough for me right now. I'm mad that they didn't give me a good childhood memory. But on the other hand, I don't blame them for all of it.

What I'm really feeling bad about is that my parents brought me up this way, and now my little brother and them, my parents are treating them the same way and they're going to bring them up just like me. Later on they're going to resent it, too. I'm trying very hard to tell my parents not to do it the way they taught me, but it's very hard for me to change them when I'm just their son.

What they're doing is when the kids go play all day, they never talk to them and say, "Don't go play because you shouldn't do this or this." Like with me, when I went to play and came back, all my parents did is just hit me. They just go, "Don't go play any more and the next time you go play I'm going to hit you harder."

I remember, I think I was in the fourth or fifth grade— you know, when I was still young I played a lot. That time I came home and—I don't know . . . my mom got so mad at me. She took out one of those clothes things, a metal hanger. She started to beat me with it. She hit me on the legs, my arms. Then—I don't know—she hit me on the head. That was when the curly end of the hanger cut into my head. It was bleeding so hard. I was so mad, I didn't care if it hurt me or not. I was so angry, I wished she would have hit me harder so I could die. This was not teaching me anything. I mean, every time they just wanted to hit me! hit me! hit me!—like that. That don't teach me nothing about not going to play.

Another thing my parents did to prevent me from going to play was chain me into my bed. The chain was just long enough for me to go to the bathroom and back into my room. I think that was bad. I'm not an animal or anything like that. That ain't going to stop me from what I'm doing for long. The only way to stop me from what I'm doing is by touching my heart and telling me the truth, telling me what I'm doing is wrong—but telling me in a nice way, not a bad way. Not trying to force me. Forcing is not the way to change a person. The way to win a person is by letting them trust you, heart to heart.

Kia Vue: *"Now we ride on their shoulders, through lands that are of gold, jungles that are of paradise—and yet I feel we're drowning, like many of our people who did not make it across the Mekong."*

Coming here, I know I have become helpless. Everything I do, I just depend on my children. Whatever I need, I just have to wait and wait until they do it for me. For example, looking up phone numbers and dialing it. I never learned how to do that. I have to be shown so many times before I could do it. Then later I have to be shown again. This was very frustrating for me and for them. When we first came and my oldest girl handed me the telephone because one of my cousins called to see how I was doing, I just grabbed the phone and looked into deep space, not knowing what I should do next. I remember everyone was laughing at me, and they were yelling, "Put it next to your ear like this and just talk."

I was shocked when I heard my cousin's voice talking out of it. I got scared and asked my children, "Wow, how did her voice come out of here?" and they were laughing at me. Now looking back, this was so silly that I laugh at me too.

Another thing is, I never got the chance to go to school over here and learn English. I mean, after about fifteen years, I don't even know all of my ABCs. I'm like my four-year-old girl—and she even writes her name better than I could write my name. My children laugh at me, and I laugh with them. But when I really think about it, it's not funny. It hurts a lot. It even hurts more if I think about it.

I feel like I should not have come to the U.S. because I never did learn how to drive. I could have if I started when I first came here. I mean, I think about other Hmong women—they came after me, and they're already driving. I feel really bad. This adds to the burden of being a helpless mother. At least if my children depended on me for driving them to places—but not only do I have to depend on them for translating for me, I have to depend on them to take me to different places. All these things make me feel I did not deserve the chance to come to America. Maybe someone should have come in my place who would be more good for the American society.

But the American society has not been good for all of us. Our children are joining gangs and getting in trouble, like stealing cars or killing someone. For me, I am very frustrated that these children don't see what their parents have done to get them here. I don't think that joining gangs and things like that is a nice way to thank us parents.

For this problem I blame both the parents and the children. I think the parents somehow must play a role in it. You see, Hmong parents back in Laos never saw so much money coming at the end of the month as here. It was just all hard work on the farm and just a little food. I think somehow this money thing has spoiled some parents. I know that many parents will say that the amount of money they're getting is not enough to pay for the rent and utilities and food and everything—but the Hmong are good money savers. Maybe for each check that comes they would probably save about one hundred to two hundred dollars. When they're saving money like this, what about the children's share of the money? The parents explain to the children, "Oh, can't you see, it's paying the rent and buying your food."

But these children here are smarter than the parents. Too many parents don't realize this: the children know how much money the parents are saving. Some of these children don't mind. They just continue on and never ask their parents for money. They're the ones that just keep on going to school and doing their homework and become good teenagers and move on to college. But there are many children who are not like that. They're the ones that get mad and jealous when they see their parents are saving so much money. They ask for some to spend, to buy some toys. And when the parents won't give them any, pretty soon the children will go out and find what they want by themselves.

When the children are seven, eight, nine years old, they have no choice but to listen to the parents. When they get older, that's when the trouble starts. First they'll go steal what they want. Then they make connections with gangs—and those gangs will give them more fun and caring and love than their parents. At this point, when the children come home, whatever the parents try to tell them, it's too late already. Now the parents see they have lost the battle, so they try to make it up by giving the children what they want, but it's no use.

These kinds of things really make me mad. To me, I see all Hmong children as my children, and to see them end up like this makes me regret bringing them over here. I always tell my children who are bad themselves that I should have just thrown them away in the jungle. It was not worth all my energy carrying them night and day, protecting them from cold and rain, for them to just come over to America to do these bad things.

It hurts me very much that these children don't see our past, our struggle for them to survive. Before, they rode on our shoulders, and we carried them through long and harsh mountains and jungles and rivers, and we brought them to freedom. Now we ride on their shoulders, through lands that are of gold, jungles that are of paradise—and yet I feel we're drowning, like many of our people who did not make it across the Mekong. How is this happening? Why? I don't know. I guess maybe I will be like others of my age, old people who die wondering what went wrong.

Zai Xiong, the Mormon elder, recalled for us the effects on him of Western education when he was an adolescent.

When I was in the fifth grade in school here, I learned that the world is round—that's what they taught us. And I came home (when you're that age you're curious about what your parents know or don't know)—I came home one day and my mom was sewing. And I asked her, "Mom, what do you think about the world, do you think it's flat?"

And she said, "Yeah, the world is flat. It's always flat."

Then I said, "Well, my teacher said the world is round."

So she said, "No, the world is flat. You can see if you look at it. It's flat."

I said, "Well, my teacher said if you can throw a rock straight like this, and if it keeps on going, sooner or later it'll come and hit your head on the back."

She said, "No, it can't be."

"They have proven their point," I said. "Have you proven yours?" I just sort of played with her. She was really firm that the world is flat.

Then I told her that there was this man named so-and-so who flew a plane all around the world and ended up where he started from. And that's how he could tell the world is round. Then I said, "And look at the earth. You look at the sky—it looks like a cup shape, doesn't it? And it covers the earth. So the earth is round."

Finally she said, "If they said so, it must be right. Because we don't have any education, we don't know." So she just accepted it.

I felt sorry, but I also felt good because I knew something my mom didn't know.

Then as I grew older, I felt even more sorry for my parents because they didn't have any education. For example, they never knew anything about computers or electronics. One day I brought home a remote control car and played around with it.

My mom said, "Oh, you got a little devil. This is a devil—how else could it move by itself?" She didn't understand, and neither did my dad.

So I told them, "It's like those walkie-talkies you saw people talking in during the war in Laos. It works the same way."

They remembered that and were willing to accept that I didn't have a little devil inside the car. But I really felt sort of sad about the whole thing.

Blia Vang (pseud.), who broke with tradition by returning to her parents' home after living with her boyfriend's family, told us she still feels pulled between the values she sees among her peers and those of her mother.

Sometimes I go with my boyfriend to the movies, but I don't tell my parents. I just say I'm going with my girlfriends because my mom and dad are very protective. If I go somewhere they're —like, "Where you going? Don't lie to us!" They just don't want us to go out that much.

I usually say, "Why not? I work most of the time or go to school. I hardly have any days off. Why can't I go during the days off and on the weekend?"

We argue and argue, and finally they'll say, "Fine! Go, go!"

But I really understand their view of not wanting us to be bad. In our culture it's very easy to get a bad name. If they think you know something, a guy's parents won't like you at all and they'll force the guy to break up with you. Girls get bad names if they go out a lot—even if they just go out with their girlfriends. They get a bad name because everyone says, "She's gone out, and who knows what she is doing. She might be sleeping with people, smoking, doing weed, crack, everything." Everytime I go out with my friends, my mom thinks I do those things too. But—if you can't prove it, then I'm not doing it.

You know, they say that your high school years are the best years of your life—where you make new friends, you get broken-hearted, find new love, all that. So I was expecting to have all of that. I had heard about all this fun from my friends, from TV, like *90210*: how everything was having fun, they don't have a curfew or it's something like 2:00 A.M. They have cars, lots of friends. They're just going out, and they're never home. I think this is like a typical teenager. I want the things they have—like fun, the cars, staying late.

But my mom will say, "Are you an American?"

Then I'll say, "No!"

So she'll go, "What are you?"

"I'm Hmong."

Then she'll say, "Well, we Hmong just don't do that. We're not like that. We can't do that."

And I was . . . like, "Why not? We came to America for free-dom. Why are you stopping us from that?"

Then she says, "We came to America, but you're still a Hmong. You got to learn that. You're not an American. What-ever happens, you may be Americanized, but you're a Hmong."

I don't really like it, but I understand she's right. No mat-ter what happens, I will always be Hmong. I would still have the same face features, the skin tone, the eyes like Hmong. Every-thing like Hmong.

At the Hmong New Year, I usually used to dress in Amer-ican clothes, but my mom wanted me to dress in Hmong clothes. My mom always said we should have the pride to dress in Hmong. The year before last I was . . . like, "Oh, I don't want to wear Hmong clothes. It's too heavy." But last year I wore it for fun, and my mom was kind of shocked.

I said, "Oh, I just wanted to wear it."

She said, "You wanted to wear it? Since when?" It was kind of shocking to her. But I wanted to wear it because it made me feel more Hmong. The old people, if they saw you dress in American clothes, they tell you that you're a punk or some-thing, or that you're a bad person. But then if you dress in

Hmong and they see you, they might have another thought . . . like, "Oh, she might be a good person because she wears Hmong clothes to the Hmong New Year. She might respect the elderly more. So if we have someone like that as our daughter-in-law she might know how to respect us because she has knowledge of our culture."

The year before I got kicked out of the Hmong New Year because we were wearing big pants . . . baggy. They didn't let us in because they think it's gang related. It wasn't gang related to me, but because of the way I dressed they didn't let me go in. By wearing Hmong clothes last year I felt much better.

Mai Moua (pseud.): "Even if I wasn't talking to David who's Vietnamese, I could be talking to someone who's Hispanic."

I think life here has been hard on my parents the most—all the changes, having to understand the language, having to learn everything new. And then as we kids grow older—I mean, we're brought up here and we want to be like everybody else. And they want us to keep our culture and all the traditions—and it's kind of hard, you know. When we want to do things they won't let us. And then they feel like . . . kind of worried about us and stuff.

For example, my older sister—she's twenty-three now—but when she was in high school, her guy friend had a prom and he invited her. In our culture we can't go out with a guy alone. We have to bring along one of our brothers or sisters. But this was their prom. She asked my parents and they said, "No, no, no."

Then the guy said, "Oh, I'll come over and ask your parents."

But they said, "No, he can't even come over."

So he never did. Eventually, after a lot of stuff, they did let her go to the prom. And when it was my other sister's turn and my turn—well, they learned I guess. . . .

Maybe they learned to trust us more. They're changing a

lot. I mean, I look at my parents and I think they're still very traditional. But when I compare them to my friends' parents, I guess they are more Americanized. They learned how to speak English more, and they associate with Americans and other people more. That kind of helped out a lot. I think that was what changed them. But for a long time it was tough for my parents and tough for us kids because we just wanted to be like everybody else, go out, have fun, and then we couldn't.

Actually, we still have some problems, like with my boyfriend, David. He's not Hmong. He's Vietnamese. And, you know, it's kind of a problem. They're still kind of like . . . when we wanted to go to the movies, they said, "No, no," even when I told them my other friends would be there. Then, finally, my older sister decided to come with us and we all went together.

But maybe their big problem with David is that he's a different nationality. Well, actually, I had a talk with my dad. We were coming home from work together, and I just asked him, "Well, what do think about him?"

And my dad said to me, "You know, I can't stop you from talking to David or seeing David, but I just want you to remember that he's different. He doesn't understand our language, our culture. He's Asian, but he's Vietnamese, not Hmong." And he said that if me and David should get to the point of marriage it would be very hard on my mom and dad to accept it because even if I'm a good person, people will look at me and say, "Oh, oh, you didn't marry a Hmong. You married someone else." And they'll look down on me.

"It'll be like you have a bad reputation," my dad said. He just talked to me a lot about that.

I understand how my dad feels, but then in a way it's kind of like . . . I'm not marrying the guy now, I'm just talking to him! This is America, you know, and there other cultures here. Even if I wasn't talking to David who's Vietnamese, I could be talking to someone who's Hispanic. It's kind of hard on me. Like, everything I do, in a way it doesn't make them happy. That's the hard part.

In America, everything is different, the whole way of our lives, everything in this society. Back there they farmed for a living. Here it's like—you go to work. Nothing is the way it used to be. But what my parents don't seem to understand yet is that here—you can date, you can go with a guy alone. There are a lot of cultures here. It's not just Asian.

Ger Yang, the dentist, told us his theory about why parent-child relations in America are so different from what they were in Laos.

There's a lot of difference between the way I was raised up in Laos and the way I can raise my four children in America. When they're under the age of two, there's no big change from the way it was—they'll listen to you, you can tell them stories, they stay with you all the time. But when they're above two years old, that's when the difference comes here: They won't listen to you anymore, they're more interested in television cartoons and even commercials on TV. They just get up very early and turn on the television and watch all the cartoons.

It's much harder for a parent here. In Laos you can control your kids 100 percent. Here you hardly spend any time with them. You have breakfast and sometimes dinner. They're at school most of the day and they come home late. Here, even if you're a good parent, you can only spend about 50 percent as much time with them as you could have in Laos. If you're not a good parent, maybe you only spend about 5 or 10 percent what you would have spent there.

Over in Laos, you see a lot of family members working together on the farm. You see children working alongside their parents. That built a stronger bond between the children and their parents. It made the children listen more, and they were more dependent on their parents. Everyone stuck together and respected each other. Over here, if you don't stay close with your kids, they'll leave and never come back. Over there, even if you didn't care that much about them, they would come back. They had to.

At a dance in the park ▷

Over here, the children get a lot more resources from their friends than their parents. And I think that's why there are so many Hmong gangs. They hang around with their friends, and they become more likely to listen to their friends than to you.

This is the way I see it: Over here, your kids who were born in this country are closer to the outside society than you are. And in many cases, such as if you don't speak the language well, you have to go through your kids to reach American society. But back in Laos, your kids were inside and you were outside. The kids had to go through you to reach society. So now, here in America, your kids are fencing you in.

When a son or a daughter in Laos wanted to go out with one of their friends, they would always ask a parent for permission first. Over here, since the kids are on the outer side, if you don't ask them who they're going out with, you'll never know. You see, you have to go to them to ask them where they're going. In Laos they would come to you and tell you where they're going and who their friends are.

Maybe there are still some girls here that ask their parents, but that's slowly disappearing, too. And the reason for that is, the girls are going to school and they think they know more than you. They spend all their time with their friends and they learn how to argue. Soon they will say, "How come my brothers get to go out and I don't?" You see, they are slowly losing sight of who they are. They are becoming Americanized.

I remember back in Laos, I had to ask my parents for permission whenever I wanted to do anything, and if I didn't they would beat me. Here, you can't beat your kids. You can only speak nicely to them. So I think the only way to control our kids here is to be friends with them more. They feel pressure when you order them to do things here, and they reject it. They need to see you as a friend, someone supporting them. The roles have become completely different. Raising children here is very, very difficult.

Gangs

If this chapter on Hmong youth gangs is a logical sequel to the chapter on family conflicts, it is also a logical prequel to "Being American." I have chosen to put these narrations about Hmong gangs into a separate chapter because at this point in Hmong American history the presence and the problem of gangs in the community loom huge, just as they have in many earlier immigrant histories. Youth gangs did not exist among the Hmong in their Southeast Asian villages. That they are ubiquitous here tells much about the frustrations and methods of adjustments of young people from a new immigrant group to American society.

The rapid proliferation of Hmong youth gangs is in large part a reaction by Hmong teens to what they perceive as their parents' social impotence in America, as Vicki Xiong describes in this section when she laments the deteriorating relationship between her father and brothers. Because they see their parents as being overwhelmed by America, Hmong teens feel desperately the need to establish their own social potency, but their means are limited by their youth and their status as children of poor immigrants. They must work with the only resources that they see as being immediately available to them, and thus they band with other Hmong teenagers who suffer as they do from what they consider their parents' inability to cope with the circumstances that America presents. To the gang members, the Hmong youth gang is a "family" that—as eighteen-year-old "Loco" Vang and thirteen-year-old Phia Lor characterize it—knows better than their birth parents how to maneuver economically, how to survive on alien turf, how to provide bonds that are more relevant to life in America than what their birth families can offer.

But such benefits come at a huge cost. The gang members

are children, yet they have available to them in their ineffectively supervised urban world the adult-caliber weapons of war; and too often these children, living in the "safety" of America, ironically replay the terrors of war which their parents suffered through in Southeast Asia. As I write this, I've just returned to campus from winter break. While I was gone one of my Hmong students who knew about my work with the community slipped under my door a local newspaper with the front-page headline, "Gang Payback Feared in Terrifying Ambush." This is about the tenth time in recent years that such news has made local headlines. The newspaper reports that a couple of days ago two Hmong teens and a woman passerby were gunned down outside a pizza parlor. Four other Hmong teens were seriously wounded. Members of the ambushed gang, MOD, which stands for "Men of Destruction," had recently had a fistfight with a rival Hmong gang, who came back to settle the score with automatic weapons.

"It was real fast," a fourteen-year-old girlfriend of one of the wounded Men of Destruction told the newspaper reporter, in terms that sound horrifyingly similar to those of our narrators who lived through the war. "Like Brrrrrrrr! It sounded like thirty, forty shots, I don't know how many." I remember now how many of our youth gang narrators said they were scared, would like to leave the gang, do something else with their lives. Only a few of them are figuring out how.

When an early sociologist, Frederic Thrasher, studied youth gangs in Chicago in 1927 he concluded that gangs generally establish themselves in neighborhoods that are poor and socially disorganized. Most of the Chicago gangs Thrasher looked at were ethnic; the parents of the gang members were often European immigrants. Thrasher observed that, first and foremost, the gang created order where there was none; it also served to provide alienated young people, who felt denied the opportunity to achieve the American dream, with a way to obtain the material goodies that seemed to be within the easy grasp of other Americans. Perhaps nothing much has changed since Thrasher made those observations seventy years ago, and now many Hmong teenagers are slipping into that well-established pattern.

It is a pattern I first saw as a child. There were no Jewish youth gangs where I grew up in East Los Angeles, in the 1940s and 1950s, though I had heard plenty about big-time adult Jewish gangsters, such as Mickey Cohen and Bugsy Siegel, and about others who had been legends when my mother was a new immigrant: the Lenox Avenue Gang headed by Gyp the Blood whose real name was Harry Horowitz, the Rough Riders headed by Kid Dropper who was born Nathan Kaplan. In my immediate environment, however, the only gangs were *pachucos*, Mexican-American teens who saw their immigrant parents as powerless, unable to get for themselves and give their children the economic advantages and status that they saw as being so prized in this alien North American world. By the time I was finishing grade school in East Los Angeles, most of the Jewish parents there were American or Americanized, since they were for the most part a generation younger than my mother, who, as I said earlier, did not give birth to me until she was forty-four. They had no accents, they knew how to read and write and maneuver in this country, and they were achieving middle-class status. When *pachuco* gangs became violent in the 1940s with the "zoot suit" riots, Jewish parents began an exodus from East Los Angeles to the west side, taking their kids out of the line of fire. Those kids had little reason to form gangs of their own because they saw safer and surer ways to success in America—ways that they could imagine, through the model of their parents or success stories in the Jewish community, were within their grasp.

The Chicano kids I went to school with had fewer reasons for hope at that time. The problem of anti-Semitism was equalled, if not surpassed all over the country, by the problem of racism. But also (perhaps one might say "consequently"), there were few role models of Chicanos who had made it legitimately, in the professions, the arts, business. Their parents were not able to "make it" in American terms. Though the junior high school I attended was at least 80 percent Mexican-

American, I don't recall a single Mexican-American teacher on the faculty (I was lucky to have had a couple of Jewish teachers who served as personal inspiration to me). And there were the frustrations connected to language: Not only parents but everyone else in the immediate community spoke Spanglish (Yinglish was my language at home, but at school I emulated the teachers I admired, whose success I felt was within my reach). If you know nobody like you who reads and writes and speaks the language of the school and the dominant culture well, it's hard to believe you can learn to do it; and so it's hard to conceive that education, which is predicated on language skills, can be the path to a better life for you. Those frustrations of my Chicano schoolmates are the same frustrations of many Hmong teenagers now.

Their response to those frustrations is also similar. As our young narrators in this chapter say repeatedly, their gangs give them what neither their parents nor society can or will: money, respect, prestige, understanding, fun, protection. They feel they must look to each other rather than their confused and powerless adult community for rewards. But the price they must pay through gang-related lethal violence has increased astronomically since I was a child; some of the narrators told us it has even increased since they first joined their gangs just a few years ago: baseball bats have been replaced by Uzis.

The self-presentation of young Hmong gangsters is remarkably like that of the *cholos* (the contemporary version of the *pachucos* of earlier decades), perhaps because many of the areas where the Hmong have settled, such as San Diego and Fresno, also have a high Latino population. Hmong teens have apparently taken the *cholos*—who are often their classmates but are slightly more oriented to American society—as their stylistic role models. There are similarities between the gangs of both ethnic groups not only in superficial attributes of dress, hairstyles, and appropriations of gang-member names such as "Loco," but also in their purpose and focus. Unlike other Southeast Asian gangs in America, and more like *cholos*, Hmong gangs are not very "big business" oriented. For example, I know of no story comparable to those told by Patrick Du Phuoc Long in his recent study, *The Dream Shattered: Vietnamese Gangs in America*, about cross-country operations that net gang members hundreds of thousands of dollars through big jewelry store heists. More typically, Hmong youth gangs engage in petty house burglaries, car theft, sale of stolen tape decks, whatever will bring them a few hundred dollars now and again.

Though Hmong gangs are not at this time involved in big-time criminal operations, the petty thievery that is common among them nevertheless provides spending money and luxuries that far surpass what their parents can give them. And more than one narrator told us, as "Loco" Vang did, of a parent adamantly disapproving of his gang activities with one breath, and with the next shamefacedly asking to "borrow" some of the money that was gotten through those activities. Most Hmong in America, whatever their generation, can't help but be aware of how little they have relative to the glamorous people they see on the television set (which appears to be always turned on in Hmong households) and how far they are from reaching the American dream that such glamour represents. With a few hundred dollars in your pocket it must be easier to believe, however temporarily, that you're in the running—that the good life is within your grasp. But if you are a youngster from an immigrant family, there aren't many legitimate ways to get a few hundred dollars in your pocket.

But even more important than the "spending money" young gangsters get through gang thievery is the emotional sustenance the gang offers. Almost all of our gang narrators related that the sense of meaningful community and structure and mores provided by gangs seem to them far more relevant than what the Hmong family in America can presently provide for its children. What the Hmong youth gang gives its members is perhaps not unlike what the village once provided for their parents (though the parents are totally bewildered by the gang phenomenon and would find such a comparision astonishing).

It is possible that our gang narrators, who were a somewhat self-selected group, are not entirely typical: that is, those who would agree to be interviewed for this book may have had less investment in underworld life than those who shunned a request to be interviewed. But almost all of our gang narrators—even those who seemed most enamored of gang life's excitement and "fun" (to use a word we heard repeatedly in this context)—talked of their desire to someday leave the gang behind them. What struck me about most of them was that they were American children, often heartbreaking in their innocence and their secret hopes that they might someday soon find emotional and economic sustenance through other, less life-threatening ways.

Vicki Xiong: "My father doesn't have any power here. He doesn't know what to do, how to get along in America. So maybe my brothers just thought they had to find another family in gangs."

My brother was involved in a drive-by shooting. He didn't shoot anyone himself, but since he was in the car he was put in the juvenile hall for about three months. At that time there was an incident there. Some of the kids in juvenile hall were beaten with bats, and because my brother was in that drive-by shooting they thought he was a part of the whole thing, and then they sent him to Sacramento for two years to the California Youth Authority. He got out last April. Now he's married and he's moved away.

But I have another brother, who is four years younger than him—he's also in a gang, and last September he got shot in the arm. My older brother told him not to join that gang, but once you're in there, you can't get out. The only way you could do it is through getting married. Then they would look on you as having responsibilities other than affiliating with other gangsters. But otherwise they won't let you out because they think that if you're out of the gang you might go to another gang and betray them, and you could even come back and kill them because you know all their secrets. That's why my older brother had to get married to get out of the gang.

I've been worried sick about both of them. I've cried a lot. Once when my oldest brother was fifteen he just left. My mom and I went to look for him every day. We had to go to all his friends' houses and ask where he was, and it was very hard. I was seventeen or eighteen years old at the time. I felt that maybe his friends would get mad at me and shoot me or something. I was very emotional—every time I met him I would cry and tell him he had to come home. I was just very scared. We found him living in a garage with his friends. They were sleeping in there. I asked him, "Is this where you've been sleeping for the last weeks?"

And he just said, "Yeh." I mean . . . I love him so much. I was just crying. My husband came with me there. He was just crying, too. I couldn't believe my brother was sleeping in a garage.

My father did try to discipline them so they would be good boys, but they don't listen to him. Every time he said something they would talk back. He would tell them to take the garbage out or something and my brother would say, "You just sitting there. You could take it out. I'm doing my homework." Or "I want to go play."

Other times, even nowadays, they turn on their tapes so loud, and my father would say, "Turn it down because I can't hear myself."

And they would say, "Well, you listen to your Hmong traditional songs, why can't we listen to what we want to listen to?" They were listening to rap, hard rock. Then he would go over and take the tape away, and they would borrow another one from their friends and do the same thing. So nothing gets solved. He ended up crashing one of their tapes. He was so mad, he threw it on the floor and smashed it. But that didn't help either; they would always find ways to bring in another one— borrow from friends or somehow get money to go buy it.

So my father just stepped out. He's really depressed for a lot of reasons. He really feels like he doesn't have any power over them, and I think that's what's causing him not to say anything to them after having said so much already. Now he says he doesn't want to have anything to do with them.

My dad was a policeman back in Laos. Then when they decided to leave he went to Thailand alone first so he could figure out everything for us. It was like a life or death thing, where he was putting his life on the line to find a route, to find a way he could bring his family safely to Thailand. We were worried sick, especially my mom, because we were so little at the time. She was worried that my dad might not get beyond the Mekong River because a lot of people that tried were killed or drowned. But he did it, and he came back for us and showed us the way. He brought inner tubes for everyone, all the relatives, about twenty or thirty. I was on my aunt's back crossing the river and she had an inner tube, and my father was the leader. We were right behind him. Everyone was connected to him by a rope from his waist and he swam first. He was the leader. I always remember him the way I saw him as a little girl. He was my hero. I still see him that way.

But his sons don't listen to him because he can't speak English and they can. Back there he could read and write in Hmong and Laotian and even a little bit of French. But here, everywhere my dad goes, he has to take one of us to help, as an interpreter. And maybe this is why they see him as stupid and like he has nothing to teach them. He doesn't have any power here. He doesn't know what to do, how to get along in America, so maybe my brothers just thought they had to find another family in gangs.

"Loco" Vang: "What we give each other is a lot of love and respect."

Whenever I'm out, I'm with my homeboys. We just go kicking around. What we give each other is a lot of love and respect. Some of them become bad because of their parents. You know, they got a divorce or something like that, or they beat them, kicked them out of the house, like that—so that they always end up with their homeboys. They're always getting caught, locked up, getting shot at—and the parents don't really care. Most of the Hmong parents, they have a lot of kids, so they don't really care. They let the children do anything they want. But when they come home to eat, the parents kick them out of the house and they have no where to go except to their home-boys. So they end up in the street. They're always stealing to get money because they don't work and they don't got no house to go to.

When I go home, I know my mother cares about me a little. But I don't really talk to her. I just say "Hi, hello." Everytime I used to help out my dad, he never showed respect to me for it. If he needed me to help him carry, I'd help him. But he never said "Thank you" or "You're welcome." So I got mad. Whenever he tells me what to do now, I don't even bother to do it. I never talk to him, except he always comes to me asking for money, and I'll give him some. I got it from stuff, stealing stuff. You need money to support yourself, you know. It's been a couple of years I haven't asked him for a dollar. He knows that I got money. He doesn't ask where I got it, but I think he knows.

He doesn't tell me not to go out. Well . . . he does tell me, but it isn't in a good way. He tells you in a bad way and with sticks. It seems like he doesn't care what you're going to do. He yells at me to don't do that stuff, and I just say, "What stuff?"

I don't like to argue with my parents, so when they argue I just go to my room, turn the radio up high and loud, lock the door. They come pounding on the door. I don't care, I just call my friends to come pick me up, and I only go out of my room to leave the house. I hardly ever go in the living room or in the kitchen. When I'm hungry I just go out and buy my food to eat.

I know there are a lot of parents who care: They'll yell at you, they'll get mad at you sometimes, but they'll always love you. But some kids, they don't think their parents love them, you know, because if they go home their parents would hit them or stick a gun up to their head. And so they go with their friends and just stay with them. They won't come home until the cops catch them or their parents report them running away. They don't want to run away, but it's like—it's hard to come home. Sometimes they want to come back home, like they got in an argument with their friends. You want to go home, and finally you go home but your parents yell at you, you go to school and the teacher yells at you. It seems like you're always confused, so what can you do? You end up in the street again, doing the same thing, trying to do something stupid so you'll forget all that stuff, you know, get it out of your mind. You go with your homeboy, and it's fun. You go steal a car. It takes your mind off your parents and it gets stress out. But then you get caught and locked up.

When I'm stressed out with my parents—I don't know— I'll go do a drive-by or something. You do things that you know you'll regret, but you're hurt too much to really care about it. You do sometimes feel sorry for the other guys too, you know— like, "Damn! I didn't know I did this stuff." You care, but it's hard. It's all so hard. They call me "Loco" because they know I'm too damaged. I do a lot of crazy stuff, that's why.

I got a younger brother, and he's smart and stuff, you know. For me, I'm not that smart. So my parents are always looking to him. Everything I asked, my parents never gave it to me, so . . . you know. When you ask them for money they start lecturing you. They start yelling at you, so you always end up going out, and you got to go out looking for money yourself. You just can't trust your parents. They're getting welfare, and that isn't enough anyway. We got a large family. Seven kids. It's hard, you know. You got to support yourself.

My set, we always dress like Mexicans and stuff, like Chicanos. And the other Hmong gangs, they don't. So everybody knows us, and almost every gang—they all respect us. We just fight other Hmong gangs, but it's not in clans or anything. We got all kinds of last names in my gang. And even your old friends, even if they're in your clan, if they're in other gangs then you still have to fight them. I had a couple of old friends who are in the wrong set now, so I can't respect them. I can't even care about them no more. It's like, someday I may end up fighting them or shooting them and stuff, so we can't be friends no more. When I was a kid we had a lot of different friends, but we all like—separated . . . one going to one gang, one joining another gang. So it's like going to war—even if you knew each other when you were little kids, even your own cousin can become an enemy, and you might have to shoot him. You know, that's hard.

Nobody going to care about you except your homeboys. That's what you always think to yourself. So of course you get mad if anything happens to them, like when somebody comes and does a drive-by on one of your homeboys. They're always there for you so you gotta be there for them. Some gang drives by and kills one of your homeboys, so the next day you just go back and shoot a couple of their homeboys. It just goes back and forth and it seems like it never ends, just more people die and stuff. It seems like you want peace for all, but you just can't do that because they shot one of your homeboys, so you can't let that go and you always end up shooting each other.

Like, there was this one time, this Min gang, they told us we can have a peace treaty, so we went over there right then. They broke the peace treaty. They jumped us and we had to fight back. Then a few days later they did a drive-by on us. They killed one of my friends. He was just driving his car and they came side by side, and they just shot him through the head. He was around eighteen or nineteen. So ever since that, we know that they'll always back-stab us. That gang back-stabbed a lot of people. We just go back and forth and shoot each other and stuff.

Back like 1989, nobody used guns. They only used baseball bats and knives. But now everybody is using a gun. It's just like, who's got the best gun, who's got the best trigger, all that stuff now. Everything is, can they do a trigger now? It's not like back then. You can kill someone with a knife or a bat but it takes a long time. With guns it's easier.

Ying Chang (pseud.): "You kick my ass today, then tomorrow I'll come back and kick your ass."

When I was small, my friends and I would usually just go around the neighborhood and steal fruits, steal candies and toys from stores, shoot birds, cause trouble around the neighborhood. Then, back when I was thirteen years old, something like November, when it was cold, me and a couple of my friends, we wanted some bikes, so we walked about ten miles in the middle of the night. We just went over there and yanked some bikes and rode them back, and that was what we did. The reason why we did it, most of my friends didn't have enough money or wanted to show off to their friends—like, I have something better than yours. Mostly this is the basis for us to do it.

Me, as I grew older, things started to get worse. Like first, when I was a little kid I stole candy from stores, then I stole bigger things like bikes, then from there breaking into cars to steal stereos and finally cars. It started with little crime, then to bigger crime and bigger crime, until I just realized I had enough. If you're lucky you can turn around and change it before it is too late.

When we go out to business to steal stereos or stuff like that, we want the money just to spend or fool around. Your friends are doing it, but you can't blame your friends; you got to blame yourself. There's something inside of you just telling you to do it, or it's like a habit. You start from little and you just want to steal and keep on stealing. Just like a drug. You got to steal to feel good sometimes. I mean, it's just like a road of stealing.

Sometimes they look at me as being tough, and they would say, "Hey, you're tough. You can steal better than I do." Most of my friends said that if I could steal very good, they would hang around with me. If you're very good they would want to be with you and stuff like that. When you're with your friends you talk different stories than when you're with your family—because when you're with your friends all you think is how tough you are, or how good you steal or something, and you just have . . . like a competition: "I can steal this better than you."

Then you just go out and show off to each other how good you steal. Stuff like that. For example, a Toyota. It's easiest. Basically, you use a screwdriver, you just yank. You stick it in the keyhole, pump it very hard—make it go up, down, sideway. Then the door should be open. You just open it and go in there and take out the stereo. But for American cars, it's very tough to open from the keyhole. You have to bend the window. Or other cars like Honda Accord—you can go under the keyhole. Use a screw driver to go under the keyhole and keep clicking up a little bit until you hit that little bar thing that will make the door open. Then when you get inside, you just take the pullout box. All they have are little pins down there. You just screw those little pins up, push it up from all of the sides, and the pullout box would just slide out, and you just cut the wires very quick with a scissors, knife, or anything like that. It just depends. If you're a neat person you can take as long as you want cutting it. But you could also do it in a couple seconds. You grab the pullout, just yank out the box from the dashboard, and run off with it in the alley or run into a friend's car. Or take your time. That's what I would usually do when I take the stereo, so customers would buy it.

When we go stealing and cops are behind us, what we are thinking about is trying to escape, and you would say, "Man, I promise myself, if I escape I'll never do this again. I'll never steal again." Then, later on when you escape, you go back to your friends and you say, "Oh, wow, how good you are in this or that. You escaped from the cops, a whole bunch of cops. They can't even catch you. You're professional"—like that. This is how many of the gangs feel. Talking tough, but really they're not professional. They are all scared.

I got out of the gang. I started gangs very young and—like, those are your friends; you don't have any other friends. You been playing with them, and if they got on the wrong side . . . wrong crowd, then you're just part of them. And you don't want to leave them, so you just go into the wrong crowd too. Everybody is like stuck in a big hole. You can't do anything about it. No one is willing to talk it out, like, "Hey, what we're doing is wrong." So everybody is just stuck and struggling and struggling. Once someone gets out, other people might get jealous, and they might try to kill you later on. Most of them think like that. That's why they never bother to get out.

But now most of my gang members are either locked up or they're dead. Some realized what was going on, too. When you get older you get smarter. You just look back on your life and you laugh at it. I know one of my good friends—both of us were in the gang, and now he's in jail. I know when he comes out, he will come looking for me, but this is what I will say to him: "Hey, come on, man. You been in there. I know you think the same way as I did. But we should know better by now. We're all full-grown adults. We're not children anymore. I'm not going to go out and have fun and do all those bad things all over again."

I'm just going to tell him straight out like this. Either he likes it or not. When he comes out, he ain't got a friend to back him up no more, just himself. And I'm gonna tell him, "You can be my friend, but you gotta be my good friend. We're not gonna go out and steal anymore because I have a job, and if you really want to work, I can hook you up with a job." When you go out there, causing trouble and stealing things—I mean, one little thing like a candy bar, you can get caught and you get locked up.

I thought I was going to be locked up forever, be a criminal forever, or get killed. Because the gangs now are more into killing each other, not just fistfighting. Because like, if you kick my ass today, then tomorrow I'll come back and kick your ass, and all my friends will come with me. This is how guns comes about. If you're gonna get rid of that person, you have to kill him. Either you kill him or he'll kill you. This is why gangs today got into shooting. Because if you don't kill that person, for sure that person's gonna come back and kill you instead. See, this is how it is.

I'm not afraid anymore, even if they come out of jail and say, "All of those promises we made as gang members—like to be friends, and help each other out, and if one goes we all go," like that. Basically all of these things were not true.

Phia Lor (pseud.): "The sheriff wrestled me to the ground and then handcuffed me. They didn't take me to jail because I'm only thirteen years old."

I don't call me and my friends gangsters, but I guess other people call us that, just because we have baggy pants, big shirts, weird hair cuts—like long in the front and short on the back. All my friends and I do is, we just cruise around the streets near our school. I'm thirteen and most of my friends are thirteen, but we have someone who's sixteen or seventeen drive us around. We don't go shooting people or anything, we're just having fun.

I don't know why we go cruisin' so much—I guess because most of the time we're bored. Bored with school and everything. We just want to go driving around, having fun. In the morning I leave the house. Then I call up my friends from a pay telephone, and they come pick me up. We just go along, all day, having fun. Then at the time when school is supposed to be over, we come home. Our parents don't know if we're in school or not. They don't call the school, and the school don't call our parents. So we just have to make it home on time, like the other students.

Sometimes though I don't make it home—I don't go home all night. I just hang around with my friends. No, I don't worry about what my parents will think. I don't think they care that much. They seem to do their own things. All they say to you is, "Don't go do gangs. Go to school and get good grades." But they don't seem to follow through. At first I was scared of them when they said that. But after a while they'll forget and I'll forget, and I just go do my things with my friends. It's only when I get in trouble that my parents remind me again of what they wanted me to do. But I just can't remember them telling me anything when I'm with all my friends. It's only when I'm alone and get in trouble that I will remember what they said.

If we don't go home, it's because we're either sleeping at one of our friend's houses—or we just go out looking for some old house where the people have moved out and we go to sleep in there. Oftentimes what we do is—maybe we might have already spotted an unrented apartment in the daytime. Then, when it's night, around one or two in the morning, we come through the window, and we just spend the night in the apartment. No one knows that we sleep in there. We have fun all night. Most of the time we only have a little rest. We sleep just a little and then wake up early and leave before they start waking up in the other apartments. Or sometimes we just sleep in and wait until everyone has left in those other apartments. Then all of us would just sneak out. Sometimes we all take our own blankets and pillows, so we just go to sleep and wake up, and then we go do our same things again.

My friends and me smoke weed a lot, but we don't do real drugs—you know, things like cocaine or heroin. We mainly smoke and drink beers a lot. We think it's cool, and it makes us feel better. When we celebrate something—like stealing something and getting the money for it, these are what we buy: weed and beers. The rest of the money we might use for car gas because we travel far. Sometimes we could go as far as up to Sacramento. We don't have girls. We just mainly have fun by ourselves. I guess we're still small, so we prefer to be with ourselves. It's much more fun.

What I really like to do? There are not a lot of things to do, so we just go stealing a lot of the time. This is how we make money. My friends and I never get money from our parents. It's useless to ask them nicely for a few dollars. So we have to make money from selling radios or tools from the cars we steal. There was one time, my friends and I went to this neighborhood in Visalia and spotted a Prelude. What we used to break in with was a flathead. When we did that I wasn't thinking about anything. Everything was cool and fun. All I was scared of was that the owner would come and start shooting at us. But we just jumped in, and one of my friends who's sixteen drove us right off.

After we drove it for about fifteen minutes, I saw a sheriff car following us. I think they didn't know that the car was stolen. It was just that my friends and I looked young. All of us together looked like an Asian gang, so they followed us. That was when I started to worry. Everything suddenly changed from laughing to worrying. Then I started to feel that I shouldn't have done it, but it was too late.

When the sheriff turned their lights on us, we all jumped out of the car and started to run in every direction. We left the car in drive mode, and I think it struck another police car. I didn't stop. I ran just like my friends. But I was caught. I ran but I didn't run too far. I hid myself behind some cardboard boxes. What I didn't know was that the sheriff was tracking me with a K-9 dog. The dog was able to find me hiding behind the cardboard boxes. I didn't try to run away from him or do anything, but I was bitten by the dog anyway. It bit me on the legs and on the side. I don't know if the sherrif did it on purpose or not, but that dog really bit me hard.

Now I'm really trying to stay away from my friends. I don't want to—but my older brothers and teachers all want me to. My teachers think that I can make it and not turn out to be a dropout. That's because even though I was absent a lot from school, I was still able to keep up a 3.0 grade point average. I guess that makes me feel different from my friends. I don't know why I keep the friends I have. I haven't been with them for two weeks now. But it's really hard to stay away from them because—sometimes, I'll see them at school, and they'll ask me why I didn't come out when they came by my house to pick me up, or how come I didn't pick up the phone when they called. What am I supposed to say to that?

Susie Chang (pseud.): "When it got to the point those other girls jumped me, all my gang girls did was, they all just stood there."

I been with the gangs since I was like twelve, and now I'm sixteen. Being with them—they always have bad things in their mind, to do something bad to other people or fight people or other gangs. Girls fight girls and boys fight boys, things like that. We smoke—do marijuana and things like that. Some of the other girls do drugs just like the guys, but I don't. We just like—kick back, everyone just like . . . talk, laugh, talk and smoke. That's about it.

For most of the girls and boys that I hang around with, we just act like brothers and sisters. There's no sexual things involved between us, but for some horny people there are sexual things involved. I seen it. This usually occurs during the night when we are either at a friend's house or one of us have rented a motel. Then everyone would just come in. You know, almost anything could happen—where a girl can be sleeping with more than one guy . . . or some girls can get raped. But what can they do? They can't complain to anyone except their best girl-friend who they really trust.

One bad incident I had was in December when I was fighting with other gang girls from a different gang. The girls in my gang said they would back me up—but when it came to fighting it was only me fighting three other girls. I could not believe it. When it got to the point those other girls jumped me, all my gang girls did was, they all just stood there. So I could not trust anybody. You can't even really trust your own cousin. Maybe if you know someone really, really close, then you could trust them to help you. But if it's just your friends, you could never trust them. Like I found out, you should always have doubts because they're going to back stab you. While I was fighting those three other girls, the boys were trying to separate us. I thought my girlfriends were going to help me, but they were just standing there.

So that all made me think about the future, and I just tried to stop what I was doing. It wasn't really worth it—it wasn't going anywhere. My gang can't help my life forever, and I saw that . . . even now, my friends are not always there for me. Friends, they're just there to have fun and play with you. But that isn't what life is all about. So now I think what I really want to do is get an education, maybe go to Stanislaus State College when I finish high school, maybe get to be a teacher. I know I can come back and try to start over again.

But it's really hard for me because I know that, when I try to quit, they're always going to come and ask me to go out. When they come, I'm always so tempted. So now, I told my parents to help me by having them say to my friends that I am not home. But it's still hard because I know that after school, they'll be right there outside the gate, waiting for me. And another thing about it is, my mind is always thinking about it. So what I'm trying to do is spend more time with my family, try to have fun with them more.

But also now it's very hard for me to quit smoking. Not just marijuana—cigarettes too. It was a bad habit, and now I'm really suffering from it. I have to try not to smoke around my parents, but it's very hard. When your mouth gets itchy and all that, you really want to smoke and get the anger or the frustration out.

What makes it all worse right now is that when I'm telling my younger sisters not to do what I did, they don't listen. All they say is, "Oh, you did that. Why can't we do it too?"

Sonny Lee: "The Mexican gangs hated us. They don't like Asians. They say we steal—not just cars and stereos but cats and dogs and that we cook them."

There are about twenty-five of us in my gang. But I'm not in contact with them a lot now. Not ever since I got married. That's how being in a gang is, you just stay there until you get killed or you jump out by marrying. I got married last year when I was eighteen and then I jumped out. Now I just leave them alone, I just don't hang with them anymore. I decided to get married and move on with my life. Sometimes they still call me, but not for gang stuff anymore. They just call like to go fishing and stuff like that.

What my gang does is mostly just play. After school, we would call each other up, you know, and we just go to the park or Holmes playground and have fun, like playing cards. We would just gamble for fun. We usually start out small, like each person puts out twenty-five cents, and then we go up to something like five dollars. We just do this for fun, but whoever wins the most money, he usually buys everyone of us beers and we all drink. Sometimes we just stay there until midnight, just playing cards, drinking, having fun.

Sometimes we used to go and pick up girls—like one time my friend and me, we went and picked up two white girls from Summerset. We just took them out and had fun. We drank, and we tried to get them drunk—but you know, we didn't get them. They didn't fall for it. Sometimes though we had girls with us at Holmes. Some girls, you know, they don't care about anything when they get drunk. They just drink too much and they don't care. This is how it is. If they have a boyfriend, we don't do anything. But some type of girls, nobody owns them. We would just line up on her there. You see everyone do it, so you do it too. You just don't think about it or anything.

Mostly the problems we had were within ourselves—like when someone wins all the time at playing cards and then the others get jealous. But another problem we had was with the Mexicans. The Mexican gangs hated us. They don't like the

Asians. They say we steal—not just cars or stereos but cats and dogs and that we cook them. They started saying we do stuff that we didn't do, and you just hate them for that. That's how the problems started. So us Asian gangs had to hang together against the Mexican gangs.

Like that Bulldog gang—they're Hispanics. They made all the trouble against us. That was the last gang fight I was in. Those guys just started cussing at these Asians who were my friends. My friends got pissed because they were outnumbered by all these Hispanic guys. So they just came back to us and told us what was the problem. Then my whole gang went over there, and we started cussing the Hispanic gang. This time there were a lot more of us than them. The next thing you know, you just hopped out of the car and started chasing after them with sticks and chains. Pretty soon there's a big, bloody fight. I was scared. I was just only the driver, but my friends beat the shit out of those Mexicans.

But for me, though, joining the gang wasn't about being tough. I just didn't feel that way. For me it was just fun, and for security. We help each other and back each other up. This is what is so great about it. Some gangs have a leader, but our gang, we just follow anybody who comes up with an idea or has the most ideas—we just follow that person.

All I ever got caught for was curfewing. I was lucky because I could have got caught for breaking and entering or something, and a lot of the guys I was with had guns. Like one dumb thing that happened at Holmes—we were playing cards and one of my friends was winning a lot and he was drunk for drinking so much beer. He got so excited, he just pulled out a gun and started shooting in the air. He wasn't himself, he was so drunk. He didn't know what he was doing. But we all ran off and the cops came and took him away.

Some of my friends, they went to jail. Now it all kinda scares me. Before, I guess you don't care. You just wanted to have fun. But now, once you're married, especially marrying at this young age, I have to support my family. I started a new life, and it's very hard.

Mike Yang (pseud.): "I died and then came back as a new person."

I was born in Honolulu, Hawaii, and when I came to the mainland I was a sophomore in high school. I'll admit it, I was a bad boy. I had a lot of fights with my parents—because when I just went to play volleyball or something like that, they thought I was into gang things when I wasn't. Eventually this got to the point where I felt they were pushing me into gangs just by accusing me all the time. They just lectured me and yelled at me even when I wasn't doing anything bad: Like I never wanted to hang around with the bad kids. To me, my friends were good, they weren't bad, but my parents saw them as bad. I hung around with Mexicans. When you're in America, Mexicans are better to hang around with than Asians because Asian people will get you in a lot of trouble. But my parents told me not to go with the Mexicans, to hang around with Asians instead.

So then I did, and my parents liked that better, but the Asians were the bad ones. They got me into doing bad things. Once I was with them I became bad myself—I was smoking, doing weed, went drinking, ditched school, got kicked out of McLane High School for fighting when I was a sophomore.

The reason I got into a gang only when I started hanging out with Asians is that usually all the gangs are just within your own race, and the problems are also just within your race— Hmong against Hmong, Mexican against Mexican, black against black, Cambodian against Cambodian. There's almost never like Hmong against Laotian or Cambodian against Hmong: it's the same against the same. Whenever I had problems it was another Hmong gang against my Hmong gang. It was rarely with another race gang.

Actually, I don't really know now why I joined the gang. Maybe it was because there were some people who didn't like me, and they said things like I stole their girlfriend so they're going to kill me. I was really scared of that, and I thought I better join some gang. I knew the gang would protect me. If someone beat me up, we would all go and beat them up. And it feels like you won't get hurt that much if you have your whole gang behind you.

In a large gang like mine—there were fifty to sixty guys—you don't really know all of them, but when it comes to team-work, everyone knows their responsibility. There's a big guy and a second big guy that the rest look up to. When the younger ones have a problem, they would come to you for help and you would help them. You just get into a routine when you're in a gang. You beat some guys up, next time their gang comes and beats you up. They shoot your house, you go and shoot their house. It just goes on and on like that.

I don't know why there's so much shooting now. I guess the main reason is, you want to be the toughest gang around. So with Hmongs, you want to be the top of all the Hmongs. You have to make the other gang be scared of you. That's the whole thing. When we started, all of us only used pencils for stabbing and baseball bats for hitting. We never shot each other. Then one day, I don't know, some guys went to Kearny Park, and one of them just took out a gun and started blasting. Since then on, it appears everyone wanted to use a gun. No one wanted to fight just using baseball bats, so it's not safe anymore.

Before, actually, I thought it was more like fun—everyone jumps in and you just fight back and forth. Now it's not fun no more. If you go bother them, there are these young gangs—kids about nine or ten—they don't care at all. They'll just shoot. They don't care. You have to worry about them much more than the older gangs.

I think everyone just wants to be top guy. You want everyone to be scared of you so you have a lot of respect. These young gangsters want to be somebody. They don't want to be a nobody. They want to be on top so they can have respect from the older guys, too. It's sad—I mean these nine- or ten-year-olds, they just point the gun at you and pull the trigger. If they get caught, they'll just be released or treated as a juvenile—whereas if the older guys do it, it'll be tough for them. So the nine- or ten-year-old kids don't think twice before they shoot you.

I got to the point where I just wanted to get out. I guess that was after some guys came and shot bullets through our house, and my father was crying and got all crazy. He didn't know what to do with me anymore. But you can't just go out of the gang because your old homeboys would come after you—and they might shoot up your house, too, or even you.

Then one day I went to some party. It was Blue's nineteenth birthday and they had a barbeque. After the party, no one wanted to get into my other friend's junky car, so we all, about eight or nine of us, piled into this girl Babe's car, which was pretty and comfortable. It was about 12 a.m. or something like that, and I was tired so I fell asleep on my friend Pheng's lap. This was the last thing I remember.

When I woke up I was at the hospital. I had already had some surgery done on my stomach, and I couldn't move. I was wondering why I was here, and then I cried and cried. I thought it was a dream at first—I tried to move and I couldn't. Then a nurse came in, but she didn't really tell me what had happened. Then Danny and Sam came. They didn't know not to tell me—so they told me: We had been in a car crash. About four of us were hurt real bad and two of us were killed. I was just crying.

I wanted to go to my two friends' funeral, but no one could take me because I wasn't healthy enough. I didn't get to see them when they got buried. When I got out, they'd already gotten a stone and everything on their graves, but I never saw them.

I think I had about twelve surgeries and it cost like two hundred thousand dollars. The insurance paid about eighty percent, and my dad had to pay the rest. I was more scared of my dad at the hospital than of not getting better. He came in crying to me and yelling, "See, when you don't cherish my words the first time, this is what happens." I started crying and begging him for forgiveness.

I guess the one good thing that came out of it was that when I had that car accident, all those people that didn't like me probably thought I died because they heard some guys were killed and I had just disappeared since I was in the hospital. So those guys just left it like that. And I said to myself that I did die in a way.

After I got out, when they saw me, they just saw me as this skinny guy: "Who wants to mess around with him anymore?

Who cares? He can't do anything anymore." And then another group of guys started causing them trouble, so they forgot all about me.

Then I started hanging around with different people because my homeboys thought I couldn't do anything anymore anyway. So I think in a way that accident saved my life. I died and then came back as a new person. That's how I see myself now. But to lose so much, like my friends and my dad's money. I don't know, that's hard, too.

Being American

Whether you are an immigrant or the child of an immigrant, whatever else your experience of America might be, it is also, almost invariably, fraught with ambivalences, pain, guilt, and confusion. For immigrants of the older generation who have come to America to escape poverty or persecution in their own country, the problems are the most dramatic and obvious. For my mother, coming to America as a young woman with tremendous expectations, hoping to "better" herself and help her family back in Eastern Europe, the disappointment must have been almost immediate as she discovered the streets were not paved with gold, neither literally nor figuratively. Because she could not read English and never really learned to speak the language with facility, she was often lost or disoriented, even during the years I was growing up, after she had already been here for a couple of decades. She could never feel totally at home in this country that was hers only by adoption. "You are an American," she would always tell me, by way of explaining why things should be easy for me here—and by way of distinguishing between us.

When she arrived in America the only trade for which my mother was qualified was in the garment industry—the "sweatshop"—where wages were low and work was seasonal. For much of her life in this country she took a trolley to work before the sun was up and another trolley back to a furnished room long after dark. When the cloak season was over she did not know where her next meal would come from. This was not the America she had dreamed of, but it was all that was to be had for an uneducated immigrant.

Nor was the failure to find her dream the only cause of her sadness. There was her loneliness for her parents and brothers

Homework ▷

and sisters, and for the shtetl where she had been born—her home—despite its poverty and its dangers and discomforts of anti-Semitism. There was the confused feeling of guilt that she had been sprung free while the rest of her family were stuck back there; and later, when her brothers and sisters disappeared in the Holocaust, there was the terrible guilt of the survivor. And though there were no pogroms or holocausts in America, she was miserably conscious of being a Jew in a country of gentiles, always aware of her looks and the accent that she never lost.

The disappointment and pain I heard in the voices of many of the adult Hmong immigrants who were my narrators often reminded me of her. Their children reminded me of me. The Hmong immigrants cannot finish mourning for their relatives who did not make it here—those who were killed in the war or while trying to escape from Laos, and those who are still alive but have disappeared from the immigrants' lives perhaps forever because they chose to remain in Southeast Asia. The feeling of loss does not lessen even with time, as Mee Vue says when thinking of her sons and daughters who remain in Thailand and Laos: "Though I eat or smile there is still one part of my heart that is hungry and sad."

But that sadness is far from the immigrants' only problem in America. Hmong people who came here as adults consistently complain of disorientation. In the mountains and jungles of Laos, they always knew where they were. On the streets of American cities, with traffic whizzing by and street signs in an alphabet they have not mastered, they are always lost, as so many of our older narrators told us repeatedly. Their only hope is in their children, who can learn to read and to drive and to take advantage of all the opportunities this country might offer those who have cracked its secrets of literacy and technology.

Yet the parents also fear what will be inevitable when their children get educated: that the children will grow away from them, that there will be an unbreachable cultural gulf. How can these immigrants not be ambivalent about the opportunities open to their children, though they have risked their own lives in order to help them to those opportunities? When I was eighteen and on my way to college my mother confided to me with confused concern that her friend Molly had warned her not to let me go to college: "Because then she'll think she's better than you are," Molly told her, "and she won't have anything to say to you anymore." Of course my mother wanted me to get an education, but how could she not be worried? I was stepping into a world where she could not follow. What would be left for us to share?

The middle generation Hmong people who were our narrators are more easily able to adjust to American ways than their parents, but they have their own set of worries. They came here as children or teenagers and were sent to school where they learned the language, though often with great difficulty. By now many of them have gotten into college and are preparing for careers. Though they have reason to expect a brighter future than their parents, their struggle is far from easy or guilt-free: They feel at a disadvantage because they learned English as a second language, and they will never speak without an accent, never be grammatically perfect as native speakers can be. They see a glaring difference between their parents' old-fashioned, ineffectual immigrant ways and how "real" Americans live, and they alternate between being ashamed of their parents and ashamed of themselves because they are ashamed. They know that they are preparing to enter another social class that will bring them even further away from the culture of their family. They are ambivalent about becoming part of a culture where life may be materially easier but morality is no longer self-evident—where, for example, the desirability of family allegiance that takes priority over everything and the desirability of rugged individualism that permits an American to forge ahead can collide brutally with each other.

However, despite the various ambivalences of the middle generation, what often came through strong in the stories they told us was their sheer hunger—their determination to realize the promise of America, to win a piece of the pie for themselves. As a teacher of young adults, I've heard so frequently from many of my white students in the last years that they can't even hope someday to own their own homes and live as well as their parents do, that the American Dream is dead. But many of the middle-generation Hmong I interviewed have not gotten word of its demise: they believe in the American Dream with as much hope and innocence and appetite as Horatio Alger's newsboys once did.

The younger generation of Hmong, those who were born in America, share many of the problems and aspirations of the middle generation—and they have additional reminders that they live in a world different from the Hmong world of their elders. For instance, they often have difficulty even conversing with their grandparents because many of the American-born know only a little Hmong and their grandparents speak nothing but Hmong. Even food becomes a wedge that divides. Through the school lunch program you learn at an early age how seductive pizza is. As eleven-year-old Susie Vang observed to us, how can rice compare? What, other than facial features and a nagging guilty feeling that you should be "more Hmong," is left? They know nothing of the home in Southeast Asia or the people their parents mourn. There is no Laos for the young, except through their parents' tales or pictures in a travel magazine. They are angry with their parents' parochialism, their unbending "Hmongness." They wish their parents would or could be more like Americans.

Sometimes in our interviews the young people tried to speculate on who they would have been had their parents remained in Laos. They could not do it. They could not imagine themselves living in a remote mountain village, marrying at fourteen, farming every day. The person who could live that life would not be them. They have not been constructed to be farmers who live in a little Hmong village in the mountains of Laos. They have been constructed to be—and they are—Americans.

Mee Vue, who ran through the jungle with her young children and later came to America to join her oldest son, told us about what keeps her from feeling like an American and what her dreams are for her American-born grandchildren.

When I stepped on that plane I was happy because I knew I would soon see my son, Cha Lee. He was in America with Ia, his wife, already. But there was another thought, and even today I'm still thinking about it. I still have daughters, sons-in-law, and other sons back in Laos and Thailand. Though my mouth said to come to America, my tears were sliding down my cheeks. If I can only stop thinking about them. But it's hard. One side wanted to come, but the other side worried about the ones that were left behind without their mother. Though I have been here for a long time already, I still miss them every single day and night. If I was to have one wish, I would wish that all my children would be here with me. But since everyone is everywhere, though I eat or smile there is still one part in my heart that is hungry and sad.

Since I have been here, I don't have much worry except for my children back in Thailand and Laos. The other worry that I have is that I'm too old. I don't speak English, I don't know how to drive a car. I can't walk alone on the sidewalk because I might get lost. I am like a little child. There are too many cars. I don't know how to cross the street. I just don't know where to go except stay home. But if I was a little bit younger, I would be able to go to school, learn how to read and write, how to drive a car like my daughter-in-law, Ia. It would not be that hard for me. But I am old, and I can't really do what my heart wants to do.

Though I do not have too many worries here, no matter what happens, I will always be a Hmong because I still have my children back in Thailand and Laos to keep reminding me of who I am. Without them maybe I would more easily become Americanized, with my sons here. But because of my children back there, I always remind Cha Lee to do the tradition, like calling a shaman when you need to and the spirit name-calling.

But what I wish for mostly is for our Hmong people here to go to school, learn the English language, get good jobs, and then help those who are behind. Before there was the war, children could not go to school as they pleased. But here in America, I hope that all of my sons' children will learn as much as possible. This is what is important to me now—to see all of my children and grandchildren here go to school and get a good education. There is not much I can do myself, but if they will succeed, then I will be happy.

Dr. Tony Vang: "A lot of people that see me as American don't understand all of it—what my history has been. They don't see the Hmong in me."

Although I have my doctorate from an American university and I am a professor now in America, and although I came here when I was just eighteen years old, in 1972, before the big migration—there are ways that I will always be Hmong. There is so much that is beautiful in the Hmong culture—the extended family, for example. Being a Hmong means you could never dump your mother to live in a nursing home. Being a Hmong, it is my responsibility to take care of her until she dies. Because I am a Hmong, I know my mother is second only to God because when she dies I will ask her spirit to help me. Her spirit will be with me all the time, until I die. When I die my spirit will be with my kids until they die too. For a Hmong these strong bonds just keep on going and going.

    If I had to say, I would say that I was about 30 percent American and the rest Hmong—though I suppose many Hmong people would say I'm mostly American because I've lived here most of my life, I have a professional job, my wife isn't Hmong. But being Hmong is for me an emotional thing. For example, when I listen to Hmong music—I'm still moved by it. I listen to American songs, but I don't understand them as deeply as when I'm listening to Hmong songs. Through ways like that I know that I'm still Hmong. Nothing will change that—it's so deep inside of me.

    And no matter where I am, if I see something that's bad for

the Hmong people, it still hurts me. The Hmong people don't always understand that when they just see me as American. When you grow up with a family that's very poor like mine was back in Laos, when you experience a lot of tragedy like we did, it's hard to forget. Like my brother—when I left Laos to come to America to study, he took me to the airport, and he was in his air force clothes. He shook my hand, and he told me—he said, "You know that my life is very short. I don't know how long I will live. But all I want of you is to come back after you have your education—and love the family and take care of my kids and be the leader of the family." I never thought this would be our last meeting as brothers, but it was. Three months later I heard he was shot down. He said he had a short life, but I never expected it to be that soon.

I was all alone in America at that time. I went through school in Hawaii with high honors and I got my doctorate, and nobody knew how I was really hurting, how sad it was. I had no father to be proud of me. I had no older brother to come and pat me on the shoulder and say, "Congratulations, you did well and I'm proud of you." None of that—but I did make it through. I didn't even have scholarships or anything. I went through school supporting myself. I used to earn $1.60 per hour. If you had a girlfriend, you couldn't even go to the movies on that. You couldn't even have a date because that might cost $10.00, and I needed that money to just make it through the week. I had to count every penny of how I spent my money.

But I always remembered what I needed to do. In Laos, I knew this person who went to study in France. He would always write and send back pictures of how beautiful France was. I remember in one of his letters he wrote something like, "The only way to become self-sufficient is to have an education." Then he lay down in the letter step by step how he was going to do things. Those messages were so strong that they made you feel that you yourself were in Paris already. For me, it was the starting point, an idea of how I could see my future. I didn't go to France though, because I always loved America. I always believed in America more than France. And you see, today my dream has become a reality.

But a lot of people who see me as American don't understand all of it—what my history has been. They don't see the Hmong in me. They don't know that I experienced what I know all the Hmong people here have faced in one form or another. They all had to leave their village in Laos, they all lost husbands or fathers or brothers or children or other relatives in the war. I'm a Hmong because deep down in my heart, where no one can see, I bear the same scar that every Hmong man or woman of my age bears. Somehow I just know of better ways to cover my scars than many of them do. But that doesn't make me less Hmong than anyone else.

Pao Her (pseud.): "I'm just stuck in between, jumping back and forth."

I'm eighteen and when I came to America I was about four years old. I didn't speak any English, and my parents still can't speak English that well. But I remember I used to watch television a lot, and I learned that way. I still like programs like *Full House*. It's a comedy about a white family. I think it's fun to watch sometimes because they have some good programs about family problems and stuff. In some ways, they're not that much different from us, but in other ways they are.

I think the big way they're different is the way they show their emotions. They're much more emotional than us—like with hugging. Americans give hugs to each and everybody in the family, but the Hmong—they just don't hug each other or . . . like, kiss you before you got to sleep. They just say, "Go to sleep." Well, sometimes now I kind of question how come we Hmong do it that way. Sometimes I feel like maybe I want to give my family a hug, too. But then I think, "Well, maybe it's not good," because we just don't do that stuff.

Or another difference that I see on American television with families is that they go out, like to restaurants. Sometimes I go with my friends to restaurants. But my parents don't go out that much. They have to stay home and watch the house. I kind of want my family to go to restaurants and eat out once in a while, just see how it's like, but they never do. My mom wants to go out, even just to a fast-food restaurant, but my dad—he goes, "Just stay home and eat." Sometimes he does take my mom and my little baby brother out, but never the whole family. When I get married I think I'll probably be Americanized, so probably the whole family will go out to a restaurant once in a while.

But the truth is, I don't really feel American and I don't feel all Hmong. I don't know that much about the Hmong culture, like my parents say; and I don't know much about the American culture, how their society works or what their laws are. Sometimes I don't feel like I fit in. So I'm just stuck in between, jumping back and forth.

My little sister, she was born here and she doesn't even speak that much Hmong. She's like, more Americanized. There's not that many Hmong families living in this neighborhood, except one across the street and they don't have a daughter her age. So she doesn't come in contact with Asian girls that much. She's—like more Americanized by playing with her American friends. She asks for clothes—like bathing suits—that American girls would wear that's different from what Asian girls would wear. She hangs around mostly with the girl next door, and she goes out to their church with them. When she gets home from school, she puts her bag down and goes over there and they just play until it's dark.

When she speaks to my mom it's mostly in Hmong, but when she speaks to us or her friends it's always in English. Sometimes she says the wrong word in Hmong to my mom, and my mom goes, "You don't know that much Hmong anymore!" I imagine this worries my mom, because in our culture, a girl is supposed to be a good daughter, like knowing how to speak her language—so that when she marries she could communicate with her in-laws in a more formal way.

Sometimes I think I'd like to have some American friends too, but—like if they invite me over to their house, I don't feel comfortable going over because I'm afraid they might think I'm different. I might get stereotyped or something by them—like they might think I would steal their stuff. So if they ask me to go, I usually end up making excuses like, "My family's going out and I gotta be there."

I don't invite them over to my house either because there's a lot of people in my family, and I know they're not used to that. And my parents are not like American families where you go over, and they really invite you in, they say "take a seat" and they give you refreshments, stuff like that. I've been over to American families, like for a party and stuff. Even though they may not know you, they kind of make you feel like it's okay. But Hmong families . . . well, they're the same way too, but they don't have that much to offer, like food or anything. So I don't want to invite kids over and then just sit around. We don't have games like in American families, where they all play board games together like Monopoly, or they have all these other games, or they say "Let's play on the backyard swings." We don't have stuff like that.

And then they might not like . . . uh, all of us speaking Hmong. They might think we're talking about them, and then that might make them feel uncomfortable—because my parents don't know that much English. I just feel like it's kind of embarrassing to invite them over to my house. But then I go, "Why should I feel embarrassed?" But sometimes I just feel that way.

When I invite my Hmong friends over, it just feels like they're my brothers and sisters. It's like they're just there. They don't expect to have games or things to have fun with. We can just talk or listen to music, watch TV, maybe do homework or something. And they don't even notice my mom and them. It's like we're all the same.

But usually I don't feel like I'm a real Hmong either because . . . for example, I don't know that much about the Hmong language. I kind of feel angry at myself because I should know what my parents or grandparents are saying to me. Sometimes I find it really hard to understand what they mean. There are a lot of words they use that I don't know. Like sometimes

Making music in America ▷

they tell me, "Go and get something in the backyard," like parsley. They say it and I go, but then I ask myself, "Wait, what did they mean? Is it this, or is it this?" . . . I didn't know what the word meant, but I didn't want to be embarrassed in front of them, so I just take my chances at guessing which. Half the time I would get the right one. But the other times I would get it wrong, and they would just think I was absentminded, like they'd say, "How can you be so forgetful? It was the same one you picked last time."

I'm not keeping my own culture, that's how I'm feeling. And I'm keeping the culture that is not even mine. It's confusing—even with Hmong kids I know, they're becoming more Americanized, and they speak more English to you than Hmong. You want to speak Hmong to them, but then you might not feel comfortable—because they may not want to speak Hmong, or they may not know as much Hmong as you and then they would feel uncomfortable.

It's so easy to forget your language and the culture because you don't come in contact with it as much as you would if you were back in Laos. Like, my parents want me to learn the bamboo pipes. Sometimes I feel that I want to, but usually I don't because I don't see much use for them everyday. If I was back in Laos, I would be learning to play the bamboo pipes, but since I'm here, I'm more into American stuff, like playing volleyball and basketball and football and going out with my friends.

Here you're in so much contact with American things, like on TV: you don't see anything about your own culture, but you see everything about American culture, so that's what you learn.

Vicki Xiong: "Maybe because I always slept with my parents when I was small, I wanted my son to sleep with me."

My husband and I decided we didn't want more than four children, maybe two daughters and two sons. And we wouldn't start until after I finished school. Four is the ideal number for most people here, because life is very hard. I always wanted a large family like my mom, but I don't feel that I can raise as many children as my mother because I'm not as strong as she is. And besides, I want to do some other things, too, like get a Ph.D. So I didn't want to get pregnant too soon.

At first everyone thought there was something wrong with me—like physically or psychologically—since I didn't get pregnant. In the Hmong culture, you get married and they expect you to have children immediately. Everyone thought I was infertile, and they began finding me all these herbs and medicines. They did everything they could. They were really pressuring me. My parents wanted the shaman to come, and I felt if my parents wanted me to do that, then I should. So they called in the shaman and he did his ceremony, and I believed I was going to be pregnant. And that's exactly what happened. I guess I really didn't want a kid right now, but they think if you postpone having a kid, then you will never have one. So that's why I had my son.

But when I was pregnant my friend at school who's American and has grown-up children was telling me that she had a crib for her kids when they were little, and all her kids slept in a crib while she and her husband slept alone together in the bed. I really liked the idea when I was pregnant, so I got the crib. But when my son was born I never let him sleep in it. I just stacked it away. Why? Maybe because I always slept with my parents when I was small, I wanted my son to sleep with me. I just thought it was wrong to put him in the crib because he was so tiny and helpless. I was so attached to him. I wanted him right beside me. I couldn't put him away in a crib.

So after I had my son, I told my American friend, "I can't put him in the crib like you did with your kids." Then she asked why, and I told her, "Well, you know, I feel that he's part of me, and he's been part of me ever since he was inside me. I just can't let him sleep alone. He might be cold or hungry or need me, and I wouldn't hear him."

So she thought about it. And after a couple of months she

came back and told me, "Vicki, I think you're right. If I would
be able to do it all over again, I would have my son and daughters sleep with me."

Chia Ton Cha: "You can see that finding myself wasn't easy at all."

My dad wanted us all to go to school and become at least somebody. But now there's a real conflict—that lack of education my
parents have. It's not only them two, it's the whole family tree
from our great ancestors to my mom and dad today. It started
from the beginning—where my ancestors have begun. But now
my mom and dad have conflicts with us children because we
have education and they don't understand us and we don't
understand them.

When I was young I expected my mom and dad to teach us
everything, but they couldn't do much to help. They don't
speak English. They are financially unsecured. Most of all, they
have so much grief about their own suffering lives that sometimes they forget about us. But I won't blame them for all the
support they couldn't provide for me and all the things they did
or didn't teach me. What they learned from their parents and
their life back in Laos was a very abusive way of acting, and they
can't stop being who they are. But they gave me some of it, and
sometimes I really hate being myself. They taught me things,
and I took it for granted that's how you're supposed to be. But
now I see it's wrong. So I try to be more open-minded, like
people at work. But then I'm still narrow-minded, and I get in
conflict with others.

I really believe our problems started as soon as we came to
this country and us kids were educated. We expected our parents to be just like the American parents, but they can't. And we
kids were becoming like an American, thinking like an American, doing things like an American. They didn't want us to do

Taking care of the baby ▷

that—they wanted us to be like them. And we can't be like that, we don't want to be like that. That old generation is too narrow-minded. It's not what we want to be. So we argue with them and they can't understand, they can't counterargue. They would just scold and put me down for who I am. They said that I can't be an American and that I'm a Hmong. That's what they said.

When I was in school it was always miscommunication with them. Every activity I was involved in—I just had to keep ignoring them to do what I wanted to do. I was in a volleyball team, a cross-country team, marching band. I played everything. I was really a volleyball freak. I played all the time. I lived for it. But I didn't want to share any of this with my parents because they couldn't understand it, and they wouldn't know how to encourage me, they wouldn't even care to encourage me.

So every time I had to bring home a piece of paper that needed my parents' signature so I could participate in something, I just went ahead and signed it myself. I forged my parents' signature on almost every document that involved me and my parents. And then when I did things like go on a camping trip to the mountains with kids from school and I got back, they punished me by tying my hands behind my back. I was already sixteen. That's how bad it got.

So you can see that finding myself wasn't easy at all. I finally realized that I had to go through the military to find myself. That was the only way I could fix the conflict of my being an American and accepting myself as an American instead of what my parents say—which is that I'm not an American and they won't accept that I'm an American. I lost myself over these conflicts. And then I chose to find myself in the military force. That's what I did. I got into the top ten of the military occupational specialties. They helped me get my A.A. degree. I really believe my critical personal moments in the Army helped me to find who I was. I was born in Laos and us Hmong originated in China. I am a Hmong. But also I can be an American. . . . I am an American.

Ia Vang Xiong, the feminist spokeswoman in the Hmong commu-
nity, also told us about her struggles to make a place for herself
and other Hmong people in the American educational system.

I came to the United States when I was about twelve years old,
so they had to put me in school right away. I felt isolated, and I
think I made myself feel like an outcast because I was afraid
nobody would understand who I am, what I've done in my life,
where I've been. So I was always very quiet. But I tried studying
very hard because that was the only thing I could do that would
. . . you know, bring self worth to me in the future. I was a silent
person, but I was trying very hard to learn. In fact, a couple of
teachers noticed and said things to the class like, "Look at this
person, she doesn't talk one word, but she does all her
homework."

I was so afraid to speak in class because I was afraid I
would speak the wrong words. After a while, I knew I could
speak English pretty well, and I spoke English when I got out of
class. But the minute the teacher would call on me in class, I
would . . . like, "Oh, no," and then all of a sudden I felt my vocal
cord close up. I was that nervous that I couldn't say a word, even
if I tried. I just felt that emotion of crying. I knew I couldn't say
what I wanted to say: the English came out wrong, I couldn't say
the pronunciation right, and in the end, when I did speak out, I
was even more embarrassed. It was that bad on me.

It went on even when I got to college. I just couldn't raise
my hand in class. But at least if I didn't understand something
by then I was able to go to the professors and ask them to clar-
ify, yet I knew in my heart that wasn't enough. I knew that if I
wanted to be a teacher, I had to break the ice. I had to be able to
speak in front of people, and I had to be able to express myself
clearly. I told myself, I've got to practice right now because
there'll never be a better time.

But I was so afraid to even raise my hand and ask questions in class. Finally, I convinced myself that even if it was a
dumb question, it was worth asking. So I got up enough guts—
this was in a geography class—and I raised my hand and asked a
stupid question. I was way in the back, and everybody in class,

they laughed. It made me even more embarrassed. But then I go, "Okay, I've just got to practice again."

The next time it was in another class, and it didn't take me as much time to get up the courage to spit the question out. I did it, and I survived that one, too. Then the next time, I decided I should just try something spontaneously. Well, I couldn't do that, but I volunteered to do storytelling in my education class since I like to tell stories, and most people said I did a good job at it.

But I still couldn't talk in class spontaneously. Then one time a criminology professor said something about the Hmong eating dogs, and that really offended me. I was lecturing myself, "Ia, you got to speak up now or I forever forbid you to say anything! Ia, if you want to practice, you've got to say it now!" So I tried to raise my hand, but I couldn't say it. I couldn't bring myself to say it. And that bothered me the whole day and the whole night.

The next day as soon as the class met again, I raised my hand and I told the professor that what she said about the Hmong eating dogs offended me very much because the Hmong do not eat dogs, and "Southeast Asians" is a broad classification. You've got to be specific about which group you're talking about.

Then she said, "Oh, okay, then which group eats dogs?"

I said, "I don't know, but if you're going to say something like that, you have the responsibility to be specific." I was shaking and fighting within myself to really bring out what I wanted to say. I didn't do it that well, and I know I could do better now, but at least I said something.

When I look back at my whole struggle in school now that I have become a teacher myself, there are a couple of classes that I had so many years ago that have really been on my mind. One was when I was in the seventh grade. A lot of the classes I had were English as a Second Language classes, so I was with Hmong students. But in this social studies class I was mainstreamed with American students, and I was the only Hmong. I didn't understand one thing they said in that class. I sat in the back, and the teacher didn't know what to do with me either. He just looked at me, and I'm sure he felt sorry for me, and I felt sorry for myself, too. The whole year I was just . . . sitting in the back in the corner. Everybody was grouping together and having conversation, and I was still just sitting in the back. Nobody talked to me and I talked to nobody. When the bell rang I would get up and just go out the door. When report card time came I got a "C" in the class—I know I didn't deserve even that because I did zero work, but the teacher just gave it to me like a present. Yet I did listen. I heard about the Revolution. I heard about Abraham Lincoln. Those names stuck in my head, although I learned nothing else. Now I have students that are like that.

A lot of my students hardly speak English. The Hmong students are no problem because I can speak to them in Hmong. But some students speak only Spanish. There was one student in particular—I had a bilingual student sit with him and tell him in Spanish whatever I said. He can write in Spanish, and he did write in Spanish. But the problem is I can't read Spanish, so I don't know whether he's writing the right things or not. It has been quite a challenge for me. I feel very sad for these students, and I feel really sad remembering the way I was when I was in their position. I feel like . . . you know, the teacher probably felt very sorry for me—but there wasn't any help for me. I wish maybe a tutor or someone could have explained things to me or could at least have made me feel part of the class.

But there's another class I remember from when I was in school. It was ninth grade English, and the teacher was a black American. He was really trying very hard to encourage the black Americans to succeed in his class, and because I was a minority, he was trying to encourage me to succeed, too. He would give us work to do, and I really had no idea what the work was all about. But I would take the book home, and all night I would look for some word that looked familiar. I would write out all the passages and complete all my homework, and I guess a lot of the black students didn't do their homework. Anyway, I met the teacher in the hallway and said, "You're Mr.

Lynch, right? Here, I finished my homework." I handed it to him and he was proud of me.

Then that day in class he said, mostly to the black Americans, "Look, you children, you know how to speak English perfectly well. You were born here, you read well, you know how to do the work, and then you choose not to do the work. And look at this girl, she hardly speaks English, but she has determination and she finished all her homework. And she just gave it to me in the hallway."

I felt, "Oh, that must be good." And that encouraged me to continue, so I could get the praise and feel self worth. So for the first time in my life, I kept working really hard like that.

Now, in comparison to other teachers, I think I feel more sympathy for the kids in my class that are struggling. I feel I understand where they came from. I look at a child and I . . . it's like, "I understand how you feel. I understand who you are. I know where you came from and how you got to be here. I understand you."

Right now I'm working on my masters in administration because I think an administrative degree will open up a lot of options for me, like to be a resource person. But in maybe ten years I want to pursue my doctorate in education and probably teach in college. I feel that by then there'll be plenty of other Hmong people teaching in the elementary schools. So I would be a better role model if I moved up. Since I've become a teacher, there are a lot of Hmong that are majoring in teaching now. I've spoken at workshops for them, and they call me on the phone to discuss problems. I have given them my service. I have . . . It's like a road: It was hard, but I made it through to the other side and have come back and pulled a lot of people with me. Now we're here on the other side and we have to take one step further. I have to go on to a higher level and then pull them again. Another way I could say it is, "You know, I made it, and you could make it, too. This is how you do it. . . . This is how I did it, and if any of this can be of help so you could make it, then use it!"

Ia Vang Xiong and her class ▷

*Bee Thao told us about how he is working in America to realize
the dreams that his mother, who died in the Ban Vanai camp, had
for him.*

Right now I'm majoring in pre-dentistry at college. But when I
came here school was very hard. I was sixteen already, so they
put me in the tenth grade so I could graduate at least when I
reached my nineteenth birthday. But I had to take seven classes,
and stay after school to have all the courses I needed, and go to
summer school every year. It was hard, but I learned from my
other experiences that giving up never helps. And besides that,
you know, my mom, when she got very sick in the camp, she
talked to me, she actually said this: "Bee, I don't know if I'm
going to live and see you in the future; but whatever is coming
next, just try your best, even though I close my eyes. You
become a successful person, a professor or doctor or whatever.
And even though I die, my spirit will always be with you, and
I'll be happy." So I think back to that, and I look back to the
road I've already had my journey on, and I know I have to move
on. I can't give up. That's the reason why I'm still fighting here
and trying my very best to make it.

I'll tell you the truth. The first years in high school were
very hard because language was a big problem. When I wanted
to say something in English, it didn't make sense to the Americans. It was hard for them to understand, and once in a while
they made fun of the way I talked, the way I spoke English.
Then, when you get turned down a couple of times. . . .

I felt embarrassed, stupid, useless. In high school we had a
study group that was supposed to study for the economics class.
Each of us had to read a couple of sections and then come up
with a theory to share with the group so they can study. I did
mine, but like I said, English wasn't my first language, so I had a
hard time trying to understand the reading. Somehow I
wrote—like half a page, and when it came my turn to speak, I
did it, but it seems like they only understood 10 percent of my
speech. There were some people who were—you know, very
nice, and they said it's okay. But there were like two friends—
one of them a . . . I think Mexican, and the other one like Ameri-

can, white American. And actually they didn't say anything in front of the kids in the study group or my teacher, but after we walked out—you know, they really made fun of my English. They did that to me for a couple of weeks. And then, I think they got tired of it and let it go. But it really bothered me . . . hurt me.

It was really hard not knowing how to explain yourself in English, not just for me. This friend and I, we had P.E. together, and he was Hmong, too. After we played basketball we had gone back to the locker to get changed and take a shower. And then somehow, his wallet in his locker got stolen. He had twenty-something dollars in his wallet, and all his textbooks got stolen, too. Since my English was still better than his, he asked me in Hmong to go with him and see the coach instructor.

When we talked to the coach, somehow we got so nervous because—you know, that's the first time I went to his office to talk to him. My friend was more nervous than I was, so I tried to speak to the coach, but somehow it didn't make sense. He just said, "Young man, I'm sorry but I do not understand what you guys are trying to tell me."

Then my friend tried to tell him again, and then I tried to tell him again. But the coach didn't care that much. So when we couldn't make him understand—my friend just cried like a baby: Think about somebody in high school just crying like a baby! And somehow . . . you know, we decided to walk out. . . .

But we were very lucky. We had another friend we saw there, and his English was much better than ours. So we told him and he went back with us to talk to the coach. And after the coach understood everything, he told us that he would talk to the other coach and together they would find out if anybody saw anything, so my friend could get his things back. But in a way the whole thing made me feel very mad. In a way it made me feel very useless and stupid—like, it doesn't matter how hard I try, I don't think I'll get there.

That's the feeling I had at that moment, but I am always telling myself that I can not give up. I'm not a quitter, I've got to fight. You know, fight is the key word that'll make me a success.

So I tried very hard, and somehow, in three years, I made it through high school.

Now in pre-dentistry, school is still hard for me, but I know I'll do it, even if it takes a long time. For example, if you're going to go from here to Stockton—you get to Highway 99, then you see all kinds of drivers. Some of them go sixty-five miles an hour, some of them go eighty-five—zoom, just like that! And maybe they can get there in one hour. But to me, I think that if I can concentrate on the road, put my hands on the wheel and concentrate and obey the law, somehow I'll get there, and for sure—maybe tonight, maybe tomorrow, but—hey, I'll get there anyway. I just have to concentrate. That's the feeling I have toward myself.

My big, big dream, that's going to make me the person I want to be, the kind of man that I want to be, and the life that I want to have, is to get my dentist degree. Back in the camp, my mom used to have a very close cousin. In Laos, he was a dentist, and he made all kinds of money. You know he's a very nice person to talk to, also. I guess my mom wanted me to take him as a role model. She wanted me to see if I can become the same kind of person like him.

When I came here, it was hard for me because no one else in my family went to high school or graduated from a community college or did pre-dentistry. But now I always talk to my nephews and my nieces. I always tell them, "If I can make it, you guys can make it. I'll be the first one to prove it. I was the first one to cross that jungle and then stay waiting for you guys to come. Now I'll do my very best to pull you, to help you."

At this time some of my nieces and nephews are married and some have jobs, but some of them are still in high school, and I'm the one that they look up to. And I feel kind of proud of myself that even though I don't have a dad or a brother or someone that I could look up to, I'm someone my little nephews, my little nieces, and my cousins can look up to. That's a great feeling that I have.

Susie Vang (pseud.): "I see myself as an American kid."

I see myself as an American kid. I was born here—that was
eleven years ago. I go to school here. I'm American because of
the way I dress and the food I grew up with. I know more about
the American culture than the Hmong culture, even though I
think the Hmong culture is important. I would like to learn
more about . . . like the dances. And I know I will learn. But I
have too much school right now, and it takes so much time.
When you're doing your homework and your parents want you
to learn things in Hmong culture—it's frustrating. I guess
that's why I didn't learn more. But my parents understand that
my education is more important. That's why they don't really
stress doing *paj ntaub* . . . you know, the quilt stitching. I don't
mind that I can't do it because there's only a few girls at my age
who know how to do *paj ntaub*, and those are the ones who just
recently came here to the U.S.

But . . . I still believe in the Hmong shaman and all that,
though for me, it's hard to understand a lot of it. But when I'm
married and have kids, I would like to call in a shaman or an
elder to come and *hu plig*, like what my mom did when I was
small. That would probably be the only thing like that I would
do because . . . mainly, if I was given a choice, I would prefer my
kids to be baptised. I would like to marry into a Christian family and raise my kids that way, but I feel there has to be something I could share with my kids from the Hmong culture, and
hu plig might be something I would like to keep.

Also I feel lucky that I can speak two languages because
when my American friends are around and I have a Hmong
friend there, and I want to tell my Hmong friend something
very, very personal, I could just speak in Hmong. I could use
this as a secret language, so other people who don't speak the
language won't understand it. That's one thing that's good
about being Hmong.

But what I don't like is, I saw a lot of my cousins marrying
so young. I don't know why they do that, but I worry about
them. I'm just scared, you know . . . that young to be married!

I would be embarrassed around my school friends. Many of them who married that young, they're very quiet at school. They won't talk to anyone. All they want to do is be with themself. I don't know why they're like that, but like I said, maybe they're embarrassed that they married so young.

I think they should marry around like age twenty or twenty-one, so they could go through high school and get their education. When you marry young, like at thirteen or fourteen, you will not have good education . . . or any fun. All you do is stay home and have a baby. It would be very tough for me. I hope to at least finish high school, at the least, because I think getting a good education is very important. Because if you want a good job, you have to have a good education.

But my parents don't pressure me. They usually let me decide what I want. The biggest fights I have with my parents are about the way I dress and sometimes about food. For example, when we have back-to-school night, where we take our parents to school and meet our teacher, I don't mind about the way they dress. Even though they dress in old clothes with slippers on, it doesn't bother me. American parents, they dress nice because they work and have money. My parents don't speak English and don't work, so I don't mind. Just as long as they come to see my teacher, it's good. But they don't like the way I dress. They always say that my pants are too big or "your shirt is too long" or "tuck in your shirt." But I like the way I dress. I think it's cool because most of my friends dress like me. Maybe they would like me to dress like I came from another country— like a dress with pants under it and then no socks, only shoes, and wearing clothes that don't match.

And my mom also complains when I let my hair go. She says "Tie it up!" because if I don't I look like those gangs that came out of somewhere. Or if I'm trying to cut my hair, like trim it, sometimes she says, "Don't cut it. You'll look like a geek, like those people on the street."

No, I don't like that, and I argue back when I get really mad. I usually say, "I could dress the way I want," or "I could do this if I want to."

Sometimes she'll say, "Don't talk back to me," or "I'm your mother, and don't talk like that back to me."

Then I don't say nothing. Then I get angry and just go outside and play two-squares. This makes me feel better, and then I'll forget about it.

And also about food: Like the Hmong, they always stay home and eat. But like the American families, they sometimes go out to eat—somewhere like a Danny's or Wendy's, and those American families order pizza to eat. But for the Hmong, they just seem to make their own food and they just eat anything that they have. I know that my parents don't have money to go out to restaurants because they need to pay the bills and pay . . . like for my baby brothers—they might need new clothes and my parents have to go out and buy it for them.

So if my mom makes something that I don't like to eat, then I don't eat. I'll wait until the next morning to go to school and just eat over there. Sometimes I just can't stand it because they don't go out. American families, when they don't go out, they would order pizza to eat at home.

Mai Moua (pseud.), who is struggling to convince her parents that it is all right for her to date someone who is Vietnamese, told us why she feels she cannot say she is a Hmong.

I wish we could get the older people to see more things about how life is in America, not just be around Hmong people all the time. Then they might be able to teach their kids differently. I want my mom and dad to see the world. I want them to experience other people, know about the different cultures. In school we're taught like that—because there are so many different kinds of people here, and we can be friends with them and understand each other. If I want to go to a friend's house for a slumber party or something, I want my parents to say, "Okay, your friend is—maybe Mexican, or something, but, yeah, I'll let you go." I want them to be able to trust me, to trust other people, to open up, to communicate. They have to see America—and feel and hear everything. That's how I feel.

I still value our culture, like the New Year—we go to toss ball and stuff—*pov pob* they call it—and we have fun. But then, in a way—to be honest—I have to say I am an American. I was raised here. My life has been a mixture of both cultures. So I couldn't really say that I'm just Hmong because it's a mixture of American traditions and our traditions—and the cultures clash together.

A lot is changing for me because although I was born back there, I came here when I was three, so though my parents might still be Hmong, I was brought up in a different land. I am hoping to go to college next year and become a psychologist. I know how things would have been for me back there in Laos if we hadn't come here. I would probably have gotten married and had kids by now because they usually get married early and have kids. I would probably be farming for a living instead of graduating from high school now.

It's sad when I think about it. Here we take everything for granted, like electricity, everything over here. There it's just very, very poor—the people working on their land, they have very little to eat. If I were to live back there my life would be very poor. Everything would be very hard over there. For me to go back to Laos and farm—I know I could do it, but the thing is, it would be very hard. I would have the feeling like—uh, I can't make it, I won't survive here. I've got to go back to America. I would probably feel like that.

Penny Yang (pseud.): "I'm an American with a mixed background, just like a lot of Americans."

My mom is Japanese and my dad is Hmong and my stepmom is American. It feels kind of different because I never met anyone who is Hmong and Japanese and American before, but I'm proud of it. I kind of get background from all sides, exposure from all different cultures. I wish, though, that I knew how to speak Hmong or Japanese really, really well. I think they didn't teach me because they felt I was going to get confused. Now, since we moved to Fresno, I've spent a lot of time with my cousins on my dad's side, but I didn't pick up Hmong. I guess that's because at home we speak mostly English. My mom and dad always spoke English to each other and to me.

When I'm with my dad's relatives, I wish I could understand more of what's going on. I wish I could communicate with them because it's kind of put a barrier between me and them that I don't speak Hmong. Even though I love them and know that we're a family and everything, it's holding me back because I don't know the language. So in a lot of ways I feel left out, and I know I would feel different if I could speak Hmong. When we have a family get-together with my dad's relatives, I can talk to all of the cousins who are about my age—that's okay. But for the adults—they'll come up to me and just talk to me, and I don't know what they're saying. I just smile and say, "Hi." And that's okay, though I wish there were more. But, really, I don't feel too, too out of it because I've asked my dad a lot about the Hmong culture, and he told me about how he grew up and things.

My biggest contact with the old culture is probably the Hmong New Year. When I was little I even used to dress up in Hmong costume for the New Year, though I don't anymore. I feel good and proud that it's part of me, but—yeah, I do feel nervous not knowing Hmong even though I might look like a Hmong: For example, there might be some Hmong boy that would offer to toss ball with me at the New Year. That's the traditional way for boys and girls to get to know one another. To look at me, especially if I were in Hmong costume, I think they can't really tell if I'm Hmong or not. But when they talk to me, I know they'll find out that I'm not. I guess they'd be surprised to find out that I'm only part Hmong. That would be a little uncomfortable.

I feel that the way I was raised, I have a lot of the American culture in me. But I don't really feel left out of the other cultures—because in a way I don't feel truly all American. But neither do I feel all Hmong or all Japanese. I feel like I'm mixed, just kind of my own person with three things together: three things just kind of wrapped up in one. I don't really want to put a label on myself like, "Oh, I feel more American." I wouldn't be able to say that . . . that wouldn't feel right.

It was kind of hard at first, until I started to really figure out how I felt about it. I couldn't say I was Hmong, so I couldn't be with that group. I couldn't say I was full Japanese, because I knew I wasn't just like the Japanese kids I saw. I didn't act just like they acted, I didn't know the language like they did. I kind of felt—you know—almost confused, like I didn't know where I fit in, until I really started to think about it. And what I realized is that I can't just put myself here or there, I just can't fit into one category. If my Hmong or Japanese relatives don't understand me, then I really can't do anything about it. That's just the way I am. I'm an American with a mixed background, just like a lot of Americans.

Epilogues

Another Personal Story

In spring of 1996 I completed the first draft of the manuscript for this book. It was not coincidental that I felt a tremendous urge at that time to retrace the particular immigrant experience that had been so crucial to my own life: my mother's journey from her Latvian shtetl, Preili, to America. During World War II Latvia was invaded by the Nazis, and after the war it was a satellite of the Soviet Union, so during most of my life it had been virtually impossible for Americans to travel there. But in 1992 Latvia became one of the breakaway Baltic republics. And now I could hop a plane, be served lunch and dinner on board, and arrive as a tourist in that country that had haunted and pained my most formative years through my mother's perpetual grief for what she had lost there.

I am not sure now what I had hoped to find in Preili, or "Preil," as the Jews who once lived there had called it. Before the Holocaust, about half of Preil's four thousand inhabitants were Jews, but I guessed there would be few or no Jews there now, and that it would look nothing like the shtetl my mother left more than three-quarters of a century ago. I knew I would find no one from her family: her brothers and sisters—all except for my Aunt Ray who came to America in 1926—were exterminated by the Nazis. Perhaps their house might still be there, perhaps someone who knew the family.

It felt important to me to share this exploration with my son, Avrom, who is twenty-one and barely remembers his grandmother who died when he was four or our Aunt Ray who died a few years later. We are a small family. My mother had brothers, sisters, cousins, but now Avrom and I are all that remain.

My son's enthusiasm for the trip surprised me. He had never talked before about any desire to know his family roots.

What had he imagined we might find? Neither of us could put our hopes into words. "Some trace . . . anything," we both finally told each other. We took a night train from St. Petersburg to Riga, Latvia's capital. A sleepless night. It was dawn as we approached the city, and we could make out graffiti on fences and the sides of buildings—some of it in English. "Fuckass police" we saw twice. Latvian punk kids, we smiled. And then swastikas here and there, the lightning insignia of Hitler's storm troopers, and a Star of David intersected by a diagonal line, the words "canabel [sic] corpse" next to it. More than half a century later and they have not changed, I thought bitterly— nothing's changed except that there are probably not more than a handful of Jews left in Latvia.

In Riga we hired a car and a driver. I was tense with bad expectations. I would make things very clear from the start, I decided. If the driver showed any hostility to my project I would get rid of him and find someone else immediately. Agris, his name was—a big blond man in badly fitting, mismatched jacket and pants. He extended a large paw to shake hands when he came to pick us up. Perfunctorily I took it, and I looked determinedly into his blue eyes as I told him without ceremony, "I am Jewish. My mother's family was from Preil. Her mother and father died there. Her brothers and all but one sister were killed by the Nazis there. My son and I want to go to the town to find whatever we can—the Jewish cemetery where my grandparents were buried, whatever remains of the synagogues." Aunt Ray had told me before she died that there were two synagogues on her street alone. "Sondergass," the street was called—a Yiddish street name. "Maybe we will find someone who remembers the family, who can tell us about their end. I need your help with the language and the detective work," I said firmly.

Agris didn't blink. He seemed to me to understand immediately not only my words but the unspoken emotional content behind them. "I help with everything you need," he promised. "I do my best to find it, everything you want."

I got in the front seat of the car next to him. Avrom sat in the back. I saw now that Agris was a gentle soul, perhaps somewhat simple, naive—but diligent and eager to please. I felt sorry for my initial abruptness. In softer tones I carried on polite conversation as we drove along. His family? His home? He has been married for five years. He and his wife have a daughter of six months. The three of them live together with his parents in a small, three-room apartment. Agris is twenty-seven. His father is fifty-seven. Recently his father lost his job in a factory: "In Latvia, you can get a job until you are thirty-five," Agris says. "After thirty-five, nobody gives you work anymore." His story comes pouring out in a tumble of words. He is the only one in the family who brings in money. He makes two hundred dollars a month (thirty dollars less than we would pay his company for one day of his services). His parents have a low-rent, government-subsidized flat, but "low rent" still means that about half of Agris's salary goes for rent. Many days he works twelve, fifteen hours. "I young, I strong," he says many times during our trip. "I can work on two jobs. I need not more than four hours sleep at night. But there is almost no work for me in Latvia. Only what gives two hundred dollars a month."

I despair when we arrive in Preil. It appears to be a modern, dull Eastern European town—one shoe store, one barber, a bakery, blond children licking ice cream cones, unimaginative little houses that date probably from the 1950s. On none of the street signs can we make out the name "Sondergass." When my family lived in Preil, Aunt Ray had told me, it was a town of only a few streets. Now it has spread out to many streets.

Agris stops the car a half-dozen times, whenever he sees someone who appears to be at least a septuagenarian, to ask if they know where Sondergass might have been. From everyone he gets puzzled looks. Those who glance into his car see us. Perhaps they recognize that we are Americans on a quest, or perhaps he has told them. They look at us with curiosity. Do they see "rich Americans"? Do they see "Jews"? I wonder why I've come on this nebulous quest and what my son must be thinking. I push down a wave of depression, hopelessness.

Finally someone directs Agris to an official-looking little building, what I imagine might be a historical society—though I can't believe these Latvians cared enough about the Jewish population that once lived there to preserve a record. Agris goes in, comes out with a large, middle-aged blond woman. She nods at us with a concerned expression. There is much gesticulating and pointing in various directions. Perhaps something is left after all, I think with relief. Another man comes out of the building, and I watch the woman talk with him; then Agris talks and the man listens. He is about forty-five, intelligent face, very serious looking. He gets in a car parked nearby. Agris comes back to us. "That man is the mayor of Preili now," he explains. "He knows where everything is. He will take us everywhere."

The mayor of Preil will take us everywhere? The idea is really amusing. Avrom and I smile at each other. My mother's father was a tailor in Preil. My mother, from the time she was ten years old, worked in other people's houses as a servant, until she learned to be a seamstress. The family lived on herring and potatoes, "and meat one time a week, one tablespoon full of meat for each person." And now the mayor of Preil is guiding her daughter and grandson around the town.

"Early in the twentieth century simple people or even ne'er-do-wells would leave their shtetlach, go to America, and then come back a few years later with a shiny motor car driven by a liveried chauffeur, their pockets stuffed full of the gold they picked up from the streets of America." Did my mother tell me such stories? Did I make them up from American myth? The "land of opportunity" story, the "rags to riches" story.

"The mayor knows what you are wanting," Agris tells us. "He will help me to help you find what you are needing."

We drive in two cars to the outskirts of Preil, which is only a few minutes away. The mayor stops his car on the side of what looks to me to be a forest. Agris stops too, and we get out. "It is an old Hebrew cemetery," he explains. We walk through high grasses, and suddenly there are ancient, moss-covered gravestones dotting the landscape. Many of them have fallen down. A few still stand, but the Hebrew letters carved on them are barely visible. Nobody has tended them in more than fifty years.

My grandfather, after whom my son Avrom was named, died of cholera during World War I. My grandmother died of cancer only months before the Nazis invaded the shtetl and

killed all the Jews of Preil. I want so much to find the gravestones of the grandmother and grandfather I never knew. My
son and I search every stone, but on most the letters are not legible. And then one stone . . . I can make out three letters only:
ל ו פ, L U F. The family name was Luft. Whose grave was it? We
can't be sure. My son takes my hand and we stand close
together.

Then the mayor leads us to a big plot with a large marker
that looks newer than the gravestones. The letters on the
marker are easily legible. Avrom and I read them in Yiddish:
"In memory of our brothers, sisters, aunts, uncles, mothers,
fathers, and children who perished here through the fascist
atrocities." So others have come back to see, just as we have, and
they erected this memorial. The mayor tells Agris to explain to
us that the Nazis took many of the Jews of Preil to this spot,
made them dig a large grave, and shot them right here—just
where the plot with the marker is. My son puts his arm around
my shoulder as I weep quietly for the misery of the past. The
mayor stands at a little distance from us. I feel him watching us,
and I am sure of his empathy. I know none of this was his fault.
He was probably born in the 1950s.

We drive back to town. Sondergass now has a Latvian
name, the mayor tells us. One of the old synagogues is now a
warehouse. The building of the other synagogue was long ago
torn down. What more is there to see? A large church still
stands. Agris translates the mayor's question: "Do you want to
go inside and have a look?" I remember my mother's stories of
pogroms that usually started from the church at Easter time—
perhaps that very same church. Jewish homes were burned,
Jews were slaughtered by the Latvian gentiles long before the
Nazis came in 1941. My family had lived in Preil for two hundred years. How many of them were murdered in pogroms after
priests told peasants that Jews used the blood of Christian children to make their passover matzos? "The pogrom"—all too
familiar lore of my childhood. I decline to go inside the church.

People who pass us on the sidewalk greet the mayor, shake
his hand. They look at us. I don't know what he tells them,
whether or how he explains his leave-taking from official

duties, but I hear a word that sounds like "American" several times.

Agris leads us back to his car, and we follow the mayor's car again, this time through a great stone gate of former grandeur, to what appears to be a dilapidated castle. The mayor, perhaps because it is the one "tourist attraction" in Preili, would like me to see it. He walks by my side. Agris translates. This was once the castle of Count Borg, a very famous nobleman. My mother's stories of the castle—full of fairy-tale wonder and fear of the gentile nobility's tremendous power—come back to me.

The castle has long been deserted. Inside, it is freezing; everything is in disrepair—crumbling ceilings, broken walls scorched black by a fire. I think I hear the scurry of rats' feet.

"Some rich people came here a few years ago and said they would make this into a hotel," Agris translates. "But they didn't do it." Do I only imagine that the mayor is looking at me hopefully? I am the granddaughter of a tailor, the daughter of a servant girl—but I am from America, he must be thinking. All things are possible for Americans. For a few moments I calculate wildly. How much could it take to renovate this colossal wreck that must have awed the little girl who became my mother? Surely not more than a few hundred thousand. Couldn't I raise that kind of money? And make a present to the town of a thriving hotel that would employ scores of people? Or live in the restored castle myself—the rich and gracious daughter of poor little Gitta Mary Luft? My imagination races. It would have been beyond my mother's wildest dreams, the stuff of fantasies, building castles in the air. Couldn't I do it if I really wanted to? But what would it be like to be stuck here for more than a few days? I clutch my purse with my blessed American passport inside.

If the gentle mayor was disappointed that I did not jump at the opportunity to purchase a Latvian castle he made no sign. "He has thought of somebody who may have known your family," Agris translates. We get back into our automobile procession again.

This time the mayor parks in front of a small house. A woman of about seventy comes out, greets him warmly. Some people on the sidewalk wave to him. "They seem to love their mayor," I observe aloud.

Agris must have translated. "He says he needs to be elected again in three months time, and he is not sure he will make it. His mother and his father are ethnic Russian, and now, since we get freedom from USSR, some people who are Latvians say only an ethnic Latvian should be mayor of Preili. He has worry." The perpetually virulent ethnic animosities of this part of the world—the form changes, but it continues to exist—sometimes more and sometimes less beneath the surface, but always threatening to explode.

The woman's name is Julia—"Yulya," she pronounces it. She wears a silver crucifix around her neck. Julia speaks to Agris and the mayor in Latvian. Then in a perfect Yiddish such as I have not heard since my Aunt Ray died, she asks me what tongue I speak. I'm astonished, delighted. We speak in Yiddish —I with my terrible American accent, Yiddish words confused with the German I learned as a university student.

What can she tell me? "Luft? Yes, they lived over there," she points vaguely in a left direction. "Tailors." She knows! I am ready to jump up and embrace her. She saw them alive—people who belonged to me, whom I never saw! "But I was only a girl," she tells me in my mother's and Aunt Ray's Yiddish. "I don't remember anything about them. Only the name and that they were tailors."

How did she learn Yiddish? She's an ethnic Pole, she explains. She speaks Polish, Latvian, Russian, German, Yiddish. She grew up in Preili with Jewish children. "Everybody loved everybody else. We had no trouble here." Not my mother's version of the story, but she is sincere. She learned Yiddish as a child from her little Jewish friends. They were all like brothers and sisters. As she says this I can't help but stare at a picture of Christ crucified on the wall above her chair.

"What happened to my family? Do you know?" I implore her for any details. She knows no specifics. The Jews of Preil had all been rounded up in the main street. She tried to go there, to see her friends. She was only a girl, fourteen, maybe fifteen. The Nazi soldiers turned her back. Her friends were not taken to concentration camps. They were killed—all of them—right there in Preili. She can tell me no more.

We hug as we part. She says we must cancel our hotel reservations in Riga and stay with her. "Then come next spring," she implores when I tell her we must go back to Riga tonight. We exchange addresses. She is very taken with Avrom. Perhaps he looks to her like the murdered friends of her childhood. Maybe there was a young sweetheart with his dark eyes or black curls. . . . "*A shane bucher*," she says about Avrom in Yiddish, "a handsome young man."

There is not much for my son and me to hold on to here. The details are lost. There is nothing more to recover. We saw the trees my mother must have seen as a child. The cobblestones of the main street must have been there when she lived in Preil. The church was there. Julia was not yet born when my mother left. The past and this faraway world will continue to be a mystery to me. It is America that is my home. Like most of the Hmong people I worked with, nothing remains for me of the other world. I have no other home but America.

Agris was a wonderful guide. He kept his promise. He did everything he could to help me find what I wanted to know. But there is little to be found out. The drive back to Riga takes more than three hours, and it is very late now. I am a little sad and very quiet. But Agris talks freely. "I am strong. I can work two jobs. Three jobs. But there is no money in Latvia. Nothing is needed that I can do. No matter how hard I work, I make maybe two hundred dollars a month. Meat is four dollars for a little piece. We never have. Fish—I must go fish myself. Furniture—my father and I make ourself. To buy good things—a nice car, good clothes—that would be a fairy tale for me. If the Communists come back it will be more worse. If that happen, I will run away."

I would like to be mulling over what we saw during the last ten hours—the cemetery, the mayor, Julia, the castle. But Agris is talking desperately—as though he must not let an opportunity escape him. I know what he wants to ask. His hunger is like my mother's must have been. "Never can we even have a vacation," he tells me. "Never can we go somewhere or stop working to rest. You are nice. I can say all this to you." Then, "Maybe you can help me. I don't know how to do. How do you get to come to America. How can you find a job there?"

I tell him how difficult it is for immigrants in America. I want to tell him about the Hmong people I have been working with, though I realize that he will not hear it. "If you could come to America," I say as gently as I can, "maybe, many years from now, life can be easy for your daughter. But for you, it would be hard. . . . It's hard there if you don't speak the language well, if you haven't been educated in America," I say, remembering my mother who—even to her death, having lived in America for more than half a century—spoke English no better than Agris does, never mastered the mysteries of written English.

"Life in America is good for me," I continue, "but for my mother—she had to work hard just like you do here. She never had anything, even in America."

But he will not hear me. "Please, you are so nice for me," Agris says again. "If you can help me to come to America . . . and find a job, I can give you three months from my salary, four months from my salary."

He is serious. I want to tell him that he doesn't understand how painful it is to leave one's culture, to give up one's language, to adjust as an adult to a whole new world, to watch your children grow away from you because they have become American while you will always remain an immigrant. I want to tell him how powerless one becomes. I want to say he is lucky to be close to his mother and father, to have a family that isn't divided by oceans or the disasters of war or the less-obvious-but-still-terrible pain of cultural splits between parent and child.

"Here everything is closed," he goes on. "There is nothing for me to become. There is nothing for my daughter to become. Nothing we can change in our lives. If I can come to America, everything will be different for us. I know America. It is the golden land." He will not let himself be discouraged.

Lillian Faderman

Ghia

Though I have been here for fifteen years, deep inside me, this American world around me feels as strange as it was when I first arrived. There is so much I have learned in these years, but there is so much that I do not know and feel that I will never know. It is as if when I learn one new thing today, it only opens up many more confusing questions that I will have to find the answers to tomorrow. Like many of my people that we interviewed, I feel that I am in this enormous "American jungle," that I have been swallowed into its deepest, thickest, innermost center. Though I try to find my way by learning about what is around me, the paths are so complicated and the denseness makes everything so dark that I often feel I am being pushed back into the blackness, as though I have not traveled very far from who I was the day I first came to this land.

Many of my people that we interviewed said the same thing. What I felt so many times when they talked was their despair. I felt that they also were lost in this enormous American jungle. As wise and determined as many of them were, they could not see their way to the light. The older people watch helplessly and hopelessly as the "strange spirits" from the American jungle cast a spell on their children who do not want to learn about their ancient and rich culture, who do not want to listen to their elders, who go to gangs or take other strange paths for their direction. The elders feel powerless because no matter how hard they try to warn their children of dangers, strange spirits seem to have come over the children. Not even with the help of the shaman spirit can the elders understand where the souls of their children have gone or why they follow alien spirits.

To many of the young ones, She-Yee, the shaman spirit their parents call on to guide them, does not have power. Their own She-Yee is the spirit they have met in the American jungle. To these young people, it is that new spirit that will guide them like She-Yee's spirit guided their parents from Laos and Thailand. It is only the new spirit, they say, that will help them survive the American jungle.

So there are not many things that bring the young and old together here in America. Maybe that is why our New Year festivals attract tens of thousands of us, and that Hmong people come from all over the country to take part in the big celebrations in areas like Fresno: The Hmong New Year festival is one of the few places where the Hmong of all generations can meet—where the young can dress in the clothes that their ancestors have worn, and where Hmong music can be played on tape through loudspeakers that can be heard all over the festival grounds. The young can be Hmong here, and the old can be happy watching them and remembering their own lost world.

But when the Hmong New Year festivals are over, the young go back to their strange spirits, and the old go back to crying over what has happened to their children. Of course they are suspicious of all the shadows in the jungle. When Lillian Faderman and I sat together in interviews, I could feel that to the older people, she was thought of as one of those "strange spirits" in the "American jungle." I always had to assure them she was not of the harmful strange spirits. That she is a "good spirit" who just wanted to learn more about our Hmong people. When they saw how much we wanted to listen to them, they talked—about their struggles and the pains that they have had to endure for so long, and about their hopes and victories and little happinesses. And so old as well as young—they told us their stories.

Ghia Xiong

Glossary

Chao Fa
People of the Hmong resistance who fought the communists
after General Vang Pao's army was disbanded (*Chao Fa* means
"God's disciples.")

choj, ib choj
Silver bars, sometimes used as high currency by the Hmong in
Laos

dab
Spirits which can be either benevolent or malevolent

fiv xov, tus fiv xov
In catch-hand marriage, the man's kinsmen who inform the
bride's parents of her whereabouts after the kidnap

hu plig
The calling of the soul to return to or stay with a person's body;
hu plig guards against an attack of evil spirits by preventing loss
of soul or restoring a soul that may be lost

Kammu
Language of the Yao

kher kong
Ritual consisting of chanting, use of incense, and various sym-
bolic devices to effect cures or cast spells

luam laws
Spice

neng
A healing spirit that lives in the body of the shaman

npaj, ib npaj
Laotian coin of small denomination

nyias, daim nyias
Carrying-pouch for a baby

paj ntaub
Hmong stitched quilt

phom gaslasbees
Hmong rifles

pov pob
Ball tossing between men and women on Hmong New Year;
a way potential mates get to know each other

pum hub
Spice

qeej
Bamboo pipes; the major Hmong musical instrument

qeej tu siav
"The Saddest Song," played on the *qeej* for the death ceremony

qos npua
"Pig potatoes," a yamlike vegetable

saub
A prophet who has special healing and fortune-telling skills

sev, daim sev
Long skirt worn by women over their pants

sher qeng
String to be tied around the wrist or neck to ward off evil spirits

suab mus tij
Edible fern

tshuaj npua
Yellow rain (chemical weapon of the Vietnam war)

txoob
Palm tree-like vegetation with an edible center

Toj Phim Nyaj
Female evil spirit

vab
A woven rattan or bamboo tray used to separate the chaff from rice grain

Bibliography

ADLER, SHELLEY R. "The Role of the Nightmare in Hmong Sudden Unexpected Nocturnal Death Syndrome: A Folkloristic Study of Belief and Health." Ph.D. diss., UCLA, 1991.

BARNEY, LINWOOD G. "The Meo of Xieng Khouang Province, Laos," in *Southeast Asian Tribes, Minorities, and Nations*, ed. Peter Kunstadter (Princeton: Princeton University Press, 1967), 271–94.

BEDARD, MARCIA E. "Maternal and Child Health in the Hmong American Community." Paper presented at 1990 conference, "An Ethnic Mosaic: Southeast Asians in Fresno," California State University, Fresno.

BISHOP, KENT A. "The Hmong of Central California: An Investigation and Analysis of the Changing Family Structure during Liminality, Acculturation and Transition." Ed. D. diss., University of San Francisco, 1985.

BLIATOUT, BRUCE THOWPAOU. *Hmong Sudden Unexpected Nocturnal Death Syndrome: A Cultural Study.* Oregon: Sparkle Publishing, 1982.

CASE, GABRIELE. "Patients and Healers: Interactions between Hmong Shamans and Their Clients." Master's thesis. California State University, Fresno, 1989.

CHAN, SUCHENG, ed. *Hmong Means Free: Life in Laos and America.* Philadelphia: Temple University Press, 1994.

DANA, ANNETTE FEDERICO. "Courtship and Marriage Traditions of the Hmong." Master's thesis, California State University, Fresno, 1993.

DANES, SHARON M., KATHLEEN A. O'DONNELL, AND DOAUNG-
KAMOL SAKULNAMARKA. *Middle Generation Hmong Couples
and Daily Life Concerns*. St. Paul: University of Minnesota Press,
1993.

DAO, YANG. *Hmong at the Turning Point*. Edited by Jeanne L. Blake. Minneapolis: WorldBridge Associates, 1993.

DONNELLY, NANCY D. *Changing Lives of Refugee Hmong Women*. Seattle: University of Washington Press, 1994.

DOWNING, BRUCE T., AND DOUGLAS P. OLNEY, eds. *The Hmong in
the West: Observations and Reports*. Minneapolis: University of Minnesota, Center for Urban and Regional Affairs, Southeast Asian Refugee Studies Project, 1982.

FASS, SIMON M. *The Hmong in Wisconsin: On the Road to Self-
Sufficiency*. Milwaukee: The Wisconsin Policy Research Institute,
April 1991.

GARRETT, W. E. "The Hmong of Laos: No Place to Run." *National Geo-
graphic* 145 (January 1974): 78–111.

GOLDSTEIN, BETH L. "Schooling for Cultural Transitions: Hmong
Girls and Boys in American High Schools." Ph.D. diss., University of
Wisconsin, Madison, 1985.

GREENE, WILLIAM LEWIS. "Identifying Cultural Values with Story
Completions: Comparing the Narratives of Hmong and American
Children." Master's thesis, California State University, Fresno, 1993.

HAMILTON-MERRITT, JANE. *Tragic Mountain: The Hmong, the Americans, and the Secret Wars for Laos, 1942–1992*. Bloomington: Indiana
University Press, 1993.

HAYES, CHRISTOPHER L. "A Study of the Older Hmong Refugees in
the United States." Ph.D. diss., Santa Barbara, California: The Fiel-
ding Institute, 1984.

HENDRICKS, GLENN L., BRUCE T. DOWNING, AND AMOS S.
DEINARD, eds. *The Hmong in Transition*. Staten Island, New York:
Center for Migration Studies, 1986.

HIMES, HOWARD KENT. "Traditional Parenting Practices and Attitudes of the Hmong." Master's thesis, California State University, Fresno, 1991.

HOWARD, KATSUYO K., ed. *Passages: An Anthology of Southeast Asian Refugee Experience.* Fresno: California State University Press, 1990.

JOHNSON, CHARLES, ed. *Dab Neeg Hmoob: Myths, Legends, and Folk Tales from the Hmong of Laos.* St. Paul, Minnesota: Macalester College Press, 1985.

LEWIS, JUDY, ed. *Minority Cultures of Laos: Kammu, Lau', Lahu, Hmong, and Iu-Mien.* Rancho Cordova, California: Southeast Asia Community Resource Center, 1992.

LIVO, NORMA J., AND DIA CHA, eds. *Folk Stories of the Hmong: Peoples of Laos, Thailand, and Vietnam.* Englewood, Colorado: Libraries Unlimited, 1991.

LONG, LYNNELLYN. *Ban Vanai: The Refugee Camp.* New York: Columbia University Press, 1993.

LONG, PATRICK DU PHUOC. *The Dream Shattered: Vietnamese Gangs in America.* Boston: Northeastern University Press, 1996.

MOTTIN, JEAN. *The History of the Hmong (Meo).* Bangkok: Odeon, 1980.

OLNEY, DOUGLAS P. *A Bibliography of the Hmong (Miao) of Southeast Asia and the Hmong Refugees in the United States.* Minneapolis: University of Minnesota Center for Urban and Regional Affairs, Southeast Asian Refugee Studies Project, 1983.

PFAPP, TIM. *Hmong in America: Journey from a Secret War.* Eau Claire, Wisconsin: Chippewa Valley Museum Press, 1995.

QUINCY, KEITH. *Hmong: History of a People.* Cheney: Eastern Washington University Press, 1988.

RANARD, DONALD A. "Thailand, The Last Bus." *Atlantic* (October 1987): 26–34.

RICK, KATHRYN. "An Investigation of the Process of Biculturation with Hmong Refugees." Ph.D. diss., University of Colorado, 1988.

STROUSE, JOAN. "The Reformation of Culture: Hmong Refugees from Laos." *Journal of Refugee Studies* 1 (1988): 20–37.

TAPP, NICHOLAS. "Hmong Religion." *Asian Folklore Studies* 48 (1989): 59–94.

THRASHER, FREDERIC M. *The Gang: A Study of 1313 Gangs in Chicago.* Chicago: University of Chicago Press, 1927.

TRUEBA, HENRY T., LILA JACOBS, AND ELIZABETH KIRTON. *Cultural Conflict and Adaptation: The Case of Hmong Children in American Society.* New York: Falmer Press, 1990.

VANG, LUE, AND JUDY LEWIS. *Grandmother's Path, Grandfather's Way: Oral Lore, Generation to Generation.* Rancho Cordova, California: Zellerbach Family Fund, 1984.

VANGAY, JONAS VANG NA. *Hmong Parents' Cultural Attitudes and the Sex-Ratio Imbalance of Hmong Merced High School Graduates.* Merced, California: Mong Pheng Community, 1989.